TEA WITH EINSTEIN
AND OTHER MEMORIES

TEA WITH EINSTEIN
AND OTHER MEMORIES

For Susan & Frank

best wishes

WILLIAM FRANKEL 20/4/06

HALBAN
LONDON
In association with
ejps
European Jewish Publication Society

First Published in Great Britain by
Halban Publishers Ltd
22 Golden Square
London W1F 9JW
2006

www.halbanpublishers.com

in association with
European Jewish Publication Society
PO Box 19948
London N3 3ZJ

www.ejps.org.uk

The European Jewish Publication Society gives grants to support
the publication of books relevant to Jewish literature, history,
religion, philosophy, biography and culture.

A CIP catalogue record for this book is available from the British Library.

ISBN 1870015 97 5

Typeset by
Computape Typesetting, Scarborough, North Yorkshire
Printed in Great Britain
by MPG Books Ltd., Bodmin, Cornwall

Contents

In loving memory
of
Anne Rebecca Frankel
1946–1989

I

'The Buildings'

My childhood was spent among the Jews in London's East End and my world revolved around family, synagogue, a few friends, school and *heder* (Hebrew school). I was born on 3 February 1917, the second son of Anna and Isaac Frankel who had come to London four or five years earlier. My father's surname was Kiesel but, on arrival in London, he was advised that the name sounded very foreign and that it would be a good thing if he adopted his mother's maiden name, which he did. Their emigration to London took place soon after their marriage which was, as was common in those days and in their Polish-Jewish society, an arranged one. My mother was the second youngest of a family of eight children living in Przemysl, a garrison town in the Galician province of Poland on the river San, while my father was born in a nearby village called Mosciska. I never saw any of my grandparents – they had died in Poland before I first visited that country when I was twenty years old. My father's mother had died when he was very young and he had been brought up by one of his sisters who later moved to Budapest; another sister moved to Montevideo and thereafter the only communication between them was a very rare exchange of letters.

When I was born, my parents were living in Eastman's Court, an alley off Wentworth Street which was more popularly known as Petticoat Lane, or simply The Lane. Eastman's Court, demolished before the Second World War, consisted of a row of tiny, terraced cottages each with one room on the ground floor, one room on the first and a small yard at the back in which the outside lavatory was located. On the other side of the street, opposite Eastman's Court, stood 'The Buildings', otherwise the Wentworth Street Dwellings, and our flat there was the first home I remember. We must have moved there when I was about three and I imagine the reason for the move from Eastman's Court was that, by then, we were three children and more space was needed. It was not very much more because our home in The Buildings also contained no more than two rooms and a kitchen but the rooms were considerably larger.

The main attraction for me in our new home was what we called the playground which was the paved courtyard surrounding the buildings. Somebody had invented a nice little earner by acquiring a few small tricycles and hiring them out to the young denizens of the buildings and I recall happy summer afternoons and evenings careering about on my hired bike and only once crashing into the vehicle of a burly kid called Sammy Segal who thereupon attacked me – this was the only occasion I remember of a personal involvement in a violent encounter. Sammy remained burly into adolescence and adulthood. Years later we became friends when he joined the Young Sinaists, the Jewish youth group of which I was a co-founder. Like most of our group at the time, Sammy was keenly interested in cantorial music but, unlike the rest of us, he took it up as a vocation. Our childhood fracas was completely out of character because when I later knew him as a young adult, he was the quintessence of gentleness and I could not possibly imagine him assaulting anyone. He later became a professional cantor and was much loved by his congregation in Leeds; sadly, he died young.

Living in The Buildings did not necessarily indicate poverty – although it did in the case of my family. A number of my father's friends who owned apparently prosperous businesses in the Lane also lived there for it was very conveniently located for their work and it was also within a minute's walk of the Old Castle Street Synagogue which they all attended. An ascetic-looking Mr Gaber had a large shop selling fabrics in front of which was my father's stall. Mr Tepper, jolly and ruddy faced – his wife shared these characteristics to such an extent that she could have been his twin – was the proprietor of a shop selling kitchen utensils, an exciting place whose abundant and varied stock overflowed on to the pavement. Their flats were far more comfortably furnished than ours and their appurtenances, crockery, decorations and the like, were richer. We did possess basic furniture, a table, chairs and beds but they all looked as though they had been acquired second-hand and a few orange boxes served as occasional pieces.

One of my earliest recollections is connected with one of these orange boxes – I must have been three or four at the time. Heating was by means of an open fireplace and on this occasion there was a fire burning with coke or coal as the fuel. But the fire was low when my father came home, and he was cold and somewhat irritable. Making his displeasure vocal, he then threw one of the small boxes on the fire. The wood was bone dry and, within seconds, huge flames were shooting up the chimney which itself caught fire. Black smoke billowed into the room: my mother quickly herded her three boys into the passage outside while my father went in search of a fireman. Fortunately, our flat was not burned out and we continued to live there, but I do vividly recall my terror at this incident.

Neither we, nor anyone else I knew who lived in similar circumstances, possessed a bathroom. We washed at the kitchen sink and once a week, generally on a Friday, my brothers and I were taken by our father to the public baths in nearby Goulston Street. For tuppence we received a towel, a small tablet of soap and the use of a bath tub the water for which was controlled by an attendant from the outside of the cubicle. Customers tended to stay for long periods in the warmth and comfort of their baths and, when the water cooled off, would yell something like 'more hot water in number twelve please' and the attendant responded until requested to stop. On some occasions, my father would take us to Shevchik's Turkish bath in Brick Lane across the street from the Machzike Hadath Synagogue and, when we moved from the Lane, our pre-Sabbath bath took place at Mr Gimmack's bathing establishment in the Cannon Street Road which, as well as the bathrooms, included a *mikvah* (Jewish ritual bath) in which we three boys, sublimely unaware of its religious purpose, happily cavorted. These baths, too, were located within yards of a synagogue.

Petticoat Lane was re-named Middlesex Street in the mid-nineteenth century but the old and evocative label hung on. When that part of the East End became the heart of the Jewish ghetto, 'the Lane' was Wentworth Street, not Middlesex Street – except on Sundays. I remember, as a small child, standing with my father at his modest stall in Wentworth Street. Business never could be described as flourishing but my father did have an advantage over other stallholders who struggled as they transported and displayed their wares. His exiguous stock did not have to travel far for the stall was within a few yards of the entrance to Wentworth Street Buildings where we lived. Almost all the residents were immigrant Jews and it was, in a sense, a classless society the only distinction being between the observant Jews with whom we associated and the others with whom we did not.

The Lane slowly fell asleep on Friday afternoon. On Saturday the silence was close to being palpable as the village rested on the Jewish Sabbath. We woke with a thunderclap early Sunday morning when not only Wentworth Street but the whole surrounding area prepared for an invasion by, what seemed to me at the time, the total population of London. As a child I found the Sunday scene both colourful and frightening. What child could resist the turbaned vendor of Indian toffee and its sickly sweet smell? Itinerant purveyors of paregoric tablets promised a lifetime cure for every conceivable ailment while the impromptu auctions of clothes or china were a constant source of entertainment. But the size and the pressure of the crowd were disturbing.

*

Synagogue life in those early days was based on the sanctuary in Old Castle Street whose rituals were those of the Lubavitch sect. Its spiritual leader, when I became aware of such things, was Rabbi Shmuel Hillman who later was appointed a Dayan (a judge of the ecclesiastical court administered by the anglicised United Synagogue). One of his daughters, Sarah, married Isaac Herzog who became Chief Rabbi of Ireland and, later, of Israel. Rabbi Hillman was followed in the spiritual leadership of the Old Castle Street Synagogue by a slight, somewhat other-worldly rabbi by the name of Gutnick who, after a few years, left for Australia. But the real leader of the congregation was its *shammas* or beadle (today that would probably be translated as 'executive director') named Chaim Rapapport. He was a dynamo, constantly ordering people about (including the rabbi), dominating the services and, particularly, the meagre meal, known as the *shalosh seudah* (third meal, more accurately known as seudah *shlishit*) eaten between the afternoon service and the conclusion of the Sabbath. He would organise the seating, pass round what food and drink there was and lead, in his piercing husky voice, the singing of the *zemirot*. He also endeared himself to me by always having some sweets in his pocket which he would hand out to the children who pleased him.

There were literally dozens of small synagogues in our part of the East End and it was only in my teens that, with the help of my more sophisticated friends, I discovered the more anglicised and decorous of them. The most illustrious was the Spanish and Portuguese Synagogue in Bevis Marks, but since the Hebrew was differently pronounced and the content of the services also differed from the rituals to which I was accustomed, I seldom went there. The Great Synagogue in Duke's Place was the most prestigious of the stately and orderly houses of worship, constituents of the highly organised United Synagogue. Initially I would only go there, sometimes to wait fruitlessly in a queue, when a famous visiting cantor was leading the service. Later on in my teens I regularly attended the Friday evening services when the musical attractions provided by the reader and choir were augmented by a sermon from a visiting rabbi. The synagogue was officially the pulpit of the Chief Rabbi who, however, rarely attended. There was also the Hambro in Adler Street (named after a former Chief Rabbi) and, in the eastern fringe of the East End, the Stepney Green Synagogue where, it was rumoured, girls sang in the choir. My father would have thought that I had embarked on the road to conversion if I had told him I went there.

My mother saw to it that her sons were always adequately and neatly dressed though money must have been terribly short. Once a year, in the autumn days before the Jewish New Year, she would take us to a clothing shop in Bell Lane, a street off 'the Lane' in which the Jews' Free School was located, to buy us new suits, each consisting of a jacket and short trousers – in our society, long trousers were only worn after barmitzvah. Invariably, after the choice was made, there would be haggling over the prices, a process which took far longer than the selection of the clothes. The proceedings concluded when my mother, with her boys trailing her, walked out of the shop only to be recalled by Mr Laufer, the shopkeeper, who would then conclude the deal on terms acceptable to both parties to the transaction.

2

A Hasidic Childhood

My parents had come to London because my mother's eldest sister, Esther, was already settled there and married to Samuel Tym, a clothing manufacturer who had built up a successful business. My father, who had had no vocational training whatever and, as far as I could gather, was not particularly interested in any gainful occupation, was offered a job in his brother-in-law's factory, probably as an element of the dowry. He did not remain long in that employment. I was told that Tym was fond of my father but, recognising after their first year together that he was making no contribution to his enterprise, he provided some cash to enable him to set up in business on his own. The sum was, apparently, insufficient to acquire a shop so my father became a stallholder in Petticoat Lane from which he tried to sell boy's short trousers.

Petticoat Lane was, at that time, the centre of the London *shtetl* (Jewish village), the first home for the thousands of Jewish immigrants arriving from Eastern Europe at the end of the nineteenth and beginning of the twentieth centuries. The community they formed was sharply divided by religious attitudes but, nonetheless, the knowledge of their common background constituted a powerful link between them all. Its members were mostly street traders, artisans or small businessmen. A high proportion of the immigrants, detached from the norms of their homeland *shtetl*, were far less concerned with their Judaism than with earning a living. Those who did not study Torah, meticulously observe the Sabbath and attend synagogue regularly, rarely mixed with the orthodox Jews. And the observant Jews, among whom were my parents, had their own divisions based both on place of origin and sectional religious loyalties.

The major religious divide was between the Hasidim and the rest. Founded in Eastern Europe in the eighteenth century, the Hasidic movement was a revolt against rabbinic legalism, narrow intellectualism and spiritual aridity. The Hasidic teachers stressed joy, enthusiasm and humility in the search for God and that made a powerful appeal to the oppressed Jewish masses at the time. One of the great centres of the movement was my parents' Galicia: they were 'Galitzianers' as were nearly all their friends.

Each Hasidic community had its own spiritual leader, the *rebbe*, not to be confused with a rabbi who is essentially a teacher. The *rebbe* was not simply a teacher but a father figure, role model, saint and miracle worker who would advise his flock and intercede on their behalf with their Maker. The eldest son of the *rebbe*, deemed to be infused with the holiness of his father, succeeded him and dynasties were founded which persist to this day.

In the course of time, some of the dynasties debased the Hasidic ideal but all of them, the good and the flawed, had their loyal disciples who re-told, or invented, stories of the wonders and even miracles performed by their *rebbes*. I was brought up on those tales. I listened to them fascinated, though taking them no more or less seriously than the fairy stories in the books I regularly borrowed from the local free library before I moved on to science fiction. I may have been too sceptical. Martin Buber, who recorded Hasidic legends, quoted one teacher, Mendel of Rymanov, as having claimed that 'if a thousand believing Hasidim were to gather round a block of wood, it too would work miracles'.

To me, in my childhood, the appeal of the Hasidim was their

jollity. At that time, these very observant Jews were not performing their religious duties with the intensity and gloom which characterises right-wing orthodoxy at the present time. The many Hasidic services and other gatherings I attended in my youth were invariably enlivened by enthusiastic singing and dancing (not to mention drinking) at the slightest provocation. All these activities were, of course, exclusively male.

My father regarded himself as a Bobover Hasid owing allegiance to the *rebbe* of the Galician town of Bobov. There was, however, no *rebbe* bearing the Bobover title in the East End during the 1920s and the closest substitute was the Sassover *rebbe* who then held court at his modest conventicle in Settles Street which was situated in the isthmus of cramped houses, small shops and overpopulated tenements where the Whitechapel and Commercial Roads met at Gardiner's Corner. The Sassover *rebbe*, gentle and soft-spoken, died while still a young man − he had always looked otherworldly to me − and was succeeded by his eldest son who was about the same age as my older brother. My father maintained his loyalty to the House of Sassov and we continued to visit but the magic created for me by the mystical figure of the real *rebbe*, as I always thought of him, had departed.

My father was short, tending to plumpness as he grew older, and I particularly remember his, only partially successful, efforts to hide his pleasure when, as was often the case, someone referred to his resemblance to King George V. Mother was equally short but slight and kept her hair in a neat bun. Most of the time she wore an all-enveloping apron and, on the rare occasions when she left the house for a visit of some kind, changed into one of the very few dresses she possessed. I never saw any signs of affection or tenderness between my parents nor do I recall their ever addressing each other by their first or pet names. I myself do not remember ever being kissed or hugged by them; shows of affection were apparently not practised in their own families and they did to their children as was done to them. That is not to say that my two brothers – Benjamin and Hyman – and I were not loved; the atmosphere must have been such that we never had any doubt that we were. My parents went through life performing the roles which their traditions and upbringing had allotted to them. My father was the breadwinner, though he was never particularly good at it, while my mother ran the house and brought up the children.

Her duties were far more demanding than his. She did everything that would now be performed by a full-time nanny, maid, cleaner and cook. In addition, she conducted the family's correspondence such as it was (her handwriting, in Yiddish, German or English, was copperplate) and attended her children's schools whenever a parental intervention was necessary. My father did his work and spent much of his spare time in the synagogue and with his circle of Hasidic Jews at the usually dingy 'courts' of some of the Hasidic *rebbes* in East London. His recreation from these activities was an occasional card game with a few cronies. That particular game was called 'sixty-six' but we always referred to it by its Yiddish name '*zeks und zechzig*'. My mother, on the rare opportunities when she had the time, read English novels (she had taught herself to read the language) and, when the cash position was easier than usual, she would see a play at one of the Yiddish theatres which then existed in the East End.

The main Yiddish theatres were the Pavilion in Whitechapel Road and the Grand Palais which was close to Gardiner's Corner. Gardiner's, a large store which nobody I ever knew could afford to patronise, gave its name to one of the major road junctions of the East End where Aldgate High Street met Commercial Street, Commercial Road, Leman Street and Whitechapel Road. Sometimes Mother would take me with her to see a play and, as best as I can recall, all the plots were essentially the same – the tensions between parents and children, a subject of unceasing interest to Jewish mothers and fathers – and generally crudely produced tragedies or comedies.

I recall the excitement when my rich cousin, Joe Tym, visited our slum house. A car enthusiast, he would always arrive in an expensive, and often new, automobile. Other than this the only adventure was the annual school excursion for a day to such exotic retreats as Chingford or Theydon Bois in Epping Forest. I do not recall ever taking part in the competitive games which constituted the programme on these outings and the most interesting elements for me were the class walk to Fenchurch Street Station under the eyes of the teachers and the subsequent train ride.

These were the only train rides I ever took as a child. For a few years after I reached the age of eleven, I did travel by train to Southend to spend a day with my mother and Aunt Esther who would be staying for a week or two at a kosher hotel in Westcliff, the more genteel end of working-class Southend-on-Sea. While there they did no sightseeing or engage in any other form of entertainment – their holiday was simply a relief from the drudgery of their daily lives and it was made possible by the generosity of my cousin Joe.

It was only when I moved schools at the age of eleven that I made my first Gentile friends for during my early childhood, English life hardly touched me. There were the Gentile cleaning women who came in to scrub after we had reached the financial heights to afford one. There were the 'goyim' I heard roistering as I hastily passed a pub and I knew a few friendly non-Jewish neighbours who came into the house to turn out the lights on a Friday evening, since orthodox Jews were not permitted to perform this task on the Sabbath. But that was about all. The Hasidic world of the East End was not quite the same as that of the *shtetl* in '*der heim*' (the homeland), but London's Hasidim still maintained the clannishness, warmth and joy characteristic of the original.

There was always an ambivalence in our family regarding birthdays. My brothers and I were growing up in a culture, of which we were learning in our schools and from reading, in which birthdays were occasions for parties, greeting cards and presents. In my family these things did not happen, possibly because that was the way things were in Poland or it may have been a way of avoiding expenditure. As we grew older, we did feel somewhat deprived at the absence of any celebration of our birthdays – the English date, of course. But my father was unenthusiastic, seeing this as an expression of assimilation and, when the subject arose, he would refer to the Hebrew dates only. My birthday, he insisted, was the 11th day of the Hebrew month of Shevat. But, with the one exception when I was given a child's tricycle, I did not receive any presents on either the Hebrew or English dates.

My own children and I inhabited the same kind of world. We spoke the same language, even though the values and attitudes it was employed to express were likely to differ radically and certainly offered fertile soil for disagreement. We read more or less the same literature and enjoyed the same kind of films, radio and television. We attended similar schools and learned similar things at them. Not so the relationship I had with my parents with whom my brothers and I had nothing in common except family affection. Our parents did not speak the same language, they had little idea of the subjects we were being taught at school and of the life offered to their children in the tolerant and open society into which we had been born.

They knew they could not direct us on specifics and so avoided the almost inevitable hostile reaction when parents are so misguided (as they generally are) in offering unsolicited advice to their adolescent children. All that my father hoped for was that I would become a good and observant Jew and that, somehow, I would earn a living. My mother who was not passionate about religion, tried to teach us to be decent people.

She ran an orthodox Jewish home and attended synagogue on the major Jewish festivals but was scornful of those who appeared to be too good or too pious. I think I inherited that characteristic.

Within their extremely limited means, my parents did not deny their children anything of importance. But what was important? That issue came up when my elementary school offered its pupils the opportunity to learn to play the violin and I was anxious to take advantage of it. But the violin was going to cost fifteen shillings and the lessons sixpence a week. I think my mother would have gone for it but my father regarded music as unimportant and vetoed the idea. If I had wanted the fifteen shillings for some specifically Jewish purpose, I have no doubt he would have found a way to help. Who knows? If his decision had been otherwise, I might have given Heifetz a run for his money!

My mother was gentle and soft-spoken and the most frequent of the references made about her was that she was a 'lady'. On rare occasions when she was deeply distressed, she would unobtrusively and softly weep and never did I hear her raise her voice in anger. She regarded it as the natural order of things that she should personally undertake every bit of the household work. I never saw my father perform any domestic activity, nor did we, her three sons. We were never asked to assist in the washing up, for instance, or in the serving of meals or in making our beds. The most we were expected to do was occasionally to run to the corner grocery shop to buy some necessaries. The most regular of these, as I recall, were broken biscuits – they were much cheaper than the unbroken variety and tasted just the same! I doubt that my mother had ever read a cookery book or followed a written recipe but, nonetheless, her culinary repertoire was delectable albeit limited. Our menus were pretty standard. Midweek lunches (all three boys came home from school for lunch) were generally a bowl of soup with lots of bread followed by something like pot roast or, as a special treat, *kreplach*, a kind of ravioli. The summer diet included a variety of dairy foods. One of the visible signs of summer was a row of glasses of milk standing on a shelf or windowsill each covered with neatly folded scraps of newspaper. A glass of cool sour milk on a warm day was refreshing as well as nutritious.

But as far as cuisine was concerned, the whole of the working week was only a prelude to the Sabbath meals which began with Friday night supper. We invariably accompanied our father to the evening synagogue service welcoming the Sabbath which was less of a bore than usual since it was short and generally enlivened by good singing. The house looked different when we returned, for the room which served as our kitchen, dining room and living room had been transformed. The table was covered with a white cloth and illumined by the Sabbath candles in glittering candlesticks, two made of silver and two of brass. Two ceremonial loaves of bread, covered with an embroidered cloth, were placed before my father's chair together with a carafe of mother's homemade non-alcoholic raisin wine.

The ritual never changed and the combination of the food, the blessings and the sung *zemirot* (table hymns) exuded a sense of confidence that the world was a good place, that the family was united and that we were following an old and colourful tradition which was superior to anything around us. Then came the food and the menu was similarly unchanging – chopped herring or chopped liver followed by chicken soup which contained the thinnest of *lokshen*, vermicelli, the making of which was an art. I used to watch fascinated as my mother prepared this delicacy. She made the dough and then rolled it out to such a thinness as to raise fears that it would tear when lifted. Amazingly it did not. The sheet was then rolled into a tube which was flattened and sliced with great rapidity into the thinnest of strands. My parents had told us that in their Polish-Jewish environment one of the most telling tests of a good potential housewife was her ability to cut thin *lokshen*. My mother passed that test with honours. The rest of the meal tended to be an anticlimax for the next course was the boiled fowl from which the soup had been made and which was therefore tasteless, supplemented with similarly overcooked vegetables. Finally the dessert was invariably some fruit compote, usually stewed apples.

Some of my earliest recollections centre on visits to the *rebbe* with my father after we had finished our Friday night meal. My mother never joined us on these occasions for Hasidic society was exclusively male and any women who insisted on attending were confined to a remote corner of the room and concealed behind an emphatically opaque curtain. My brother Ben and I (Hyman was too young), each holding one of our father's hands, would push our way into the over-filled, shabbily furnished and usually foetid room of which the focal point was the *rebbe* sitting at the head of a long table, wearing a *streimel* (a velvet cap trimmed with fur, the celebratory headgear of the Hasidic elite) and shimmering long silk coat.

The disciples wore their Sabbath best. The de rigueur outer garment was a shabby, Edwardian, dandy-style frock coat pronounced 'frackot' by the Yiddish speaking congregation, or sometimes abbreviated to 'frack'. Like the *rebbe*, a few dressed in a long silk coat, which looked like a dressing gown, and wore a *streimel*, but most heads were covered with black *yarmulkes* (skullcaps). Since orthodox Jews are not permitted to carry anything on the Sabbath (that was regarded as work), my father did not carry his *yarmulke* in his pocket but wore it on his head en route covered by his bowler hat.

Some Hasidim had succumbed to a measure of acculturation and, like my father, had taken to wearing suits. But all the adult males had, tied about their waists, a black silken plaited cord, long enough to cover the circuit two or three times and secured by tucking it in, not by knotting. There must have been some reason for this procedure which I may have known at the time but it escapes me now. This girdle, in Yiddish *gartel*, divided the lower (carnal) part of the body from the upper half in which the heart and mind were located and was a symbolic separation of the profane from the sacred.

My father's arrival in the *stibl* or small house of prayer (literally, little room), was invariably spotted by one or other of the Hasidim in attendance on the *rebbe* and he would be ushered to a respectable place at the table. By the time of our arrival, there was very little food to be seen there other than ends of the twisted challah loaves or some uninviting remains of boiled chicken or salted herring. The *rebbe* kept a food plate before him from which he would, from time to time, extract morsels with his fingers and give them to honoured guests. To share the *rebbe*'s food was an act akin to communion.

Children were left to hunt for some kind of refreshment during the proceedings. There was not much food about at the best of times. The *rebbe* was sustained by the gifts of the faithful and they rarely possessed the means to provide more than the necessities for a, generally large, family. We children might be given occasional nibbles of food but, more often than not, our hunger as the long evening wore on was relieved by delicious salted chickpeas that must have been cheap because they were plentiful. The thirst they created was assuaged by lemonade and, when that ran out, water.

But the event which made the evening so enjoyable was the singing. The Hasidim were ready, at the drop of a skullcap, to throw themselves into boisterous renderings of Hebrew table hymns and, occasionally, Yiddish songs with a religious theme. Those blessed with strong voices waited to be begged to sing and, overcoming their seemly hesitation, then performed a liturgical musical solo.

These arias were often those which had achieved popularity by being recorded. The great cantors of the day, most of whom had by then emigrated to the 'golden land' of the United States, were the pop stars of that milieu. Their records, on some of the best-known labels in the industry, were international best sellers and in the East End their distribution was a lucrative business for Levy's record store across the road from Aldgate East station. The earliest luxury I can recall in my parents' home was a hand-wound gramophone, the gift of Joe Tym, and our first records were of cantors like Rosenblatt, Chagi, Kwartin and Sirota.

But it was not all singing on Friday nights. Alternating with the jollity was the boredom of listening to the *rebbe*'s homilies, in Yiddish, of course. What was said was clearly well above the heads of the children and I missed these irrecoverable opportunities to gain spiritual and intellectual inspiration.

3

Beyond the Lane

My father, as I have indicated, was not cut out to be a businessman. His first attempt on his own, the stall in Petticoat Lane,
was a failure and so he turned to the only area in which he had
experience and expertise, the synagogue. He became the
shammas and collector of the weekly membership subscriptions
for a small synagogue in Sander Street, a short thoroughfare
which ran parallel with Commercial Road linking Berner
Street and Back Church Lane. In the courtyard of the synagogue stood a tiny cottage, the 'tied' residence of the *shammas*
and his family. So we moved there, for the first time out of the
familiar and friendly environment of Petticoat Lane. The
cottage had, it seemed, never been adequately maintained and
the roof leaked. On one occasion the rainfall into the single
bedroom on the first floor in which we all slept was so heavy
that Mother wrapped up her three small boys and we all moved
into the ladies' gallery of the synagogue until the cottage roof
was patched up and we could return to our 'home'. Our move
not only brought us nearer to the Sassover establishment
(although by this time the Sassover *rebbe* had died), but also into
the catchment area of a newly arrived Hasidic *rebbe* who had set
up practice in a converted public house in Umberston Street,
near the Jewish market in Hessel Street, and within five
minutes' walk of our new home.

That opened up fresh vistas. The newcomer, the Przemyslaner *rebbe* (another Galician *shtetl*, nothing to do with my

parents' town of Przemysl), was a more earthy figure than had been the saintly Sassover. What was more, he had a flock of engaging children with whom my brothers and I could play in the spacious ex-pub, or in the street if something was going on inside. However, what established an almost familial, intimate relationship between the Frankels and the Przemyslaner clan was the *rebbe*'s *shammas*, Reb Mordche Leib.

When, a number of years later, I began to practise at the Bar, I immediately identified my relationship with that formidable and invaluable functionary, the barrister's clerk. He was my *shammas*. A barrister, precluded from advertising or hobnobbing with solicitors, his only possible clients, must rely on his clerk to establish a connection with them and to take care of all the mundane necessities like the collection of fees. Similarly, the *rebbe* was dependent on his *shammas* for the practicalities of life. The *shammas* was not only the major-domo at all public appearances of the *rebbe*, he was the organiser of the household, the collector of the contributions, the marriage broker for the children and everybody's friend and confidant.

Mordche Leib was all of these things and more. Tall, good-looking, black beard neatly trimmed, smartly dressed, he was the mainstay of the Umberston Street ménage. Because he was a *landsman* – his Galician *shtetl* was close to those of my parents – he was a frequent visitor to our home and a particular favourite of my mother. She enjoyed his gossip and his wit and was ever hospitable, providing unlimited glasses of tea with slabs of her delicious yeast cake, even occasionally going so far as to dispense more substantial fare, despite the poverty of the house.

We made infrequent sorties to the *stibls* of other Hasidic *rebbes* in the area. The Trisker *rebbe*, who lived in a more prosperous neighbourhood than most, not far from the Pavilion Yiddish Theatre, was the most imposing. A tall, well-built and impressive figure, his discourses, though as incomprehensible to me as those of his colleagues with which I was more familiar, nonetheless held my attention because they were always delivered with authority and without the diffidence and hesitations I sometimes recognised in the pronouncements of the Sassover and Przemyslaner *rebbes*. But it is possible that I formed that favourable impression because the food there tended to be more ample than elsewhere.

The Kotzker r*ebbe* was at the other end of the economic spectrum in his down-at-heel premises near Truman's brewery in Brick Lane. A colourful character, he achieved some notoriety after making an exaggerated war damage claim and, before the war, when he accused the *Jewish Daily Post* of libel.

That English-language newspaper, which had a brief but lively life, came into existence in the 1930s when the impact of Hitler and the rise of his British counterpart, Sir Oswald Mosley, had deepened Jewish apprehensions. There were already two Jewish newspapers published in the East End but they were both in Yiddish. For the more acculturated, the main source for Jewish news was the weekly *Jewish Chronicle*. It could not have had a large circulation in the East End but the copy displayed in the newspaper section of the Whitechapel Public Library was always surrounded by a dense pack of readers. The *Jewish Daily Post* came into existence to give the non-Yiddishists the same daily news service as was available to their parents in *Die Zeit* or *Express* and it occupied a splendid office in Whitechapel High Street. Above the door was a bronze coat of arms which, many decades later, was still to be seen over a shop front next to what was a notable East End institution, Bloom's kosher restaurant.

The *Jewish Daily Post* never had the remotest chance of survival. It lost money from the beginning and, in a panic bid to attract readers, began to publish stories of real or suspected scandals. And one of them was a lurid description of the alleged indiscretions of the Kotzker *rebbe* in the neighbourhood of

Piccadilly. The *rebbe* sued but, since publicity would have reflected badly on the Jewish community at a troubled time, the parties agreed to arbitration.

Neville Laski, KC., then President of the Board of Deputies of British Jews and a distinguished barrister, was the arbitrator and he found in favour of the *rebbe*. The paper, which was foundering financially, could not possibly pay the damages and went into liquidation. Had the *rebbe* recovered his award, he might possibly have been spared the later encounter with the law over his war damage claim which led to his precipitate departure to the United States.

It restored one's faith in Hasidic leadership to meet the Bialer *rebbe* who lived quite close to our Sander Street home. He struck me, even as a child, as an individual set apart from our mundane lives for he radiated piety and accepted without question an existence of utter poverty. Unlike some of his colleagues, he seemed totally innocent about money matters which may have been either the reason for, or the consequence of, the absence in his household of a masterful *shammas*.

The Dzikover *stibl* in Dunk Street off Brick Lane was a Hasidic synagogue for disciples of the rabbinic clan from the Polish *shtetl* of Dzikov and it was without a *rebbe* – none of its legitimate representatives had settled in London. The followers of the absent *rebbe* had nonetheless acquired premises for a synagogue and the atmosphere there was always cheerfully chaotic. On rare occasions, the *rebbe* came on a state visit from Poland to bring good cheer to his followers and collect their dues. These were always occasions for frenzied shenanigans.

A stranger looking in at a service at the Dzikover *stibl* would have regarded the exuberant scene with bewilderment for it was unlike any other place of worship with which he might have been familiar. Every worshipper, when not talking to or arguing loudly with his neighbour, would be engaged in private supplication, his body weaving and bending, arms often raised, assertively demanding the personal attention of his Maker. Before the Ark stood a lectern for the use of the individual who was formally leading the prayers. He could be seen swaying, wreathed in his large *tallith* (prayer shawl) but his words were totally lost in the tumult.

Most of the worshippers were impecunious immigrants who must have found the seedy *stibl* a welcome alternative to the insalubrious tenements in nearby Old Montague Street or Flower and Dean Street in which they lived. Some earned a pittance as small traders or peddlers and one I knew followed the dual occupations of Hebrew teacher and vendor of tickets for the Irish Sweepstake.

What now would be called (at least in America) the sanctuary served all purposes. It was the synagogue, classroom and dining room, for communal eating and drinking were staples of Hasidic life. Almost every Sabbath service ended with a blessing recited over a glass of whisky which would have been donated by one of the more prosperous congregants to mark a family event or anniversary. The traditional *shalosh seudah* was the highlight of the week. The celebrants sat around a table set on one side of the synagogue before a meagre repast consisting of salt herring usually eaten with a dry egg biscuit and washed down with lemonade. If any whisky was left after the morning service, it was finished off then.

But the focus of the meal was neither the food nor the drink but the rousing and companionable singing of *zemirot* and liturgical pieces. Of all the impressions that remain of my Hasidic childhood, none is fresher or more abiding than the memories of the Dzikover *stibl*. The small conventicle in Dunk Street knew nothing of parish pump politics or the ambitions of office seekers or, if it did, I was happily in ignorance of these blemishes of religious life. In those days of innocence, it seemed to me the place where good, pious but poor Jews served their Lord with gladness.

In a cheerfully disorganised congregation like the Dzikover there were bound to be endless entertaining anecdotes. The one that comes most readily to mind is the occasion when an affluent member of the congregation – there were a few – wanted to give one of his sons the experience of a ministry before deciding to take up the profession. There was, as far as I can recall, no committee or board which ran the synagogue. It seemed to me that the few individuals who had gained the respect of the majority of the congregants made the decisions. In this case, the powers-that-were had agreed to the request of the father but limited the functions of the son to the recital of the only prayer that was read in English, that for the Royal Family. It was not recited at the daily prayers but was limited to the Sabbath and festival services and began with the words, 'He who giveth salvation unto Kings ...' The young man was thereafter only referred to in the congregation as 'Der Hee Hoo'.

*

Sander Street, to which we had moved from Petticoat Lane and which no longer exists, was no more than a hundred yards in length, probably less, and its population was completely Jewish. Along one side of the street was a brick wall, either a factory wall or the backs of shops on Commercial Road. The wall was very useful for the resident children who used it for ball games and, during Passover, for pitching nuts, a popular item of the Passover diet, in some sort of contest. The other side of the street consisted of a row of cottages each comprising one room on the ground floor and another on the first, a basement kitchen and small backyard. The synagogue was the outstanding edifice of the short thoroughfare, and a grocery shop stood on the corner with Back Church Lane – but this was more than a shop. It was the social and welfare centre of the immediate vicinity and was presided over by a large and good-natured lady named Mrs Bloom. Mrs Bloom's was tiny but crammed with groceries from floor to ceiling. Commodities like sugar, rice and barley were kept in sacks and sales were weighed on scales which stood on the counter. Prunes and other dried fruits came in sticky blocks, as did salt which had to be scraped before being sold.

Running over to Mrs Bloom's early in the morning before leaving for school was a treat for the purpose then would be to buy some fresh rolls, light and crisp. That was also something of an extravagance because rolls cost more than bread and yesterday's bread had to be finished so that these jaunts were not too frequent. Milk was also sold at the grocery (as it was invariably called) where it was poured out of a milk churn into a saucepan brought by the customer.

But we rarely bought milk there. Our milk was brought to our house daily by our orthodox Jewish milkman whose piety ensured that his product had not been in contact with anything that might make it unkosher. He was *Mordche der Milchiger*, Mordecai the Milk, who played a double role in our lives. Six days a week he would come to our door with his horse and cart which carried milk churns and with a ladle would dispense some pints of milk into my mother's utensil. She would immediately take the purchase to the gas stove and boil the milk to avoid it going sour since, I need hardly mention, we did not possess anything like a refrigerator or even ice box. In his other life, on Sabbaths and festivals, our milkman was the *Baal Koreh* (reader of the appropriate passage from the parchment Torah scrolls) at the Dzikover *stibl*. He was a better milkman.

Wherever we lived, the door of our home was always hospitably open. Coming back from school, there always seemed to be someone in the kitchen/living room keeping my mother company. The visitors (the conversation with them was in Yiddish) would usually be recent arrivals from my parents'

Galician area of southern Poland. They were either immigrants who had not yet settled in and were looking for an occupation and somewhere to live, or emissaries collecting for impoverished Jewish institutions in that part of the world. There would always be a welcome and a glass of tea for them in our house.

One of the favourite and most frequent of these guests was a wiry gentleman named Noosan Abramovitch who was often with us for Sabbath meals when we were favoured with his rendition of *zemirot* and cantorial selections. His enthusiasm was not matched by his voice, the chief characteristic of which was its penetrative quality. During the Jewish High Holydays he found employment as a cantor either in a small provincial synagogue which did not possess a permanent staff or at the overflow service of one of the London congregations. For the rest of the year he tried his hand at a variety of occupations.

I particularly remember his foray into the world of wine making. He had installed a large tin washtub in his lodgings and there he concocted a beverage which he then bottled and tried to sell. He called his product *echter Ungarischer Tokay* – real Hungarian Tokay – and, at his request, I designed a label for his bottles. I thought I did rather well in applying my minuscule knowledge of lettering and typography to produce a label which looked, or so I thought, quite professional.

It was during our sojourn in Sander Street that my reading began with comics, obtained second-hand because we children, at that stage, did not receive any regular pocket money, just a penny or two when we made an appeal to one of our parents. It is probably an exaggeration to say that thus began my reading because the comics, with names like *Chips* and *Funny Wonder*, consisted mainly of crudely coloured strips with the minimum of explanatory words. When I grew out of the these I moved on to the *Boys' Magazine* and the *Magnet* which contained tales of public school life and characters like Billy Bunter. I devoured these stories, particularly because they presented an upper-class

English life-style which could not have been more removed from that in which I was living.

Father gradually moved up the job ladder and his last appointment was at the Artillery Lane Synagogue, an imposing building topped by a lofty dome, not far from Petticoat Lane and close to Bishopsgate. By then we had moved from Sander Street to 29 Well Street, a narrow, terraced house comprising four rooms, one on each floor, and a basement (an extended coal cellar which became my play room). The ground floor was the kitchen/living room behind which, in a tiny backyard, was the outside lavatory. My widowed Aunt Esther, my mother's sister, occupied the first floor room. She was living with us because she did not want to live with either of her two sons and hated living on her own. Once a month she would walk to the Whitechapel Road premises of S. & J.H. Tym and collect her monthly allowance which, on her return to our house, she would share with my mother, in what proportion I do not know.

The second floor was my parents' bedroom – in which my younger brother also slept – while my older brother and I shared the attic. Climbing to the top of that house was strenuous but reaching the attic induced a sense of well being, of being cut off from the world, for few would climb that height for an inconsequential purpose.

Unlike Sander Street which had been completely Jewish, Well Street had a mix of residents of whom Jews were a minority. It was a pretty rough area. The dockers and labourers who lived there spent many of their evenings in the pub and quite often we would hear the sounds of fighting and, after the pubs had closed, there would be the screaming which accompanied conjugal quarrelling. Nor were the local Jews our type, all of them being un-religious. But there was an exception – Mrs Newman who ran the grocery shop. Like Mrs Bloom's grocery, Mrs Newman's shop became a second home. She was a gentle lady, always kind and solicitous to my mother and respectful of our religious way of life though she was not particularly observant herself.

*

Some time before the Second World War, both the Przemysl-aner and the Sassover *rebbes* followed their upwardly mobile flock to the greener pastures of north-west London. They and their families undoubtedly lived there more comfortably than they had in the East End but, with their departure, the White-chapel *shtetl* virtually came to an end.

My father remained the *shammas* of the Artillery Lane Synagogue for many years – the man who really ran the show though acting deferentially to the Honorary Officers who thought they did. When the East End was subjected to the ordeal of almost nightly bombing and much of the population was evacuated, the then rabbi of the synagogue invited my father to join him in a business. The rabbi had made the acquaintance of a young refugee from Austria who knew how to make zip bags, a novel product in those times. The three of them rented premises on the ground floor of a small building in Cobb Street, off Wentworth Street, and set up a factory for the manufacture of these bags. It did well and, for the first time in his life, my father's income warranted the payment of income tax. He was not in the least discomfited by this. To him, as he often explained, paying income tax was a recognition of achievement and, he would add, '*eppes bleibt*', something remains. I always regarded my father with respect rather than with the affection I so deeply felt for my mother. Nor did I see him as a role model. But there is one characteristic that I think I inherited from him, for I have always shared his attitude to the payment of income tax.

When the business became so successful that it had to move to new and larger premises, my father's two partners decided that he would not fit in with the new arrangements and he was unceremoniously removed from the partnership. It hit him badly and he never really recovered. Shortly after this disaster, in 1946, my mother had a stroke and died at the age of fifty-six. It was the first time since childhood that I wept. My brothers and I were all in our early teens and our mother in her forties when she had her first hospital sojourn after a coronary thrombosis and I vividly remember my sense of desolation when she was taken away in an ambulance. She was never strong and healthy but almost to the last continued the labours which had ground her down. My father spent the remaining years of his life in a one-room apartment in the Home for Aged Jews in Nightingale Lane, Clapham, where he was extremely happy. He knew a number of his fellow residents and took a daily interest in the synagogue on the premises. He died there, peacefully, in his sleep.

4

Schools

The first school I attended was the Jews' Free Infants, a minor, very minor, adjunct of the important Jews' Free School in Bell Lane, just a few minutes walk from our home in 'the Lane'. The short walk from my home to school involved passing Ostwind's, then the premier Jewish bakery in the East End which housed a popular tea room upstairs. To this day I can recall the fragrance of the freshly baked bread and the sight of the heaped luscious cakes and pastries. For two hours after school on four days a week as well as on Sunday mornings I went to *heder* but I found the curriculum, the mechanical translation from the Hebrew into English of the Pentateuch and the Prayer Book, completely uninspiring.

While in the Infants School I was selected to light the Hanukkah candles at a ceremony which was attended by the then Chief Rabbi, Dr J.H. Hertz. He was a squat figure with a bushy square beard and I have a mental picture of him sitting upright on his chair enduring the proceedings. After I had lit the candles and recited the Hebrew blessings, I was taken to this imposing figure who put his hand on my head, said that I had done well or words to that effect, and prophesied that one day I would be the Chief Rabbi. I reminded Dr Hertz of this incident many years later when we had become good friends, but, alas, he had no recollection of it at all.

Our family had moved to Sander Street at the age when I was due to leave the infants school for a proper boys' school.

Two boys' elementary schools, Fairclough Street (the East End pronunciation was Fairclow) and Berner Street were close by; the latter was my parents' choice.

Berner Street School was a Victorian brick building, gloomy and damp, set in a spacious playground. Mr Murphy, our tall, gaunt headmaster, conducted morning assemblies in the large hall. Pupils – most of them Jewish – were grouped class by class under the surveillance of their master (male teachers were called masters, the females – there were none at boys' schools – were teachers). These morning assemblies took the form of a non-denominational religious service after which we moved to our large and lofty classrooms and started the series of lessons which went on until lunch. That was before the era of school meals and, since all the boys lived in the surrounding streets only a few minutes walk from the school, we all went home for lunch. Then came the afternoon session and blessed relief at about four. Because the Jewish Sabbath began at sunset on Friday evening, we only had to attend a morning session that day during the winter months, called, why I do not know, a double-session. The school closed for the Jewish festivals.

The male teachers were all figures of authority, respected and sometimes feared for the cane was never far away. Indiscipline in the classroom was consequently a rare occurrence and the boys were able to give vent to their natural exuberance only when in the playground. Most played organised games like football and sometimes cricket; the others just loped around, watched or chattered among themselves. I was in the latter category. Sports were never my thing and it was only in later life that, primarily under the influence of my son, I acquired an interest in cricket, purely as a spectator.

I made a few friends at Berner Street school, the closest being Max Caplin, a member of a large family living in Langdale Mansions, a small tenement building nearby. Max and his siblings were unusual in that they were always neatly dressed, well spoken and ambitious. We parted at the age of eleven when the examination we all took at that age, called the 11 plus, sorted us into streams. The brightest were selected for grammar schools and destined for university and the professions. The dullest continued in elementary schools until the leaving age, which was then fifteen, and they could be expected to become artisans or unskilled workers. Those who were neither one nor the other were sent to central schools which prepared them for desk jobs, the educational emphasis at these schools being on bookkeeping, shorthand and typewriting.

Max Caplin was clearly in the top category and duly left Berner Street for a grammar school. I did not do so well and was classified as only of central school quality. My older brother Ben had done no better in the 11 plus and so I did not really feel too badly about my mediocre performance. Max and I went our separate ways and I only caught up with him again many decades later when he was a distinguished physician and I was the Editor of *The Jewish Chronicle*.

The school to which I was sent in 1928 was St George's-in-the-East Central School in Cable Street and, since that was on the border of the Jewish ghetto and the non-Jewish area of Wapping, its population was about equally divided between Jews and Gentiles. Moreover, to add to the sense of strangeness to me (for at that time I had not really talked to any non-Jewish contemporaries), the school was co-educational and, since I had no sisters and had never before had any girl friends, this was also a novel experience. At first I was not at ease with the girls in my class and formed no friendships with any of them A year or two later, there was one girl, Rachel, on whom I had a crush, but I never gave her any indication of my feelings, nor do I recall ever talking to her.

The school building was in the same style as Berner Street but the distinguishing feature was that its hall was dominated by a large mural of St George on his steed lunging with a huge spear at the drippingly open-jawed dragon beneath him. Pupils remained at the Cable Street School, as it was generally referred to, for only four years and, during that period, were under the general control of what would be called elsewhere a form master or mistress. Unlike the elementary school, different subjects were taught by different teachers. I had the good fortune to be in the class of Mrs Fels, a sprightly and vivacious lady, at that time probably in her forties, who taught with such enthusiasm as to inspire all but her most vapid pupils. Jewish and living in the Hampstead Garden Suburb, she did more than teach; she was interested in those of her charges she thought possessed some promise and I was fortunate enough to be considered by her to be in that category.

In addition to being the form mistress, she taught English language and literature. She tried to teach us the rules of grammar but I was never clear about such things as past participles and, though I was reasonably smart in recognising an adjective, I was not so happy with adverbs. When set the task of analysing sentences, the same mental block assailed me that invariably came into play during shorthand lessons. I think part of the cause was that Mrs Fels was not herself particularly interested in the nuts and bolts of the language but only in the richness of the finished product.

Mrs Fels gave me an inkling of life outside the ghetto. Just before my first Christmas at Cable Street School she invited me and one or two others to see a performance of *Peter Pan* at the Scala Theatre which was on or close to Tottenham Court Road. I was dazzled by this first venture into the English theatre for the only theatrical performances I had previously experienced were those at the Yiddish playhouses in the East End. Never before had I seen a professional and enchanting theatrical performance with props, scenery, effects and convincing acting. When we were taken to tea at a Lyons café after the show, I remember that I sat tongue-tied, totally bemused by what I had just experienced.

On a couple of occasions, she invited her selected small group to her house and I observed the luxury in which the other half lived. By the time I began attending Cable Street School, we were living in Well Street not far from the London Docks' area. Mrs Fels' house in Thornton Way, Hampstead Garden Suburb was, by comparison, a palace. It was large and detached, there were separate rooms for dining, lounging and sleeping, and there were bathrooms too as well as a fragrant garden. The only house I had previously known with its own bathroom was that of my cousin Joe Tym, who lived in Stamford Hill. Since I did not know him at all well and only visited on rare occasions when I accompanied his mother, my Aunt Esther, his house seemed to me more like a museum than a place where people lived. But Mrs Fels' house was a proper lived-in home and she was a real person who talked to me and was interested in me.

Her house and the theatre were not the only taste she gave me of life outside the ghetto. In the classroom she also introduced me to poetry and literature way beyond what the syllabus demanded. Mrs Fels was not beautiful, nor sexy, but she radiated joy particularly when, eyes closed in ecstasy and sitting on the edge of the teacher's table, she recited a poem. She possessed that un-English characteristic of enthusiasm which I found infectious and later in life when I read *Howards End* I identified her with the novel's character, Helen Schlegel, who was only half English. It was Mrs Fels who encouraged me to sit for the supplementary examination which gave another chance for a place in a secondary school to those who had been unsuccessful in the 11 plus. Without her interest I do believe that I would have risen no higher than an office help.

I was fortunate enough to have another teacher at Cable Street School who stimulated the small stirring of ambition I was beginning to feel. He was Abraham Wiener, known by all the school as Tubby Wiener for obvious reasons, and he was our history teacher. Tubby was born in Tredegar, Monmouthshire, one of the small Jewish communities which used to exist in Wales and which are no more. They somehow managed to retain a deep Jewish consciousness and produced many outstanding figures in the Anglo-Jewish community.

Tubby Wiener possessed the degree of Master of Arts and was, I think, the only member of the school staff to have been to university. Clearly he was over-qualified for the job. I was told later that he had been a lecturer in history at King's College London but had been dismissed during the First World War because he was a conscientious objector. He taught other classes German which was the second language offered at the school, rather than the more usual French, because the large proportion of Jewish students were thought to have a head start in German through their knowledge of Yiddish. His teaching of history was uninspiring, consisting in the main of his reading out aloud at dictation speed from a book listing dates and events.

Tubby was very knowledgeable on Anglo-Jewish history and had written on the subject. He must have found in me a kindred spirit for there was no other Jewish boy in our class as connected with synagogue life as I was. I recall one occasion when Tubby asked a question and one of my non-Jewish fellow pupils offered an inadequate answer. Tubby addressed himself to me in Hebrew, '*va tiftach adoshem es pi ha-osson*' (and God opened the mouth of the ass – from the Balaam story in the Book of Genesis). 'Frankel,' he said, 'tell him later what it means.' At the time I knew him he was a widower and lived in a spacious, but by no means affluent, flat on Southampton Row where I visited him from time to time after leaving Cable Street School. I met both his daughters, one a literary agent and the other an author, both successful in their occupations.

These two teachers were the real benefits I received from the

Cable Street School for I did not take to the vocational subjects that were taught. I did not need to learn typewriting because I had long had the use of an ancient Remington typewriter that had been deposited in our home by a cousin. I had taught myself to use it with two fingers of each hand and I am still fairly proficient using the same digits. At school they insisted on touch-typing to which I could never adapt myself. Book-keeping was a bore. I was not interested in the technicalities and all I remember is the principle of double-entry which I suppose has been useful. The third vocational subject was short-hand. I liked the idea and would have loved to be able to use it but I must have had some sort of mental block because I was an absolute dud, looking bemused and uncomprehending at the other boys and girls who were quickly scrawling shapes which, miraculously, they were afterwards able to read.

Cable Street School also introduced me to classical music which has enriched my life ever since. During my second year in the school, when I was thirteen, our form was taken to the People's Palace on the Mile End Road to attend one of the Robert Mayer concerts for children. The hall was crowded with chattering children who suddenly fell silent when the conductor of the orchestra, Dr Malcolm Sargent (as he then was) strode on stage. The first item on the programme, he informed us, was the overture 'Fingal's Cave' and he sang the few theme notes to the words 'how lovely the sea is'. I was so enchanted by the whole performance that I saved enough pocket money to buy a recording of that piece of music. Many years later I met Sir Robert Mayer and we immediately became good friends when I told him what he had done for me. He lived to be over a hundred and on his centenary came to dinner at our house after a more public celebration at the Festival Hall when the Queen bestowed a second knighthood on him. Robert also joined us for a Passover *Seder* where the youngest present asks the Four Questions to which the rest of the service is a response. I asked him to recite the questions, which he did in English with gusto, since I insisted that he was the youngest in spirit among us. Characteristically, his autobiography was entitled *My First Hundred Years*.

Before the end of my four-year sojourn at Cable Street, I sat for the supplementary examination for admission to a grammar school. I was clearly a late developer for I was successful this time. I think I must have assumed that I would be, for I can recall no excitement, neither mine, nor anyone else's, at this result. From the education authority at the London County Council I received a list of schools which were available to me. There were three secondary schools in or close to the East End which were most favoured by upwardly mobile young Jews, the Davenant Foundation School on the Whitechapel Road, Raine's School, a little further east and the Central Foundation School in the City. I was, I think, making a statement that I was not simply going to follow the conventional procedures when I decided that I would not go to any of these and instead chose the Polytechnic Secondary School in Regent Street. One of the reasons for this choice was that an ex-pupil of Tubby Wiener was a teacher at the Regent Street Poly and I was commended to him. Another, I am sure, was the glamour I attached to the name of Regent Street, synonymous with the West End and as far away as I could reasonably get from the East End.

I was still at Cable Street School when I first heard of the Sassoons, a distinguished and fabulously wealth Sephardi family as well known to every East End Jew as the Rothschilds. I became acquainted with Solomon Sassoon, a scion of that family, because we both received Talmud lessons (I much less frequently than he) from Rabbi Dessler, the most eminent rabbi to have occupied the pulpit of the Artillery Lane Synagogue. Flora Sassoon, the materfamilias, was a legendary figure who not only ran the family business in the Middle East – principally, I believe, in banking – in remote and glamorous places like Baghdad. When she was in residence in her London home she devoted herself to her family, to philanthropy and Jewish studies. When I was growing up, a steady stream of *meshullachim*, representatives of Jewish institutions in poverty-stricken Eastern Europe, came to London to raise funds. When Flora Sassoon was at home, the collectors were almost always admitted and I heard that those claiming to represent schools or other places of learning were subjected to an oral examination by her on their religious knowledge to ensure that they were really what they purported to be rather than merely the possessors of impressive receipt books.

On one occasion, Solomon Sassoon invited me to his home for tea. I was familiar with the City of London and neighbouring areas like Bloomsbury because walking with friends was the only activity permitted on long summer Sabbaths. Affluent Mayfair, where the family lived, was too distant for a Sabbath walk and I never had the money to spare for bus fares. But a visit to the reputedly fabulous Sassoon home could not be missed and, after a bus ride for a penny or two, I walked down Bond Street for the first time, admiring the shops, and eventually ringing the bell at the splendid mansion in Bruton Street. A dark-skinned gentleman wearing a frock coat, who I took to be the butler, opened the door and ushered me in to the splendour of the Sassoon drawing room where I was introduced by Solomon to his grandmother. A succession of servants, I took them all to be Indian, handed me tea and cake while Flora asked me about my family, my Hebrew studies and my school. I was in a daze as I made my way back to my slum dwelling – a new world had opened up for me.

Regent Street Poly, on the upper floors of an uninspiring building in the less fashionable end of the street close by Broadcasting House, was anything but glamorous. My route to school was by underground from Aldgate East Station changing at Trafalgar Square for Oxford Circus and I had a season ticket which was paid for out of the small grant all poor secondary school pupils received from the local authority.

My first objective at the new school was to sit for the matriculation examination which I duly passed and then, having had my grant extended, continued at the school in the sixth form to prepare for a pre-medical examination since at that time I had decided that I wanted to become a doctor. But after a year of study I came to the conclusion that I was not cut out for that profession and, in any case, medical training was such a lengthy business and the grants were so small that it would not be fair to my penurious parents for them to have to wait for so long a time before I could be expected to bring any money into the house.

Nor was I particularly impressed by, or attached to, the Regent Street Poly. There were no teachers who took a personal interest in me nor did I make any new friends, so I decided to change both career and school. This I did with regret mainly because I was reluctant to give up chemistry and biology, subjects which appealed to me. But I had no regrets at giving up the third subject I had chosen for the examination, then called Higher Schools, which was physics; I hadn't the faintest idea what it was all about. I had no problems with either chemistry or biology, and still possess one of my note-books of the period containing rather good Indian ink drawings of plants and dissected segments of animals. I had also, for a number of years past, played with a rather large chemistry set in the coal cellar at home and used all my exiguous pocket money to buy chemicals and simple equipment – I thoroughly enjoyed my 'experiments'. But I could not see myself as a professional chemist or biologist. The other professions, like law or account-ancy, did not even enter into my calculations because I had no inkling of what they were all about. The only remaining profession of which I was then aware was the Jewish ministry and, in consultation with my closest friend Abie Baum, we both decided that we would become ministers of religion.

At that time, anglicised synagogues appointed ministers; only the 'foreign' synagogues appointed ordained rabbis. Jews' College, the institution for the training of Anglo-Jewish clergy, granted a minister's diploma to its graduates and that qualified them for a pulpit. But to pass the entrance examination for Jews' College I would not only have to possess some knowledge of Hebrew texts but also gain matriculation passes in various arts subjects.

What better then that I should join the Davenant Foundation School whose sixth form taught Greek and Latin which I should need for the degree course at London University, which accompanied the specialist training at Jews' College. Abie Baum had been a pupil of Davenant since his 11 plus and I joined him there for about a year, bored to distraction with my main areas of study and relieved only by my friendships at school and by the English literature classes given by the headmaster, Mr J.R. Evans who, on the name board outside the school on the Whitechapel Road was described as 'M.A., of the Middle Temple, Barrister-at-law'. It was the first time I had ever heard of the existence of the Middle Temple or, for that matter, of any of the Inns of Court and it was the recollection of that description which prompted me, many years later, to apply to the Middle Temple when I decided to read for the Bar.

Mr Evans (he was known to all the schoolboys as Gobby for his strongly Welsh accented speech was delivered with such sibilance as to spray many of those about him) had another charm for me and that was his love for A.E. Housman's *A Shropshire Lad*. It may have been because Shropshire is so close to his homeland that Gobby taught and declaimed Housman's poems with such passion. Whatever the case, I was infected by his enthusiasm and can still recite a half dozen or so of them from memory.

I must have communicated my boredom with school to

David Bier, a friend who was associated with an orthodox youth group called Chevra Ben Zakkai which was attached to the Adath Israel Synagogue in the north London suburb of Highbury. David was some years older than I and was in business with his father in a firm called I. Bier & Son (Iron & Steel) Ltd. He asked me whether I would be interested in coming to work for the firm and, at a meeting with his heavily Germanic father, I was offered a job which would pay me fifteen shillings a week. It was disappointing; I had expected at least twenty-five shillings but, nonetheless, I accepted,

Having done so, I started work on the Monday of the following week and wrote a letter to Mr Evans telling him what I had done. He was not at all happy and wrote back to me: 'Boys do not just fade out of school. There is a certain procedure to be gone through and, though I cannot associate you with discourtesy, it was not courteous of you to have acted as you did.' Nevertheless, Gobby wished me well and I responded by inviting him to talk to the Young Sinaists and he did so with great gusto. I took the precaution of sitting in one of the back rows.

5

The Young Sinaists

During my teenage years there was no focus to my activities and certainly no thought of what I wanted to become. I had no ambition because I was totally unaware of what the world outside the East End ghetto had to offer. The closest I came to thinking about a future occupation was when, prompted by my success and my first earnings which came from being a choirboy in the synagogue on High Holydays, I thought that, maybe, I would become a cantor. That was, apparently, what my father thought I'd be suited for. His ambitions for my siblings were more grandiose. Ben, my older brother, would be the Chief Rabbi, while the youngest of the three, Hyman, he proudly forecast, would become the Lord Chief Justice. In fact, Ben became a successful businessman and Hyman a left-wing writer and communist intellectual.

I mention this vague and unfocussed life during my early youth to emphasise the contrast with my attitudes and outlook when I first met Abie Baum – we were both twelve years old at the time. One of my street or *heder* friends had told me of a Jewish boys' club called the Junior Section of the Sinai Association which met at the Brick Lane Talmud Torah. At that time, I knew nothing of organised Jewish activities outside the synagogue we attended and the cheerfully disorderly *shtieblech* of the *rebbes*. I did not even know of the existence of *The Jewish Chronicle*, for the only newspapers to enter our house was *Die Zeit*, a Yiddish daily and, occasionally, the picture section of the

New York Yiddish paper, *Forward*.

I went, or was taken by my mentor, to the club and learned that it was an offshoot of the Sinai Association, a men's club founded after the First World War by Rabbi Dr Leo Jung, then the spiritual head of the Federation of Synagogues. He later emigrated to New York where he became a considerable figure in orthodox religious circles. His younger brother, Julius Jung, remained in London and for very many years was Secretary of the Federation. He was the best part of what had become, in my time, a disreputable organisation led by one Councillor M.H. Davis who had made it his personal fiefdom.

After the departure of its moving spirit, the Sinai Association disintegrated leaving one remaining vestige, a group consisting of a few dozen young orthodox males who met on Saturday afternoons in the prayer hall of the Brick Lane Talmud Torah. There they spent some time in Bible or Talmud study followed by the Sabbath afternoon services separated by an alfresco meal, the *shalosh seudah*. For that purpose, the rather dingy room was converted from a sanctuary to a club room furnished with benches and a couple of long tables on which were deposited loaves of challah, herrings plain, pickled and sometimes chopped, and bottles of R. Whites lemonade.

The meal was frugal but the atmosphere was exuberant. Table hymns were sung robustly if not musically and the grace after meals, a lengthy procedure in Hebrew, was an oratorio in itself, enthusiastically rendered. By the time I came on the scene, the 'elders' of the Sinai Association (they were then in their twenties or early thirties, but we youngsters saw them as a much older generation) had formed a Junior Section which I joined and of whose activities I have little recollection except that we participated in the *shalosh seudah*. I was particularly keen on the varieties of herring and remain so.

When I joined, Abie was the leader of the Junior Section. He was my age, shorter and tubbier, but infinitely more worldly.

Our schools were different at that time but our backgrounds were similar, his father being a regular worshipper at the Hasidic Dzikover *stibl* close to their home, a tenement in Heneage Street, which was even poorer and more humble than that of my family.

My frequent visits to his home were generally confined to brief sojourns in his cramped, untidy and minimally furnished kitchen (which was also the family room) before we went out. But on occasion I had seen one of the other two rooms of the tenement in which he lived with his parents and siblings. It served a dual purpose as a bedroom at night and a *heder* at other times which was conducted by Abie's father. He was a bearded and venerable gentleman, whose voice I rarely heard (for it was generally Mrs Baum who held forth), who earned a modest living partly from teaching a few boys Hebrew texts after school and partly as a vendor of Irish Sweepstake tickets. He was generally respected as a pious and scholarly Jew, a retiring figure who appeared to be totally dominated by his wife.

Abie had not inherited any of these characteristics from his father but, on the contrary, was articulate, eager and ambitious. At that time his ambition was not channelled in any particular direction – he just wanted to achieve. We shared a desire for better things but, strangely as I now look back, it was not money we were after; as far as I can recall, we never discussed how we could make money – we just wanted to be successful doing something or other. It was assumed that we would earn enough to live comfortably. He was the leader and I followed, infected by his enthusiasms. I learned from him that there was a Jewish community in London outside the tight Hasidic circle in which we had both been brought up. It was he who introduced me to *The Jewish Chronicle* (*JC*)which neither of us could afford to buy but read in the Whitechapel Public Library. We would go there after school on Friday when the paper appeared and, in the winter, made the weekly pilgrimage on Saturday. Never, or hardly ever, did we use the word Saturday; that day was invariably referred to in our circle as *Shabbes*, the East European pronunciation of *Shabbat*, the Sabbath.

From the *JC* we learned that there were Jews who had made their way to the higher socio-economic ranks and some even had titles, inherited or earned. From Abie I also learned about the existence of universities and the academic degrees they awarded. He had a round, well-formed and elegant handwriting which I did not try to copy, but he did infect me with his enthusiasm for typography and calligraphy. I enjoy lettering to this day and that, in turn, led me to an interest in typography which proved to be useful in the career that I was eventually to follow. And, after my retirement from the *JC* editorship, that interest was an introduction to the joy of book-binding.

Abie's doodles, which also became mine, though his were always more precisely executed, generally consisted in lettering our names in different calligraphic styles with prefixes like 'Professor' or 'Sir' and, adding after our names, a string of degrees beginning usually with MA followed by PhD and, as our knowledge of these things and our imaginations waxed, we might add ScD or DCL (Hon) culminating in CH or even OM. How we were ever going to attain these degrees or honours was never a subject for discussion – in our imaginations they were going to come to us, somehow.

After a year or two of our friendship, we felt that the Junior Section of the Sinai Association, being under the authority of the seniors, was too limiting and did not provide us with real opportunities to exercise what we instinctively felt, though never expressed, to be the leadership qualities we possessed. We decided to form our own orthodox youth club under our own management, not that of our elders, for we both fancied the idea of running things ourselves. We would call the club The Young Sinaists, meet on Sunday evenings for lectures, debates and discussions, a week-day evening for Jewish studies and on

Sabbath afternoons for the traditional services which we would conduct ourselves, and for the *shalosh seudah*.

Because it was the most prestigious Jewish institution in the East End, we decided that we would aim at obtaining the use of the communal hall of the Great Synagogue, the flagship of the community's premier organisation, the United Synagogue. Abie and I went to see Dr Israel Feldman, a medical practitioner, who was then the Warden of the Great Synagogue and we found him extremely sympathetic. He offered us the use of the Ernst Schiff Hall of the synagogue, free of charge, for our Sunday evening meetings.

We told our friends and soon had gathered a membership of some thirty Jewish teenagers willing to come to the Sunday meetings and also to a Sabbath afternoon session which was held at the Buxton Street Welfare Centre of the United Synagogue. The subscription was two or three pence a week which was to pay for printing, postage and other incidentals. Abie was the chairman and I the secretary. I soon found that our subscriptions were woefully inadequate and wrote a letter of appeal to Mr James de Rothschild, then an MP and a notable philanthropist. The response to the first begging letter I had ever composed was overwhelming. He sent a cheque for ten pounds – to us a fortune! With that I purchased a primitive duplicating outfit and had some letterheads printed so that I could write to well-known figures asking them to come and lecture to us.

We had an interesting succession of lecturers, none of whom requested any payment or even travel expenses. I had kept in touch with Tubby Wiener after I left Cable Street School and he was one of the first speakers I invited to talk to the Young Sinaists. The others included the Secretary of the Board of Deputies of British Jews, Mr Adolph Brotman, Professor Selig Brodetsky, a leading figure in the Zionist Organisation and later President of the Board of Deputies, Mr Neville Laski, K.C. and other eminences of the Anglo-Jewish community. There were, of course, questions after each lecture and I learned to think quickly and formulate a question to avoid an embarrassing silence while others were collecting their thoughts. I was also almost always the proposer of the vote of thanks, all of which gave me a grounding in public speaking which was to be useful later.

The Sunday evening meetings were, usually, educational but far less enjoyable than our Sabbath afternoon jollity at the *shalosh seudah* table in Buxton Street. In addition, I organised classes in Jewish history and Bible study and, being associated with the Great Synagogue, every year or so we were allowed to conduct a youth service in the big synagogue. But the event of the year was the Sinaists Camp and the first, in 1936, was held at East Dean in Sussex. How I did it all I cannot now imagine; it must have been a time-consuming activity – visiting the site, renting it from a farmer, hiring tents and other equipment, enrolling campers and preparing a programme for the two weeks. The first camp hosts were Dr and Mrs Bernard Homa, he a leader of the orthodox community as well as a medical doctor, his wife an ideal mother figure for the teenage campers, and they had with them their two young sons. Miraculously, nothing untoward happened and the event was encapsulated in a song written by Mrs Homa which was sung round the last night's camp fire. The text was given to me some sixty years later by her son Ramsay Homa. I am the Wee Willie referred to in one of its verses on the sheet headed: 'Sung at the Sinaist Camp on 22 August 1936 to the tune of "He was a Handsome Young Soldier"

> Wee Willie's very far from being weary
> Thoughts of girls keep him awake
> To the charms of gay Pessie he's yielded at last
> He gave her a tender glance

This was her first romance;
He had a gay charming manner
He made love so dashingly too;
Use your imagination what happened, because,
He was a very handsome young fellow, he was.'

*

After a couple of years, I succeeded Abie as chairman and moved into a wider circle of Jewish communal life. The Young Sinaists had become affiliated to the Association of Young Zionist Societies and that involved me in meetings at the Great Russell Street headquarters of the World Zionist Organisation and some of its subsidiaries. There I met a band of Zionist enthusiasts some of them, like Aubrey (later Abba) Eban destined to become outstanding figures in the Jewish world. I also took the lead in forming an Association of Orthodox Jewish Societies which, however, did not prosper. I discovered that orthodox Jews were even more contentious than Zionists.

The Young Sinaists continued its existence until the outbreak of war in 1939.

6

From Scrap Iron to Mizrachi

The offices of I. Bier & Son, my first employers, consisted of two rooms in a Victorian office building on City Road close to Old Street tube station. Father and son occupied one of the rooms while the secretary (my friend David's sister), a breezy young office boy and I shared the other. I spent little time in the office; for most of the working day I travelled with father Bier to various parts of London looking at piles of scrap iron for which he would make an offer, either verbally or by letter. The skill was to estimate the weight of the scrap and calculate its worth depending on the metal's composition and condition. He must have been good at it because, as far as I can recall, most of his offers were accepted. When that happened, he or David would sell the metal to a foundry in the Midlands and one of the three of us in the outside office would get on the telephone to a list of hauliers and seek the best price for transporting the scrap.

But that wasn't all the business. I. Bier & Son owned a subsidiary company called the Walthamstow Iron & Steel Company. After some months I was seconded to Walthamstow as manager. That was no great promotion because there was no other staff to manage. My job was to wait for the arrival of the men who walked the streets pulling their hand-drawn barrows, yelling 'any old iron', and purchasing for a few pence whatever was offered. They would bring the scrap metal to my depot, I would weigh it, calculate its value and make them an offer

48

which was usually accepted. I was left to my own devices for long periods and spent the time reading and associating with a delightful German-Jewish refugee who was a chemist and had been given space at Walthamstow by the Biers to do his work. We did some imaginative cooking over his Bunsen burner.

After about a year of this uninspiring occupation I came to the conclusion that I would never be a successful entrepreneur, that business was not my calling and that I needed time to think about my future. So, after some words with my bosses I left and joined the ranks of the unemployed. I recall mournful moments walking the streets without a penny in my pocket – at that time there was no such thing as unemployment benefit, or if there was, I was unaware of it.

In the event I did very little, if any, thinking about my future. A short time after I left Biers, tired of the inactivity of unemployment, I seriously went about looking for a job and eventually found one assisting in the warehouse of a company founded by German-Jewish refugees which imported Japanese goods of a bewildering variety. My task was to unpack consignments of samples, check the contents against a list and then tag them with a description and price. The pay was very much better than the miserable wage I had received at Biers but the work was undemanding and there was obviously, even to me, no future in it. At this point I came to a decision. My only degree of expertise was in the field of Jewish organisations in which I had gained a good deal of experience through my activities for the Young Sinaists; I knew which were the main institutions of the Anglo-Jewish community and had become acquainted with some of the people who were running them; I was always a pretty good organiser (indeed I remember feeling somewhat deflated when I heard one member of my youth group complaining to another that I was bossy) so I thought I could run one of the Jewish organisations as well as anyone.

I had also had a little experience of professional work within the Jewish community. When I was about eighteen one of my friends recommended me to Rabbi Bisko whose home was in Lithuania. He was, in the disparaging description of my Polish-Hasidic milieu, a Litvak (a pejorative term for Lithuanian Jews). His interest, and I suppose his profession, was in organising an orthodox Jewish youth movement called *Tifereth Bachurim* (the glory of young lads) in his home country and now he wanted to extend it internationally. Short, lightly bearded and courteous, he was always immaculate in his well-cut suit and, when he first called at my house he made a very favourable impression on my mother. I was more concerned with the job offer and the payment and, since both were agreeable, I took on the job as part-time secretary while he travelled around the provinces organising his youth groups. That was to lead to another, more interesting, part-time job.

It came at the invitation of the most colourful personality I had, until then, ever met. He was Dr Alfonso Pacifici, a member of a prominent Italian Jewish family, who had emigrated to Palestine and there become involved with a school for the education of orthodox children from the Jewish communities of the Middle East. He had been advised by Rabbi Bisko to seek me out and the task for which I was hired was to assist in fund-raising for this institution. He was a tall, authoritative and elegant man with a resonant voice and, since I spoke neither Hebrew nor Italian and he spoke no English, our language of communication was German. He was acquainted with John Sebag-Montefiore – there was some distant family connection – who put him in touch with other prosperous Sephardim (Jews descended from pre-Inquisition Spain and Portugal) with whom he had, before I met him, developed a network. We set up an impressive committee and did quite well. That led me to decide to enter full-time employment in the Anglo-Jewish community and that was, I think, the only career decision I have ever made. I put it into effect almost immediately when I responded to an advertisement in *The Jewish Chronicle* inviting applications for the newly-created post of Assistant Organising Secretary for the Union of Orthodox Hebrew Congregations. I was then nineteen and, after an interview, was appointed at the munificent weekly wage of £3, almost as much as my father was earning.

The office was in an outbuilding of the Adath Israel Synagogue in Highbury which was shared with the burial society of the Union. I have no recollection of what the job entailed, but the office was a theatre. The secretary of the Union was a cheerful incompetent who must have secured the position because of family connections – there could not have been any other reason. But the main character was the blunt and lugubrious sexton of the burial society whose conversation was almost completely limited to discussing the size of the coffins that were to be in use that day and the skill, or lack of it, of the volunteers who prepared the corpse for burial.

The Rabbi of the synagogue and of the Union of Orthodox Hebrew Congregations which now employed me was Rabbi Dr Solomon Schonfeld, a tall, handsome man, energetic, determined and forceful. We did not have much to do with each other in my job in the office, but had had some arguments in the past in the Association of Orthodox Jewish Youth Societies which I had helped to create. Its first constituents were my Young Sinaists and the Chevra Ben Zakkai associated with the Adath Israel Synagogue. During the discussions which had preceded its formation, Schonfeld, the religious head of the latter group, had insisted that the constitution of the new organisation should list him as its spiritual authority. I was reluctant to give him the power of veto, objected to his proposal and we had words about it.

Years later, in my early days as a practising barrister, I was nominated by the London County Council (LCC) to be a member of the Board of Governors of the Jewish Secondary

School, also attached to the Adath Israel Synagogue which received some LCC funding. Dr Schonfeld, one of whose considerable achievements was the creation of the Jewish Secondary School movement, was its religious authority. While I was on the Board, Dr Schonfeld proposed that the headmaster be dismissed because he was said to have acted irrationally towards fellow members of the staff and towards some pupils. Behind those allegations was the claim that he was not, in the opinion of Schonfeld, sufficiently religiously observant. The other members of the committee (mostly his congregants) accepted this recommendation, but I and the other LCC nominated governors objected on the ground that, on a matter this serious, we should set up a committee to investigate the complaints rather than accept the word of one man, even though he was the religious authority. We were supported in this by the LCC educational office. But Schonfeld and his supporters persisted; the headmaster was dismissed and thereafter initiated legal proceedings for wrongful dismissal. The case was duly heard and the headmaster succeeded in his action which ended in the Court of Appeal. In his judgment, Lord Justice Romer had this to say of the Rabbi, 'He possesses a forceful personality and character and a somewhat overbearing egotism. His general view would appear to be that if he thought a thing was right, it is right and that is the end of it ... ' Rabbi Schonfeld never forgave me for my part in this debacle and, on one occasion when he had to communicate with me during my years at *The Jewish Chronicle*, began his letter 'Dear Machiavelli'.

I did not stay long as Assistant Secretary of the Union of Orthodox Hebrew Congregations for I soon landed a much more interesting, and better paid, job as Secretary of the Mizrachi Federation of Great Britain and Ireland. The Mizrachi party was the religious constituent of the World Zionist Movement and my task was to assist in the growth of Mizrachi societies, organise the annual conference and raise funds for the organisation and its projects in Palestine. The President of the Mizrachi Federation was the Chief Rabbi, Dr J.H. Hertz and I saw a good deal of him at that time. All in all, the work was varied and interesting. Until then, I had seen very little of England, but now I was able to travel to the Federation's branches in the provinces.

7

Early Travel

In 1937, as Secretary of the Mizrachi Federation, I made my first journey out of Britain. The Zionist Congress was being held in Zurich that summer. Although my employers were not prepared to pay for me to go there, I decided that I would make the journey under my own steam and from Zurich travel on to Przemysl in Poland to meet members of my mother's family for the first time. I had saved £25. Half of that bought me a return third-class rail ticket from London to Przemysl, stopping wherever I liked. The other half would, I calculated, cover my expenses. I planned to travel by night whenever possible, thus saving the cost of hotels or, more likely, bed-and-breakfasts.

For the first stage of the journey, that to Zurich, I enjoyed the company of a friend, Myer Silverstone, a young solicitor and at that time chairman of the Young Mizrachi, who, much later, emigrated to Israel. He was making the journey to attend the Zionist Congress as a member of the British delegation. We took the train from Victoria Station to Dover, crossed the Channel by ferry and then took another train to Paris. 1937 was also the year of the great Exposition Internationale in Paris and, after a night's sleep at a small inexpensive hotel we had found on the Rue Ste Lazare, we metro'd to the Exposition early next morning and spent the day marvelling at the exhibits, particularly the great buildings of the United States and the Soviet Union which faced one another symbolically in, it seemed to me, mutually threatening postures. We had neither the cash nor the time to stay in Paris more than one day and moved on to Zurich on the night train. In the early morning the train stopped at Basle. I shall never forget the appetising aroma of coffee which greeted us as we stepped on to the station platform nor the almost intoxicating flavour of the beverage nor the crispness of the rolls which comprised our breakfasts.

The Zionist Congress of 1937 was mainly devoted to the contentious issue of partition, following, as it did, the recommendation of the Peel Commission earlier that year that Palestine be divided between the Jews and the Arabs – at the time there was no such entity as the Palestinians. The atmosphere at the Congress struck me as chaotic with masses of Jews milling around in lobbies and corridors while the speeches were being made in the main hall. I have a vivid memory of listening, awed, to some of the passionate and lengthy speeches for and against partition. I could not afford to stay in Zurich more than one night but, before leaving the city, spent some time with Myer on a rowing boat on the lake in glorious sunshine.

I could afford even less time in Vienna, which was my next stop, only from early morning, when the train arrived, to the evening when I boarded another to take me on to Poland. I spent that day with my cousins, Mitzi and Sidi Lecker, the two daughters of one of my mother's brothers, at that time in their twenties. Both of their parents were dead, neither of the girls was married and, as far as I could gather, had no prospects in that direction. My recollection of them is of their gaiety and laughter, of our incessant chatter in German and of their optimism that they had nothing to fear from Nazi Germany – this was a short time before the *Anschluss*. After my return to London I wrote to them suggesting that they emigrate and that my family would do what it could to get them into England but we heard little from them until almost the outbreak of war two years later when it was too late. Both ended their lives as victims of the Holocaust.

The train moved on to Poland. Coming from the comparative grandeur of the cities in Western Europe that I had visited, the poverty of the smaller Polish towns and villages was something of a shock. My itinerary went through towns like Ropcyze and Kielce which had a familiar ring since they were the designations of Hasidic '*Wunder-Rebbes*'. A note I made on the train described the scenery on entering Poland from Czechoslovakia as undistinguished – a vast, flat and uninteresting plain. What was of interest, and surprising to me, was the number of women, their heads wrapped in large handkerchiefs, working in the fields. It was so different from home!

At one of the small stations, attractively framed in floral decoration, at which the train stopped very early in the morning, a middle-aged but old-looking Jewish lady entered my carriage. She wore a *shaitel* (a wig worn by orthodox Jewish women) as well as many and varied petticoats and carried a large bundle of farm produce she was presumably taking to a market town. After disposing of her belongings in various parts of the carriage, she produced a Jewish prayer book from one of the recesses of her garments and began to recite the Hebrew morning prayers in an audible whisper. The other occupants of the carriage, some soldiers and other non-Jewish Poles, did not even exchange glances let alone make the comments I nervously expected.

As she stood up to begin the lengthy silent prayer called the *amida*, the conductor entered to inspect tickets. I sought to remember all the Polish words I knew so as to be ready to join in the altercation I felt sure would follow. But the conductor, after checking the other tickets in the carriage, calmly looked out of the window and waited until the old lady had taken her three steps backwards to end the prayer and taken her seat.

Przemysl, where I ended my trip, had at that time a population of some 20,000 Jews, many, possibly most, living in what seemed to me abject poverty. I was staying with a cousin, Lulek

Frankel, the only relative I knew for he had come to London a year or two before but, having failed to earn a living there, had returned to Poland. He, his wife and baby son Genek all perished in the Holocaust. The morning after I arrived, the news had somehow spread that an English Jew (of course he must be rich!) was in town, and a queue of beggars formed outside the apartment building making pitiful appeals for alms. During my stay, I was continually being approached by mendicants. Nor was it only foreigners who received their attentions. Standing in my cousin's shop one day, I counted no fewer than twenty Jewish beggars in one morning. I concluded at the time, after making the most careful enquiries of which I was capable, that about half the Jewish population was dependent on the generosity of relatives abroad.

There was little mixing between the Jews and Gentiles. Many non-Jewish shops displayed a sign reading 'This is a pure Polish business' and in practice, the Jews and non-Jews only patronised the shops owned by their co-religionists. Not all Jews were shopkeepers or living on relief. In Przemysl there were, I was told, hundreds of Jewish doctors and lawyers, far more than the 20,000 Jews needed. Nor were the professions particularly lucrative and most practitioners were lucky if they could scrape up three or four pounds a month, even then barely enough for subsistence.

A large proportion of the Jewish youth had rejected the orthodox Judaism in which they had been brought up. There was no reform movement either. Young Polish Jews, including my own relatives, cared little for compromise – they were either orthodox or completely a-religious. On the Sabbath I was struck by the number of Jewish shops that were open – in London's East End at that time practically all the Jewish businesses were closed on Saturdays. A few streets away from the shopping area, Hasidim were trudging their way to their *stibls* wearing the traditional fur hats and white stockings. One short street contained several of these small synagogues vying with each other in the fervour of their devotions which could be heard by all passers-by.

Nothing of the Jewish life I had seen in 1937, nor any members of my family, survived the war. Within just a few days after the town fell to the Germans, the invaders had killed some 500 Jews. They then handed Przemysl over to the USSR forces who deported 7000 Jews to Russia, and after the German attack on the Soviets in 1941, the remaining Jews were murdered or sent to the camps.

In 1939, prompted by the fact that the early reports in the press of the invasion of Poland mentioned that one of the towns where the invading armies met was Przemysl, I made my first venture into journalism. I imagine that the name Przemysl had not appeared in the British press before this time and readers were given advice by one newspaper that it should be pronounced 'Primrose Hill' spoken quickly. I sent an account of my visit to that war zone to *The Jewish Chronicle*. It was accepted as from 'A Special Correspondent' and I received a fee of two guineas.

*

In April 1939 I married Gertrude Reed whom I had met at the Young Sinaists. The wedding was performed at the Great Synagogue and a reception was held at the Ritz Hotel – an act of grandiloquence, not to mention ostentation, on my part. I could not possibly afford it and neither could my wife for neither of us had any money. But I wanted to make a statement and calculated that we would, in all probability, receive enough cash as wedding presents to be able to cover the bill – as well as pay for the expensive, engraved wedding invitations on which I had insisted because of my enthusiasm for typography. Happily my hope was realised. We did not take a honeymoon – our resources, such as they were, had been exhausted by the cost of the wedding and, neither then or at any later time, was I willing to get into debt. But by the month of August I had saved enough to allow us to spend a week in Paris which was unmemorable except for the sight of the sandbags in position at the railway stations we passed through on the train from Dover to London – an ominous intimation of the cataclysm to come.

Our first home was a small flat above a greengrocer's shop in Marchmont Street, Bloomsbury, whose main attractions were, first, that it was not the East End and, second, that it was close to Woburn House, the Jewish communal office building which housed the office of the Mizrachi Federation where I was working. We did not have much time to enjoy our first home. War broke out less than five months after our marriage and the Blitz that followed made life there extremely uncomfortable.

8

Cambridge

Before the Second World War, I had been to Cambridge only once, in 1937, when Sir Robert Waley Cohen opened the new students' synagogue on Thompson's Lane. My friend Abie Baum, who was then an undergraduate at Trinity College (he was the recipient of a scholarship for future Jewish ministers), had become the Honorary Secretary of the Cambridge Union Jewish Society, the CUJS, and was the organiser of the event. Aubrey Eban (later Abba, and Israel's Foreign Minister) was President of the Society. Located near the Union building, the new synagogue which was small and attractive, comprised a compact sanctuary seating some fifty or sixty, a small raised section at the back for about twenty women and an adjoining hall and kitchen. I made the journey to and from Cambridge in a Morris Oxford two-seater car which I had recently bought for the sum of £15. It was the first car I ever owned and the first time I had driven any car that distance.

My next journey to Cambridge came four years later. My wife and I were both comfortably ensconced in our Bloomsbury flat where, on Sunday 3 September 1939, we listened to Neville Chamberlain's broadcast in which he announced that Britain was at war with Germany. Until London was relentlessly bombed in the Blitz which began in 1940, we stayed in the flat and went about our normal activities as far as possible. I was rejected for military service having failed the medical examination on the grounds of a heart murmur. With the onset of the nightly bombings, most nights were spent in air raid shelters and living conditions became so uncomfortable and trying that we came to the reluctant conclusion that the time had come for us to get out of the way.

By then Abie had graduated from Cambridge and was serving as Jewish tutor to a school which had been evacuated to King's Lynn. He had been there since the outbreak of the war and had regularly assured me that, if things became too difficult in London, we could find a haven there. So that was what we did and, loading all our possessions on to a hired van, we travelled to King's Lynn in September 1940. After a few days, we found a house which we rented jointly with Abie and his sister and I continued working from there, as best I could, for the Mizrachi Federation. Our co-existence was not a happy one and, moreover, after the rigours of the Blitz had yielded to the uneventful placidity of King's Lynn, it seemed too remote a place in which to live for the rest of the war, nor did it make sense to return to London still then under attack. Cambridge was half way between King's Lynn and London and we had a friend there, Monty Richardson, who was an undergraduate. Monty, an intelligent and amiable young man, was notable in his youth for his mellifluous voice — at the Young Sinaists he was the most proficient and popular of the aspiring cantors who conducted our Sabbath services, one of the group's most agreeable activities. So we re-packed, hired a van and drove to Cambridge. Once there we stored our belongings and rented a bedroom in student's lodgings until we found an unfurnished flat we could afford. My job at the Mizrachi had ended — it simply could not be conducted other than from an office in London. But now that we were in Cambridge, what was I to do?

At the outbreak of war, the London School of Economics had taken refuge in Cambridge and was, loosely, attached to Peterhouse College but its real home was the nearby Grove

Lodge. I talked about my situation with some new acquaintances, among them Helmuth Lowenberg, an engagingly exuberant and thoughtful Palestinian Jew of German extraction, who was a second year law student at the LSE. From what he said it seemed to me that since the war was likely to continue for some while, it would be a good idea for me to join the LSE and also read law, not that I knew anything about it but Helmuth had made it sound interesting. I called at the LSE office, they checked that I had matriculated and readily enrolled me (the fee was a negligible amount which, impecunious though I was, even I could afford) despite the fact that the academic year had begun the previous September and this was February or March. I attended lectures, discovered that I loved the subject and easily passed the Inter LLB examination three or four months later.

I did not then realise my good fortune, but when I later contemplated the event, it was almost miraculous. I had, completely fortuitously, fallen into a situation where I was not only to acquire a profession but also to benefit from some of the most eminent academics in the field I had chosen. In addition to the lectures given by the faculty of the LSE and University College, London (the law school of which had also come to Cambridge) I was also free to attend the lectures of the Cambridge dons. Among them were Professor W.W. Buckland the outstanding authority on Roman Law, Professor Percy Winfield, ditto on Torts, Glanville Williams on Jurisprudence and, best of all, Hersch Lauterpacht, Whewell Professor of International Law. With the assistance of all that wealth of talent, it was hardly surprising that I graduated as LLB with upper-second-class honours – there were no firsts that year! During that two and a half year period, I had no regular job or income. We lived partly on my wife's occasional earnings as a secretary, my half-a-crown an hour fee for giving Hebrew lessons to youngsters and occasional handouts from my parents.

I rapidly learned that Cambridge was not only about study and my years there were the most broadening of my life. Of course my legal studies made the greatest impression on me and, more than any other factor in my life, influenced my future. They were also tremendously enjoyable – the only subject which caused me a little concern was Roman Law, a compulsory item for the Inter LLB examination. It involved the study of *Justinian's Institutes* in Latin and my earlier attempt at the Davenant Foundation School to learn something of the language was entirely irrelevant to this new challenge. My solution to the problem was to analyse the examination questions on the subject for the previous five or ten years and choose the half dozen or so topics which had appeared most frequently. I then memorised the passages in Justinian relating to those subjects and, to this day, I can recite parts of the Latin text.

Study did not, by any means, occupy all my waking hours. Cambridge, during that wartime period at any rate, was a very open society where both students and teachers were accessible and friendly. I usually worked, when I was not at lectures, at the Squire Law Library just behind the Senate House, in the most beautiful part of the university. En route to the library, I would halt my bicycle when entering King's Parade and stop to gaze at the sight of King's College Chapel, the Senate House and Old Schools, the corner of the oldest part of Gonville and Caius College and, in the centre of the picture, the spreading chestnut tree. It was, and still is, one of the most elevating sights I have ever seen.

At the Squire, Professor Lauterpacht would occasionally invite me into his room for a chat, not always limited to my studies, or I would go to the Rose Cafe for an eleven o'clock coffee break with some of my fellow students and talk about the world. But the most interesting of my encounters was on the street, usually on King's Parade, where on a few occasions I ran into the Very Rev. Dr J.H. Hertz, the Chief Rabbi. During the heavy bombings of London he sought refuge in the Bull Hotel which was next to King's College and, weather permitting, took his daily constitutional walk along the Parade. When we thus met, he would ask me to join him and he would walk and talk and I would listen very happily.

Hertz was short, stocky, square beard neatly trimmed, and with a reputation for belligerence. At that time he was working on his Prayer Book commentary which was in its final stages. 'Frankel,' he once assured me, 'my *siddur* [prayer book] will be so simple that even my ministers will understand it.' He talked, with much relish, about his fights with Moses Gaster who, in Hertz's early years as Chief Rabbi, was the eminent spiritual leader of the Spanish and Portuguese community. But his most regular antagonist was Sir Robert Waley Cohen, the chairman of the Shell Transport & Trading Company who was, for a long time, the leading spirit of the United Synagogue of which the Chief Rabbi was the religious head.

Sir Robert personified the mores of the United Synagogue. Although it was the largest and most important association of orthodox synagogues in the United Kingdom, it had been influenced by the tolerant English environment and had become a broad church, theoretically committed to orthodoxy, but in practice hospitable to all who wished to join it. At that time I mentally compared the attitude of its leaders with that of Sir Roger de Coverly towards the Church of England as described in Addison and Steele's *Spectator*. Sir Roger regularly attended church service on Sunday, made his way to his seat and immediately fell asleep. The United Synagogue manifested the same easy, almost casual, attitude towards religious observance that was the distinguishing mark of the Church of England and, by no stretch of imagination could Sir Robert be described as an observant Jew. His successor as United Synagogue President, the Hon Ewen Montagu, once confessed to me his love of oysters, strictly non-kosher, but he hoped (successfully, it appears) to avoid discovery because he was sure that no orthodox Jew would venture into an oyster bar.

Hertz and Sir Robert differed particularly in their attitudes towards the Zionist movement, of which the Chief Rabbi was a strong supporter while the President of the United Synagogue, and technically his employer, was, if not anti-Zionist, cool towards this expression of Jewish nationalism. During our walks Hertz talked often about some of these arguments but concluded, sadly, that life was now much less exciting with Gaster dead and Sir Robert no longer the forceful figure that he was.

When he was in Cambridge, Hertz always attended the synagogue in Thompson's Lane for its Sabbath services and sat as an ordinary congregant. On one occasion, a barmitzvah took place of the son of a German refugee couple who were temporarily resident in Cambridge. As the service neared its end, and it was apparent that there was to be no address to the barmitzvah boy, Hertz stepped up to the reading desk, said that it was an omission that should be remedied and proceeded to address the lad. The following day, some of the officers of the Jewish Society which controlled the synagogue, called on Hertz at his hotel and politely informed him that his jurisdiction as Chief Rabbi did not include our synagogue and would he please wait to be invited before again addressing the congregation. He took it in very good part and, thereafter, painstakingly obeyed the injunction.

In addition to the synagogue business, the Society also arranged lectures and many of the most prominent members of the Jewish community were happy to come up to Cambridge and talk. One of those who spoke not long after my arrival in Cambridge was Neville Laski, QC, then heading the representative organisation of the Anglo-Jewish community, and we spent much of his weekend visit together. He knew me as a member of the Board of Deputies (before the war I had represented the Artillery Lane Synagogue and, later, the Cambridge University Synagogue). Neville enjoyed his Cambridge visit so much that, thereafter, he would occasionally come up for a weekend and sleep on the sofa in our flat.

His brother, Harold, an eminent professor at the London School of Economics and a leader of the Labour Party, came to Cambridge on Mondays and always lunched at the same restaurant on King's Parade. When I spoke of this to Neville, he told me that he rarely saw his brother and I suggested we both lunch at the same restaurant. Harold turned up with a young lady who might have been one of his students shortly after we were seated. He saw us, waved his hand to Neville, and moved to his own table. Neville was affronted. 'That's not right,' he said to me bitterly, 'I'm the older brother, he should have come over to our table.' Nevertheless, when we finished our meal, Neville stopped to talk to his brother who invited him to come to his room for a chat. Neville and I walked about for a while and, when we thought that Harold had finished his lunch, made our way to his room. Before entering, Neville asked if I could call for him in half an hour, 'That's as long as I think I can stand Harold.' I duly knocked at the door half an hour later. Neville and Harold were sitting at a distance from each other, and talking as though they were addressing a public meeting with no sign of any cordiality. Neville was clearly relieved when I came and left with me immediately.

My circle of close friends in Cambridge included Vivian Herzog, also a law student. One day in 1941, he buttonholed me in the law library to say that he had just received a message from the Zionist offices in London's Great Russell Street that David Ben-Gurion, then the leader of the World Zionist Organisation, planned to visit Cambridge and would Vivian shepherd him around? He asked if I could help him with this chore and I said I would. Vivian met Ben-Gurion at the railway station, accompanied him on some sightseeing, lunched with him and then handed him over to me for the afternoon and evening. BG was exactly as I had imagined him to be. I had, of course, seen innumerable pictures so he was immediately familiar. Short and squat, brisk in manner, what distinguished him was that hallmark shock of white hair which seemed to add to his stature. He was extremely talkative – not on any subject on which I was anxious to seek his views, but in asking interminable questions. Neither then, nor at any subsequent time, did I ever detect any trace of a sense of humour in him.

Having walked him through some of the colleges he had not seen, I asked him if he would come to my lodgings in the evening and talk to a few Jewish dons and students on how he saw the Zionist future. He readily agreed and I rounded up an interested group of a dozen or so. I can still see BG, legs akimbo, hands vigorously and expressively gesticulating as he spoke with his back to the coal fire.

Whether roused by the fire or an inner heating system his speech, which had started as a calm and analytical review of the tragic Jewish situation at that stage in the war, warmed up as he launched into his forecast of the post-war scene. His theme was simple and, to most of his audience, startling. The Jewish community in Palestine was, of course, lined up behind Britain in the war with Germany. He had famously observed, at the outbreak of the war, 'We must assist Britain in the war as though there were no White Paper [the 1939 document which drastically limited Jewish immigration into Palestine] and we must resist the White Paper as if there were no war.'

He told his small and attentive Cambridge audience that, after the defeat of the Nazis, Britain, the mandatory power for Palestine, could not be depended upon to support Zionist aspirations. Consequently, he saw no other course than that, when the war ended with the defeat of the Nazis, the link with Britain would have to be broken if the Jews of Palestine were to become a self-governing nation. But he warned it would be tough going. The British would not give up Palestine passively;

the Jews would have to fight for it, there would be a bitter struggle and blood would be shed. He was passionate and impressive. It was a Zionist programme that had not, as far as I was aware, been expounded in Cambridge before and his audience was both electrified and depressed. One don, a Fellow of Gonville and Caius College, muttered to me as I helped him on with his coat, 'If that's the leader of the Jews in Palestine, then God help them.'

BG told me that he had come to Cambridge mainly because he had learned that the library of the recently deceased Sir James Frazer of *Golden Bough* renown was up for sale in some Cambridge bookshop and he was interested in making some purchases. I directed him to the bookshop and there he went, on his own, and then returned to London. Some thirty years later, when he was living in retirement at Sdeh Boker, a kibbutz in the Negev, and as I was about to leave after one of my intermittent visits, he burst out with, 'I've a bone to pick with you' (or words to that effect). I asked him what that was about and he replied that when he had asked me in Cambridge to send him to the bookshop that was selling the Frazer library, I had sent him to Deighton Bell – it should have been Galloway & Porter.

*

Towards the end of my sojourn in Cambridge, I became the President of the Law Society which had hospitably included the London evacuees in its membership. The most memorable lecture over which I presided was that given by Lord Calde-cote, then the Lord Chancellor, which took place in one of the Fellows' rooms in Trinity College. It was a lofty room, panelled and dimly lit, an ideal setting for the Lord Chancellor who was a solemn and, I thought, a rather lugubrious character. He talked about the practice of law with illustrations from his own experiences. I think that all who were present will remember his illustration of the techniques of cross-examination and the danger of asking too many questions.

This was his story. He had been defending counsel in the trial of a man charged with the murder of an elderly lady, his employer, at her country home. One of the witnesses for the prosecution was a young woman who worked at the local post office and who gave evidence identifying the accused. He had come to the post office and had asked her to send a telegram which she had read. It was a request for a nurse to be sent to the elderly lady. This identification was, apparently, an important issue and counsel for the defence sought to challenge this witness.

So, Lord Caldecote said, I asked the witness how many telegrams were brought to her during a normal working day. She thought about fifty. 'I should have stopped then,' said his Lordship, 'and used it as a matter of comment in my closing speech, questioning the validity of an identification of one out of the numerous customers visiting the post office daily. But I went on and said, 'How could you possibly be sure about identifying this man out of so many others you had seen or dealt with that day?' to which she replied that she was sure because of an unusual circumstance. She said that when she read the telegram and saw it was a request for a nurse, she was minded to ask the sender if she could address the telegram to her sister who was a nurse and who she very much wanted to see. 'But then I looked up at his face and saw that it bore a scar which made him look sinister and so I did not make the request.' Everyone in court, continued Lord Caldecote, instinctively turned to look at the man in the dock and saw the scar. I am sure that all in that gloomy room at Trinity must have felt a chill in the spine, as did I.

In my Jewish context, the most riotously hilarious occasion was the Purim *spiel* which was presented by some of the members of the Jewish society in its premises in Thompson's

Lane. The festival of Purim, recounted in the Book of Esther, marks the salvation of the Jews in Persia from a massacre planned by Haman and is celebrated joyously in Jewish communities. One of the traditional forms of celebration is a staged production of the story, often humorously, and that was our programme at the Cambridge synagogue in 1941.

Helmuth Lowenberg played the part of Esther, mainly because at that time he was acquainted with an Indian undergraduette and could borrow her sari. Vivian Herzog was the *shadchan* (marriage broker) and Monty Richardson took the part of Mordechai, the Jewish leader. I was the producer and we made it into a musical by writing parodies of the popular songs of the time. One of them was 'The Persian state it ain't wot it used to be' to the tune of 'The King's Navy' and another 'Heil Haman' to the tune of 'Run Rabbit Run'. Monty Richardson had been as successful in leading the synagogue services in Cambridge as he had those of the Young Sinaists in the East End of London, and a tribute was paid to him in a song entitled 'When Montague sang in Thompson's Lane' sung to the tune of 'When a nightingale sang in Berkeley Square'. My favourite was a parody of a then popular song 'Chattanooga Choochoo' which included the lines,

'Is there a rabbi or a *shochet* or a *mohel* in town,
Does he wear a kippa or a square mit a gown?'

The quality of the dialogue can be gauged from the following exchange:

Shadchan: Knock, knock
King: Who's there?
Shadchan: Adonovitch
King: Adonovitch who?
Shadchan: Adonovitch you like, blonde or brunette. But I got for you a peach.

The capacity audience loved it and some, almost literally, rolled in the aisles. To this day when I meet a Jewish Cambridge contemporary, more often than not, the 1941 Purim *spiel* will be happily recalled.

9

Cambridge University Jewish Society

Among the faculty and students of the two London colleges evacuated to Cambridge, a goodly number were Jews and they were cordially welcomed by the members of the Cambridge University Jewish Society (CUJS) whose home was the Thompson's Lane synagogue. At that time, practically every Jewish undergraduate joined the Jewish Society. Most Jewish undergraduates were not particularly observant and few attended the Sabbath services but at some point during the term almost all of them would attend one or more Friday night suppers, the most popular activity of the CUJS. They were rousing occasions replete with *zemirot*, traditional cooking and the lengthy, sung, Hebrew grace after meals. During term, some of these suppers were followed by talks given by invited guests. It was remarkable how many Jewish leaders were happy to come to Cambridge, usually at their own expense, to spend some time at the CUJS

The Sabbath services were conducted by students and the congregation was augmented by a few dons and Cambridge residents as well as a number of refugees from Nazi Europe. The most notable of these – and the most regular in attendance – was Professor Samuel Krausz who had been the Principal of the famous Jewish Theological Seminary in Budapest. I had occasion to visit him at his lodgings, a humble bed-sitting room in which books occupied more space than furnishings. He showed me a copy of his bibliography, a sizeable volume listing his numerous books and the articles he had written in learned journals.

The members of the CUJS cordially received those evacuated London students who were interested. I was soon on terms of friendship with the most active of the members of the CUJS many of whom went on to distinguish careers. Helmuth Lowenberg who, with his parents, had emigrated from Duisburg in Germany to Israel (then Palestine), became one of Israel's most notable District Judges. Cyril Domb, an engaging, gangling, Londoner, rigidly but tolerantly orthodox, later occupied Chairs in Mathematics in London and Israel and was elected a Fellow of the Royal Society. Lionel Wolman, a delightful northener, unassumingly benevolent, was to hold a Chair in Medicine in Sheffield until his untimely death. But the member of our Jewish circle to reach undreamed of heights was Vivian Herzog who, as Chaim Herzog, became Israel's sixth president.

Vivian was a charmer. His looks, ready smile, good nature and engaging Irish accent all combined to make him the ideal companion – and he was a hit with the girls too. He had been born in Belfast and then moved with his family to Dublin when his father, Isaac Herzog, became Chief Rabbi of Ireland. Vivian's nomadic existence came to an end when his father was appointed Ashkenazi Chief Rabbi of Palestine and, subsequently, of Israel. When we met, Vivian was a second year law student at University College, London. He subsequently gained his LL B and was later called to the Bar.

We became close friends and our major interests, apart from our studies, were the Law Society and the CUJS. At one point, when I chaired a meeting of the LSE Law Society which was held at Grove Lodge, LSE's Cambridge headquarters, a fellow student, a burly Palestinian Jew named Ashkenasy stood up and proposed a resolution that 'the power of the Jews in the Law Society has increased, is increasing and ought to be diminished'. Ashkenasy had barely finished these words when Vivian leapt from his seat, ran to him and delivered a precise and powerful punch to his head. Down he went, pandemonium followed and the meeting hastily came to an end. Ashkenasy had not been seriously hurt and he was not, thereafter, seen at meetings of the Law Society. Vivian took it all in his stride.

Many years later when Vivian was President of Israel and I was in the country on one of my regular professional visits, his wife Aura gave a luncheon party in the presidential residence for me, my wife Claire and her youngest daughter Tricia. There must have been a dozen or so Israeli dignitaries present and the luncheon proceeded in normal fashion until Vivian referred to the Purim *Spiel* and we both launched into the singing of some of the songs. The lunch thereafter became highly informal. Vivian had kept the script of our Cambridge production and gave me the copy which, unfortunately, did not include the musical parodies.

In 1943 the horrifying news of Hitler's gas chambers and crematoria shocked a hitherto incredulous world. On behalf of the CUJS I consulted Norman Mackenzie, an LSE contemporary, who was then the Chairman of the Labour Club, and we agreed to organise a joint protest meeting in the Cambridge Guildhall. Canon Raven, then the Master of Emmanuel College, presided and well-known speakers represented all three of the major political parties. The hall was filled to capacity and an overflow was improvised outside in Market Square.

After I left Cambridge, I spent a year as Assistant Secretary to the Foreign Affairs Committee of the Board of Deputies of British Jews, the representative body of Anglo-Jewry. There I came across a letter written to the President of the Board by Dr David Daube, then a Fellow of Gonville and Caius College and an authority on Roman Law with whom I had become very friendly. He was a refugee from Germany and he was proud to recall that his family had lived in the university town of

Freiburg for centuries. In this letter, he complained about the protest meeting and about me in particular saying that I was misleading ill-informed students with atrocity propaganda and he asked if the Board could do anything to persuade me to desist. I do not know if the Board replied to this letter but, needless to say, I heard nothing from them on the subject, nor did I ever discuss it with David.

Daube later reached the eminence of Regius Professor of Roman Law at Oxford and became a Fellow of All Souls. It was in the hall of that distinguished institution that I joined David, his family and friends in a celebration of the barmitzvah of his son when I was the editor of *The Jewish Chronicle*. David was most observant (though he described his position as orthoprax rather than orthodox) and the menu was, of course, strictly kosher. Hands were ceremonially washed before the meal, *zemirot* were sung and the lunch in that impressive college hall concluded with the traditional lengthy grace after meals. At its conclusion, when it was announced that the Sabbath afternoon service was about to be conducted, Professor Gershom Scholem, my neighbour at the table, rose and told me in mock disgust that he had had enough of this and was leaving to get a ham sandwich.

Some years later, David endured a particularly harrowing divorce which ruined Oxford for him and he accepted an invitation to occupy a chair at the University of California at Berkeley. Early in the 1980s, I had occasion to visit San Francisco and called David from my hotel. He appeared pleased to hear from me and invited Claire and me to lunch with him on campus. En route to Berkeley, I prepared Claire for the encounter. Being a direct and forthright American she was, I said, unlikely to enjoy the occasion for David was the quintessence of the reserved Oxford don – jacket and tie, of course, restrained and formal in conversation.

Arriving at the designated rendezvous, we looked around for

a gentleman in a dark suit who would stand out in the throng of casually attired students. Nobody responding to this description was visible and I was beginning to think that I had misunderstood the arrangements when there was a tap on my shoulder and I looked round to see David who was wearing a bright check shirt and blue jeans. At lunch he was charming and witty, thoroughly relaxed, the complete antithesis of the preview I had given my wife. He had recently visited Oxford, he told us, and had found the atmosphere so stifling that he could not leave soon enough. He found the informal atmosphere of Berkeley much more to his taste. His Oxford students could parse a sentence perfectly, spell beautifully and construct elegant essays. His Berkeley students could not do any of that but 'they think and produce original ideas' and he found that far more stimulating.

Before we parted, I asked him teasingly whether he still walked to synagogue on the Sabbath wearing his *tallith* (prayer shawl) as he had done in Cambridge. He responded with a nonchalant shrug. His life, he told me, had taken a new turn here for this was an environment which encouraged re-evaluations and change. As we parted for the last time, the gentle smile of this scholarly, committed but complicated Jew remains in my memory, an enigma and inspiration.

*

It was during my first year at Cambridge that I met Hersch Lauterpacht. Passover that year occurred during vacation time but there were a number of Jewish residents, some refugees and some service men, who would be in town during the festival, as well as a few students who, like me, lived there all year round and who wanted to participate in a communal Seder. The synagogue hall was available as was, even more importantly, the kitchen, and a few of us decided that we would organise the event. Everything was available except the money to pay for the necessary food and labour and we decided to organise a whip-round.

I, like others involved in the organisation, had a list of possible contributors, one on my list being Professor Lauter-pacht. I rang the bell of his house in Cranmer Road feeling some trepidation for he was, I suppose, the most eminent Jew at the university. He opened the door himself and, when I told him the purpose of my visit, cordially invited me in and immediately gave me a generous contribution. He had a request to make of me. When we received our supplies, would I let him have a carton of matzos so that he could tell his wife who, with his son Eli, was evacuated at the time, that he had the obligatory Passover unleavened bread in his house. Of course I concurred and, when our supplies were delivered, I took him a box. The first morning of the Passover festival, to my surprise, he attended the synagogue service; it was the only time during my sojourn in Cambridge that I saw him there.

We continued our acquaintance because he had a room in the Squire Law Library where I pursued my law studies and, from time to time, he would invite me into his room for a chat. He was interested in Jewish affairs and, as a member of the Board of Deputies representing the Cambridge synagogue, I was able to tell him a little of what was going on. We had something else in common. He had been born in Lwow, a city in the south-eastern part of Poland called Galicia where my parents had lived before their emigration to London. The members of its large Jewish population were known, sometimes pejoratively, as Galilitzianers, and were the subject of an exten-sive mythology based on their alleged simplicity and religiosity.

Lauterpacht had come to London to study at the London School of Economics and had done so well that, after gradu-ating, he was immediately offered a teaching post at that distinguished institution. So rapid was the recognition of his outstanding scholarship that, only a few years later, he was appointed to the most prestigious chair in this field, and became the Whewell Professor of International Law at Cambridge.

During one of our chats in his room at the Squire, he told me of the visit he had received from his father soon after his move to Cambridge. He had taken him to see some of the colleges and ended the tour in his room at Trinity College. When ensconced there, his father had asked him what his duties were. Well, said Lauterpacht, I give a couple of lectures each week. How long do they last? An hour each. And what else? I see students in my room here for three hours or so each week. And what else? That's all I am obligated to do, the rest of my time is taken up with my own research and activities. Father pondered a while then observed, 'Hersch, it can't last.'

Some time later, when we had got to know each other better, I flippantly suggested to him that he change his given name. As Whewell Professor, he was an adviser on international law to the Foreign Office and I was sure that, sometime or another, he would be offered a knighthood. 'Sir Henry would sound so much better than Sir Hersch.' He laughed, did nothing about it and did become Sir Hersch and, later, the British Judge at the Permanent Court of International Justice at The Hague.

We kept in touch after I left Cambridge and I met him on several occasions when he came to London when we would meet at his club, The Athenaeum. On one of these occasions I recall his pointing out to me the recumbent figure of Stanley Baldwin on one of the sofas. Later still we met when I became the London Correspondent of the American Jewish Committee and I was required to sound out Lauterpacht on his willingness to be retained as legal adviser to its delegation at the Peace Conference which opened in Paris soon after the end of the war. That did not come about but the negotiations and the further intimacy they engendered provided me with the opportunity of meeting him and enjoying his lively conversation and his irrepressible wit for some years after my Cambridge sojourn.

10

American Jewish Committee

Cambridge had been home for almost three years and had opened up a new world to me, a fantastically exhilarating and broadening experience. Although I had moved out of the London ghetto on my marriage, my life before Cambridge was still bounded by the Jewish community. In Cambridge I had, for the first time, moved socially, professionally and intellectually into the wider British society. So it was with sadness and reluctance that I packed my bags and left for London during the summer of 1943. The next hurdle to be overcome was the Bar final examination for which I sat later that year. By that time, my wife and I were living in a somewhat poky top-floor flat whose only merit was its convenient location in Warwick Court, a passageway leading from High Holborn into Gray's Inn. That meant that I did not have to walk far to reach the Old Hall in Lincoln's Inn where the examination was being held. All I can remember about that event is its conclusion and my exuberant state of mind as I left the examination hall after the last session. I would never, I told myself, ever sit for another examination. Nor did I.

From the moment I first attended a law lecture at LSE's wartime Cambridge refuge, I knew that I wanted to be a lawyer, preferably a barrister. I never seriously contemplated becoming a solicitor though the earning possibilities in that branch of the profession were far more promising. Being articled to and then joining a firm of solicitors seemed to me to approximate to being an employee and I'd had enough of that. Becoming a barrister was not only appealing because of the inherent interest of the occupation but the profession also attracted me greatly because every practitioner was self-employed – no firms, no partnerships. And finally I had the most romantic notions of participating in the dramatics of courtroom life.

I had instantly taken to the study of law, it fitted my kind of mind, always (and often to the irritation of others) inclined to turn to what I saw as logical reasoning and reliance on facts – at least that was how I flattered myself. At that time, all I knew about the life and work of a barrister had been gathered from novels, usually thrillers, and from films, and I had in my mind a picture of a glamorous and exciting occupation. It was only later that I learned from friends and teachers that the prospect of earning a living during the first few years at the Bar was not great. Given my financial circumstances there was not the slightest possibility that I could start on that new career immediately after I was called to the Bar. First, there was the cost of pupillage which at that time was a hundred guineas, a sum of money I did not possess. The greater deterrent was the knowledge that had been dinned into me by those who knew that, given the normal amount of luck, it would take something like three years in practice before I could expect to earn a living.

So I came to the unavoidable conclusion that I had to find a job and save enough to keep me for a reasonable period of time during which I would try my hand at establishing a practice at the Bar. But what was I to do? I was not qualified for any kind of job in the legal profession and my only area of expertise was the world of Jewish organisations.

It so happened that during my years at Cambridge, I had got to know Selig Brodetsky who, at that time, was Professor of Mathematics at Leeds University and, more importantly to me at any rate, later became the President of the Board of Deputies, the representative body of British Jewry. Brodetsky had been brought to England by his parents who had emigrated from Russia at the turn of the century and they settled, as most Jewish immigrants did, in the East End of London. Young Selig attended the Jews' Free School. A child prodigy showing early signs of mathematical aptitude, he won a scholarship to Cambridge, then an extremely rare phenomenon for those with his background. But what brought him into the public eye was that, in his final examination at Cambridge, he topped the list and was accorded the distinction of being named Senior Wrangler, a designation which has since been abandoned but which, while it lasted, was one of those awards which attracted public attention even outside academia.

The arrival at that time of large numbers of impoverished Jews from Eastern Europe was becoming a matter of national concern and strong opposition developed to the admission of so many aliens. An Aliens Bill to restrict immigration was being actively promoted, its advocates claiming that the Jews coming in were shiftless, brought disease, compounded the problem of unemployment and were a worthless lot who only damaged national interests. In this atmosphere, the academic success of this immigrant East End Jewish boy was a resounding refutation of these arguments and Brodetsky was held up by leaders of Anglo-Jewry as a glowing example of the opportunities that Britain offered and the benefits that immigration could bring.

Selig was feted as a hero by the Jewish community. He became an academic, but his first love was the Jewish people and the Zionist movement of which he eventually became a leader. I had first met him when he came to talk to the Young Sinaists. He was a fine speaker with a common touch enhanced, at least in my circle, by his familiarity with the Yiddish language with which his speeches to Jews were peppered. Our paths crossed again when his son Paul came up to Cambridge during the war years. Selig visited Paul from time to time and, since I had become a friend of Paul, I would generally see him on these occasions.

By that time, Brodetsky was in his fifties, a short, rotund man possessed of indefatigable energy and presenting a somewhat self-satisfied persona; he had, I suppose, good reason to be pleased with himself. I gathered from my conversations with Paul that his father was a difficult man to live up to. Selig expected great things from his only son but the diffident Paul, like so many sons of famous fathers, had no intention of competing. I saw a reflection of this one evening at Cambridge in their company. We were talking about Paul's studies and the Tripos examination which was coming soon. Brodetsky senior was expressing his ambitions for Paul's achievement at this examination and I remarked that he need have no anxiety for I was sure that Paul would gain a First. His response was that that would not be good enough; he expected his son to be first of the Firsts. Paul visibly winced. In the event, he gained a Second. Paul never really found himself. He tried several careers and while he was by no means a failure, he never achieved notable success. To the great sadness of everyone who knew him, Paul died young.

During my years in Cambridge I was a member of the Board of Deputies representing the Jewish Society's synagogue. Professor Brodetsky, then not yet President, represented a synagogue in Leeds and he was as prominent as I was insignificant. At that time, the Board of Deputies was technically a non-Zionist body and as such was a member of the Jewish Agency for Palestine, an institution created to represent the Jewish people vis-à-vis the British government which held the League of Nations mandate for Palestine. The Jewish Agency included both Zionist and non-Zionist representative organisations and the Board of Deputies was recognised as one of the latter. Many of the lay leaders of the Anglo-Jewish community, members of long-established and wealthy families, were anti-Zionist before the Second World War.

But the rank and file of British Jews and the great majority of the membership of the Board of Deputies were keenly Zionist and in 1943, to ensure that that the representative organisation of Anglo-Jewry would support the Biltmore Programme which called for the creation of a Jewish state when the war was over, the Zionist caucus at the Board staged a coup which ensured the election of Selig Brodetsky as its President, the first prominent Zionist to hold that position.

At the time I graduated, one of the main functions of the Board of Deputies' Foreign Affairs Committee was keeping in touch with the governments-in-exile, then based in London, of the countries occupied by the Nazis. Its major concerns were the fate of the remaining Jews on the continent when the war was over, support for the Zionist aim and the promotion of provisions for the protection of minorities to be incorporated into the peace treaties which were expected to be signed after the war. Since I was then specialising in public international law, Brodetsky, who knew that I was looking for a job, asked me if I would join the Board of Deputies as Assistant Secretary of the Foreign Affairs Committee at a salary of £600 – a very attractive proposition considering that, at that time, a junior lectureship at London's University College which may have been open to me paid £250. I accepted his offer.

I worked there happily because I liked my colleagues and had the feeling that I was doing something useful. But after a year my impatience to start my Bar career supplanted more practical calculations and I tendered my resignation. Brodetsky was sorry that I was to leave the Board but understood, so much so that he was a little later responsible for launching me on my long association with the United States.

The American Jewish Committee, the oldest and most respected organisation in the United States for the protection of

Jewish interests, had since its foundation in 1906 maintained contacts with the major Jewish communal bodies in Europe. During the war years the lines of communication had been broken and, in 1944, when the successful conclusion of the conflict could be envisaged, the AJC sent a representative to London to re-establish contact with the Board of Deputies and to appoint a British correspondent. The visitor was Dr Max Gottschalk, the Director of its Foreign Affairs Department, who had been a leader of Belgian Jewry before the war, had escaped to the United States before the Nazi occupation and was there recruited by the AJC.

Max Gottschalk was the personification of the cultivated West European Jew. Courtly in manner, multilingual and sophisticated, he was the kind of person headwaiters instinctively show to the best table in the restaurant. He was a lawyer by training but I do not think he ever actually practised. He may have had money of his own, I do not know, but his wife was a Phillipson, a prominent and affluent Jewish family in Brussels often referred to as the Rothschilds of Belgium, and it may have been this factor which afforded him the opportunity to spend much of his time on Jewish affairs.

Gottschalk visited London in 1944 just as I was leaving my job at the Board of Deputies and about to embark on my Bar career, and he asked Brodetsky if he could recommend somebody who could act as the AJC correspondent. He would prefer, he said, a young lawyer interested in and knowledgeable about Jewish affairs. Brodetsky recommended me. Gottschalk got in touch, we met and I was appointed, thus beginning my association with the United States which was to lead to my involvement with *The Jewish Chronicle* and much else.

Initially, my task was to send the AJC's New York office reports on Jewish life in Britain, on the activities being pursued by Jewish organisations and on the representations they were making to the governments-in-exile to ensure the protection of the rights of the Jews who may have survived when the war was over. As a briefless barrister, I had the time to engage in this activity, while the stipend I received from the AJC, particularly valuable since it was in US dollars, made it possible for me to be much more relaxed about my hasty exposure to the hazards of the Bar. It was, I believe, a good deal on both sides.

With the end of the war came the Peace Conference in Paris and, recalling the important achievements of Jewish organisations after the First World War in obtaining treaty provisions for the protection of Jewish rights, all the major Jewish organisations sent lobbying delegations to Paris. The American Jewish Committee was one of the most notable and its delegation was an impressive one headed by Jacob Blaustein, an oil magnate, then its Vice-President and later President, and Judge Phillip Forman, Chairman of the AJC's Foreign Affairs Committee. Phil was a Federal Judge based in Trenton, New Jersey, a man of great wisdom, simplicity and generosity who, until his death in 1976, remained one of my closest friends. Equally impressive were the members of the professional staff of the Paris delegation headed by Dr Simon Segal, a Polish Jew from Lwow and an expert in international law, who had succeeded Max Gottschalk as the head of the AJC Foreign Affairs Department. Accompanying him was the colourful Zachariah Shuster, an archetypal Lithuanian Jew from Vilna. He looked like Charles Boyer and spoke like him in a rich baritone. Zack was lovable, highly intelligent, entertaining and extremely literate. His native language was Yiddish and before he joined the AJC he had been a journalist on the staff of the New York Yiddish daily, *Der Tog*.

The AJC delegation stayed at the elegant Royal Monceau Hotel and I joined the delegates at weekends by courtesy of the American Embassy in London, travelling back and forth on a US Air Force plane from an airfield in Bovingdon in Hertfordshire. The AJC delegates spent most of the time talking to each other and to other Jewish representatives, occasionally meeting with members of the American and other delegations.

At weekends, when I was there, professional activities occasionally took second place to the pleasures that Paris had to offer and, despite the austerity and shortages, and the reminders everywhere of the ravages of war, there was a great deal to enjoy. Restaurants flourished and we patronised many of them. Few native Parisians (other than those who benefited from the black market) could afford the prices and the customers were therefore almost exclusively foreigners, powerfully augmented at that time by the Peace Conference delegations. And there were also the night clubs and cabarets.

One Saturday night, Simon Segal, Zack Shuster and I returned to the Royal Monceau from such an entertainment at around one in the morning and, collecting our keys, found accompanying them a message from Jacob Blaustein to the effect that he needed to see us and would we telephone him immediately on our return. Simon duly called Jacob's suite asking whether our meeting could wait for the next morning; it was late and we were all tired. 'No,' said Jacob, 'I won't keep you long but do come up now.'

Bleary-eyed we made our way to the nocturnal meeting. Jacob Blaustein, in pyjamas and dressing gown, was sitting at a desk which was covered with papers. He waved us in and we lounged about waiting for him to finish a business telephone call. He did not take long – in my experience he was always brief on the phone – and as soon as his total attention was focussed on us, Simon asked what was the subject on which he so urgently wanted our views at that somnolent hour. 'We have been here two weeks,' said Jacob, 'and we haven't yet seen Molotov (then the USSR Foreign Minister). When are we going to see him? It's urgent and important,' to which Simon wearily responded that we had been trying to see Molotov but that apparently he did not wish to see us. Slapping his hand on a pile of papers, Jacob concluded this momentous meeting with, 'Right. So we'll decide not to see Molotov. We've got to decide something!'

This uncharacteristic incident might make Jacob Blaustein seem fatuous which he certainly was not. He was shrewd and hard working, greatly respected for his dedication and perspicacity (and, I must add in the interests of objectivity, his wealth) by such as Ben-Gurion with whom he engaged in an historic correspondence on the relationship between Israel and the Jewish Diaspora. He was also kind and thoughtful. On the first occasion on which I stayed at his colonial mansion just outside Baltimore, he flew in from Chicago where he had been attending a board meeting of Standard Oil only in order to spend the evening with me. The following morning he flew back to Chicago. In the end, the AJC did not remain long in Paris as the Peace Conference collapsed and no treaties were ever signed.

In 1946 the AJC convened a conference in London to which it invited representatives of the surviving European Jewish communities to consider revival and reconstruction. I was deeply involved in the organisation of that occasion which will surely remain in the memory of everyone who participated in it. A few days before it opened, my mother had died and so I was not able to be present at the inaugural ceremonies. But when I put in an appearance after the seven statutory days of mourning, I encountered in the lobby the gaunt figure of Jules Braunschvig whom I had last seen in Paris early in 1939. He was then a young bachelor of means (my first view of a Sisley was of one in his apartment on the Boulevard Haussmann) about whom I had heard nothing since the outbreak of war. I learned from him that he had been taken prisoner-of-war and that during his incarceration had met a French rabbi who had been an army chaplain. Jules was impressed and influenced by this rabbi, studied Hebrew with him and deepened his Jewish commitment to the extent that, on his release, he had immediately associated himself with the Alliance Israelite Universelle, had become it's Vice-President (Professor René Cassin, later a Nobel Laureate, was the President) and in that capacity was leading the French delegation. We had an emotional reunion and remained friends until his demise.

One of the results of the 1946 conference was the creation of the United Jewish Educational and Cultural Organisation (UJECO) whose task it was to assist the small and impoverished Jewish communities in Europe rebuild their educational facilities. I became the Honorary Secretary of this organisation and, since at that time most of the organisations working for the reconstruction of European Jewry had their headquarters in Paris, I continued to make frequent visits to that city. My main purpose on these trips was to maintain contact and exchange ideas with the American Joint Distribution Committee (JDC) which provided most of the funding for UJECO. The new organisation only lasted about three years before its funds ran out. The JDC had come to the conclusion that it could provide the educational services more effectively and economically itself and, as a result, UJECO decided to disband but with the consolation that it had initiated an invaluable contribution to the revival of Jewish life in Europe after Hitler.

The Joint, as the JDC is generally known, was rendering a service which it would be impossible to laud too highly. It was and is, in my opinion, the surpassing Jewish organisation in the world. Not only does it raise millions of dollars in the United States for Jewish relief but also it recruited personnel of the highest calibre – able, motivated, resourceful and untiring in their devotion to the cause of Jewish survival. The organisation at that time occupied a large building in Paris on the Rue Ste Dominique close to the Invalides while another American organisation, the Hebrew Immigrant Aid Society (HIAS), also had an office nearby, and from it facilitated the emigration of survivors of the Nazi camps.

The official exchange rate in France for the dollar at that time bore no relation to its real purchasing power and a black market in currency exchange flourished. Both these American organisations were funded in dollars and, had they exchanged them for francs at the official rate, they would have received only a fraction of what they needed to spend. Like most foreign organisations operating from Paris at the time, they therefore exchanged their dollars on the black market. They assumed that the authorities must have known about it and the lack of any action against the practice was taken to imply their tacit acquiescence.

But then the unexpected happened. The Paris police raided the HIAS office, impounded its account books and arrested the local director, an American named Lewis Neikrug. That night there was a great burning of papers at the Rue Ste Dominique offices of the JDC.

The gregarious Lew Neikrug, had been happily settled in Paris for a few years and, not unusually among the American community in the city, was living a comfortable pro-consular existence. With a dollar income, the good things in life were readily available. To pursue its operations, his organisation was bringing into France substantial quantities of dollars and, of course, exchanging them at black market rates From his insalubrious cell in the Sante prison, Lew Neikrug made desperate representations to his New York headquarters for urgent action to be taken to secure his release. The American lay leaders of HIAS concluded that since this crisis had occurred in Europe, a territory whose mores, customs and procedures were mysteries to them, they would ask a European to intervene on Neikrug's behalf.

Their choice was the same Max Gottschalk who had been responsible for my appointment with the American Jewish Committee. French speaking, diplomatic and with friends and contacts among French officialdom, he seemed the ideal man for the task. Of particular relevance was his acquaintance with the wife of Daniel Mayer who, at that time, was the Minister of Finance. As I was told the tale of events by Zack Shuster, then attached to the Paris office of the AJC, Dr Gottschalk flew to Paris and, after he had settled in his hotel, sent a bouquet to Madame Mayer informing her that he was in town and how pleased he would be to see her. After a day or two he received a cordial note from Madame Mayer thanking him for the flowers, regretting that she would be very busy during the next few days but would be in touch with him as soon as possible. In the meantime, as Zack put it, 'Lew was rotting in jail.'

Madame Mayer was as good as her word and, some days later, Dr Gottschalk received an invitation to tea with the lady. He presented himself at the residence, naturally with more flowers, and in the course of the encounter mentioned that he would be grateful for the opportunity of an informal conversation with M. Mayer about the HIAS affair. His hostess promised to relay this message to her husband. More days passed with Neikrug fretting in durance vile. Eventually came a note from the Minister acknowledging the request for a meeting but regretting that his schedule prevented an early date. By that time, not only was Neikrug becoming frantic but his employers in New York had become impatient with the leisurely European pace of Dr Gottschalk's representations.

They decided that the Chairman of HIAS, who was a prominent figure in New York local politics, should himself fly to Paris and take over. Immediately after landing at Le Bourget airport, the new emissary drove to the American Embassy, saw the Ambassador and asked him to request an immediate interview with the Minister of Finance. Soon the American was in the private office of M. Mayer.

He put his case to the Minister very bluntly. If Neikrug was not immediately released, HIAS would close its office in Paris and France would lose the large sums in foreign currency it was bringing into the country. Within hours, Lew Neikrug was set free. For all the foreign non-governmental organisations then operating in Paris – and all of them knew the story – it destroyed the hitherto unquestioned belief that in Europe things could only get done in the old-fashioned European way.

*

I set up an office in London for the AJC in Old Burlington Street which served me and the constant stream of American visitors, both lay leaders of the central organisation and its chapters throughout the States as well as visiting members of the organisation's staff. One of the strangest of these visits was that of George Mintzer, a New York lawyer who was retained by the AJC to keep a watch on anti-Semitic organisations and one such was the British Fascist Party led by Sir Oswald Mosley. Purporting to be a wealthy American anti-Semite, George had entered into a correspondence with Mosley offering financial support and trying to ascertain the uses to which his money could be put in Britain. At one point in the correspondence, Mosley had intimated that the time had arrived for the two of them to meet since the information was too sensitive to be put into writing and George agreed.

Judge Forman, Chairman of the AJC's Foreign Affairs Committee, knew of this plan and asked George to bring me a large kosher salami since food rationing at that time was still severe. George and I met surreptitiously soon after his arrival and he told me that he was leaving London immediately for Mosley's country residence where he hoped to learn of the fascist leader's plans. He made no mention of the salami and, at that time, I knew nothing about it. By the time George returned to London on his way home, I had received a telephone call from Phil who asked me whether I had received the salami and, of course, I mentioned this to George who was full of apologies. He had forgotten about it when we had first met and had only remembered when, unpacking at the Mosleys, the pungent odour had hit him. Since he was not sure that he would be seeing me again and did not feel he should take the item back to the States, he had decided to present the kosher salami to Lady Mosley who had gratefully accepted it. I have occasionally speculated on Lady Mosley's thoughts as she was offered this essentially Jewish comestible. Did she accept out of politeness or had years of rationing softened her family's anti-Semitism?

It was in my comparatively early days as the correspondent of the American Jewish Committee that the demand for the creation of a Jewish state in Palestine became violent. The British forces in the area over which they had the United Nations Mandate responded forcefully to the violence of extreme Jewish groups like Begin's Irgun and the conflict reached its peak with the hanging of the two British sergeants in 1947. That provoked an unnerving bout of anti-Zionist and anti-Jewish incidents in Britain and I remember Neville Laski telling me at the time that he had been ostracised by several of his colleagues at the Bar. Since one of the main purposes of the AJC was to combat anti-Semitism, I kept them fully informed about the situation in Britain.

The main rioting had taken place in the north of England, particularly in Liverpool and Manchester, the latter containing the second largest Jewish community in the country, where, I reported, the number involved in the disturbances were no more than a few hundred, mostly youngsters. In London windows of Jewish-owned shops were smashed and there was some looting. This was the first time in the twentieth century that anti-Jewish riots on such a scale had occurred in Great Britain.

I concluded my report with my own view which I offered, as I put it, 'with considerable diffidence'. It was that hooliganism of this kind would not become a permanent feature. If Jewish violence in Palestine were to continue, I surmised that there might be more trouble in Britain but I was of the opinion that it did not amount to a permanent increase in anti-Semitism. 'All the talk about Palestine and the Jews has made it possible for the existing hard core of fascists and anti-Semites to express their views more openly and gain a temporary audience which will agree with something of what they say.'

My formal association with the AJC continued until I became Editor of *The Jewish Chronicle* in 1958. I cannot assess what benefits the arrangement brought to the organisation, but I was certainly a beneficiary. Most important to me were the friendships I established with both its lay and professional leaders. When I began my association in 1944, its President was Judge Joseph Proskauer who had presided over the conversion of the AJC from an organisation cool to Zionism to one enthusiastically, though not uncritically, supportive of a Jewish national home. One of the more arcane interests I shared with Joe was a love of Gilbert and Sullivan. He had memorised many of the wittiest and most popular songs and, at the slightest provocation, would perform them enthusiastically if not very musically. His successor as President was Jacob Blaustein, whom I had met in Paris during the Peace Conference and, of the lay leaders, none was closer to me than Philip Forman to whom I became, as he once put it, an intimate member of his family. Of the professionals, the outstanding member was the Executive Vice-President John Slawson, whose vigour, enthusiasm and vision were in marked contrast to the shortness of his physical stature. His second in command was Selma Hirsch, with whom I have maintained a lifetime affectionate friendship. There were many others with whom I kept in touch happily for long after my formal connection with the organisation had ended.

11

At the Bar

After resigning from my post at the Board of Deputies, I became a pupil of Herbert Garland, a veteran 'junior', that is to say, a barrister who had not taken silk, i.e. been appointed a King's Counsel, a KC. When Queen Elizabeth II ascended the throne, KCs became QCs. Head of a busy set of chambers at 1 Essex Court in the Temple, Garland had practised at the Bar for many years and had a flourishing and varied junior practice which made him an ideal pupil master. For six months, at a cost of a hundred guineas which I borrowed from the bank, I was to follow him around in the courts, read his briefs and, when requested, prepare drafts of pleadings or opinions. I quickly learned what the latter involved. The first time I was asked to draft an opinion on one of his cases, I wrote an 'on the one hand and on the other hand' kind of thing. Garland read it and commented that the solicitor client wanted an opinion, not doubts. It was an important lesson.

I travelled with him to county courts and police courts but most thrilling for me was to sit beside him, wigged and gowned, on his fairly infrequent appearances in the High Court mostly on undefended divorce cases. On the days when he was not in court, we went for coffee together to the ABC café in Fleet Street, opposite the High Court, or to the Kardomah Café, also on Fleet Street. Other barristers were there and we joined them to chat about this and that (as a pupil I, of course, remained silent). These mid-morning breaks were a time for gossip about the judges and other barristers and for the exchange of legal anecdotes which did as much for my education in the ways of the Bar as the more formal aspects of pupillage.

Towards the end of my period as a pupil, on a Saturday morning in early November 1944, our Warwick Court flat was hit by a V2 rocket. Normally at this time I would have been attending a synagogue service but, on this occasion, I was suffering from a heavy cold and had decided to stay in bed. It was while I was in bed and my wife was in the kitchen that, in deathly silence, the walls and ceiling caved in. The blankets with which I was covered must have saved my body from injury but my head was bleeding and covered in debris. I had no idea what had happened but got out of bed as best I could and moved in the direction of the kitchen where I found my wife buried under roof timbers. I did my best to release her but without success and, since my efforts only caused her greater pain, I desisted.

After what seemed like only minutes the top of a ladder appeared and air raid rescuers climbed in. They assured me they would take care of my wife and placed me on a stretcher which was then gently lowered to the ground. Some spectators had gathered, among them an American GI. While I was lying on the stretcher awaiting an ambulance, the GI strolled over, wordlessly took out a pack of Camel cigarettes from his pocket, put one between my lips, lit it and walked away. It was the most flavourful cigarette I had ever tasted.

I was taken to St Bartholomew's Hospital, Bart's as it was generally referred to, and my stretcher was carried to a queue awaiting an anti-tetanus shot. When my turn came, the doctor holding the needle was none other than a Cambridge friend, Marco Caine. Covered as I was in muck, he did not at first recognise me. I asked him if he could find out where and how my wife was and later that day he came to my hospital bed to tell me that she had been taken to another hospital and was in reasonably good shape.

I remained at Bart's for a few days and, for my discharge, was fitted out with hand-me-down clothes since all my possessions (including my work on a Ph.D. thesis in the field of international law which I never did never complete) were under the rubble of what had been my home. Fortunately, my friend Lawrence Rose, who was about my build, gave me the run of his wardrobe until I had obtained the necessary coupons, for clothing was rationed. I had nowhere to live and Ray and Sol Sklan, old friends from pre-war London days who had evacuated to Cambridge where they had a large house, invited me to stay with them. I arranged for my wife, whose injuries were much more serous than mine, to be transferred to Addenbrooke's Hospital in Cambridge where she remained for a number of weeks.

During the period I lived with the Sklans I took the train daily to Liverpool Street to continue my pupillage. Under a government scheme to assist bombing victims, I was able to acquire the tenancy of a flat in Dolphin Square and, with the aid of furniture coupons and £300 war damage compensation, bought some basic items of furniture and household necessities. A month or so after the bombing, I was invited to visit a salvage depot to see if I could recognise any of my belongings. I did see some items of clothing but in such a state that there was no point in claiming them. However, as I was about to leave, I saw projecting under some garbage the corner of a leather-covered book which I recognised as my photograph album and I retrieved it.

Towards the end of my pupillage, I was the beneficiary of a very happy accident. The same Lawrence Rose who had very generously let me have the use of his wardrobe after the bombing, was a pupil of a highly successful barrister named Constantine Gallop. From time to time I would look in to see

Lawrence in his chambers which were close to Essex Court and I thus got to know his clerk, his *shammas*, the all-important functionary of every set of chambers. Because a barrister is forbidden to hobnob with solicitors, his only clients, his clerk maintains these indispensable contacts. Moreover, since barristers are above handling anything as gross as money, the clerk is also the business manager.

The happy accident occurred one evening when a brief arrived for a member of Gallop's chambers to appear at Kingston Magistrate's Court the following morning. The barrister for whom the brief was intended had already left and there was no possibility of getting it to him that day. Gallop's clerk told the solicitor's clerk who was delivering the brief that there was a young man named Frankel in nearby chambers who might be available to take it on. The solicitor's clerk came over, I was there, and happily accepted my first brief.

It was marked with the handsome fee of £2 4s 6d, that is, two guineas for the barrister and two shillings and sixpence for his clerk. I travelled early the next morning to the Kingston Court where I was to meet a representative of my instructing solicitors, a firm named Dale & Newbery of Feltham, a town close to Heathrow Airport. A barrister does not appear in court without being accompanied by a representative of his instructing solicitors. Since my brief was merely to make a plea in mitigation for some driving offence which was admitted, I was told that for a case of this magnitude, I should expect only the most junior of the solicitors' clerks to be with me. However, to my surprise, Dale & Newbery's representative that morning was an impressive middle-aged gentleman named Lewis, the influential managing clerk to the firm. He hastened to inform me that he would not normally have come for this case but that all their junior clerks were otherwise engaged.

Evidently I had impressed Mr Lewis with my advocacy for, over a cup of coffee after the hearing, he asked me whether I was interested in taking on small cases in magistrates' or county courts because his office had loads of them. Making every effort to control my excitement, I told him I would be interested. Then he continued by telling me that the reason for his enquiry was that most of their small work had been going to a barrister (later an MP) with whom they were not terribly happy and 'is a Jew, you know'.

I was, of course, deeply disconcerted by that remark but decided not to respond and risk losing an opportunity of acquiring my first client. Sure enough, Dale & Newbery thereafter kept me busy. In my first year at the Bar, I earned several hundred guineas from that firm alone and their work continued for many years until, with the growth of my practice, I was receiving bigger and better briefs and had to give up most of the smaller cases. Some time after our initial conversation, I was again attended by Mr Lewis and in the course of conversation after the case had finished, he remarked that he was a lay preacher at his local church. That gave me the opportunity of telling him that in the synagogue to which I belonged, lay preachers were not allowed, only ordained rabbis. He seemed to blanch a little at that, but quickly recovered and our conversation continued without any reference to my remark. In the event, it did not diminish the flow of work that came to me from his firm.

After my pupillage ended, I became a tenant in the chambers of Acton Pile at 4 Paper Buildings. He was an elderly barrister, a Victorian presence, courtly but distant in manner, whose practice was exclusively in the Probate, Divorce and Admiralty Division of the High Court. When I joined his chambers I was the only other tenant, but in the course of the next few years, another two or three young men came in and I no longer had a room to myself. My practice flourished, helped initially by the efforts of Charles, the clerk, who had persuaded some of Acton Pile's divorce clients to brief me in common law cases. Life was good then. I loved my work, loved eating in Hall when I was not in court and was stimulated by my annual lecture tour of the United States which had begun in 1947. But, after a few years at Paper Buildings, I found those chambers did not suit me for the clerk was no longer giving me his undivided support and, not unnaturally, sought to obtain work for the new young tenants. On one occasion after I had complained about his directing one of my regular clients to another member of chambers, the atmosphere became disagreeable and I decided to leave. My first application was to Cyril Salmon, QC, a distinguished barrister who later became a Law Lord and took the title of Lord Salmon of Sandwich, a designation which aroused considerable mirth at the time. He interviewed me, said that he was impressed with my progress at the Bar but was unwilling to let his chambers be known as Jewish and regretted, therefore, that he was unable to take me. I subsequently approached Leonard Caplan, QC, who was the head of chambers in one of the post-war Temple buildings and he offered me a place which I gratefully accepted. I remained a member of Leonard's chambers at 2 Harcourt Buildings until I retired from the Bar.

I appeared only once in one of the highly dramatic courts of the Old Bailey, the Central Criminal Court. I was defending a businessman who had engaged in some questionable financial transactions and was being prosecuted for embezzlement. While sitting on the barristers' bench waiting for my case to be called, a meek looking man was brought into the dock and the judge was informed that he was pleading guilty to a charge of bigamy but wished to be represented. The judge courteously told him that he could choose any one of the robed barristers sitting in court and, to my complete bewilderment, the accused pointed to me. I was then a novice with little knowledge of, or experience in, criminal law and it was a measure of the unfortunate man's lack of judgment that he had chosen me rather than Valentine Holmes, one of the leaders of the criminal bar and later a High Court judge beside whom I was seated.

I was then ushered by an official to the cells below the court and, before being allowed to interview my unexpected client, I was handed the sum, in cash, of £2 4s 6d for what is called a 'dock brief', two guineas being my fee and half a crown for my clerk. From there I was taken to meet my client the bigamist, heard his story and returned to the court, confirmed his guilty plea to the judge and followed with my plea in mitigation.

The tale I told the judge was pathetic and I tried to put it as sympathetically as I could. My client, who was originally from a small country town, had some years ago contracted an unhappy marriage and, when he became unemployed, had left the marital home for London with both spouses agreeing that, in all probability, he would not return. Try as he could, he was unable to find a job in London and, one evening, sought some relief from his misery by a visit to a pub. There he entered into conversation with a fellow patron of the opposite sex who, it turned out, was also having a rough time. The two kindred spirits had much in common and their relationship continued after they had left the pub. They were so drawn together that, at one point, the lady informed the accused that she was pregnant. To his credit, he was ready to do the honourable thing and proposed marriage in the belief that his previous alliance had been dissolved in practice if not formally. And now, I pleaded with the judge, for doing what he thought was the right thing, he was standing here in the dock at the Old Bailey and deserved leniency. The moment I concluded and sat down, the judge, without any hesitation, intoned 'six months'. I went over to commiserate with my client but he appeared relieved and thanked me profusely adding, 'I hope to see you again, sir.'

Another lighter moment occurred only a few days later when I was appearing in a civil action in the High Court before Mr

Justice Evershed. In the course of my opening remarks on behalf of the plaintiff, I asserted that the defendant should not be permitted to 'blow hot and cold'. The judge interrupted me to say that I should employ the correct legal phraseology which was 'approbate and reprobate'. I responded to this correction with the conventional 'If your Lordship pleases' but I wasn't pleased and, during the lunch adjournment, I went to the Bar library and checked a judgement I remembered in the course of which Sir Rufus Isaacs (later Lord Reading), the then Lord Chief Justice, had used the phrase blowing hot and cold.

I brought the volume containing that law report into court and, rising to my feet after the judge had taken his seat, I reminded him of his correction that morning and then read him the relevant passage in the law report. Mr Justice Evershed listened smilingly and, when I had ended, leaned forward and said, 'Mr Frankel, when you have been at the Bar longer, you will know that it does not pay to correct the judge on an immaterial point.'

I retired from the Bar in 1955 to take up my appointment with *The Jewish Chronicle* and, before doing so, I wrote to all my solicitor clients telling them what I was doing and thanking them for their support. That produced a telephone call from Mr Lewis. Would I accept a final brief from his firm at the Feltham Magistrate's Court where, from about 1945 to 1950, I had appeared so frequently that I was known to the regulars as its Attorney-General? I had also become personally acquainted with several of the magistrates who sat there and, in fact, had acted for two of them. I was touched by the thought, said I'd be happy to accept and duly turned up at the Court. All the magistrates sitting were known to me and, after the case ended, I was invited to their room where I was offered a glass of sherry and a brief speech of good wishes from the chairman.

12

Tea with Einstein

The United States became more than just another place on the map for me when, in or around my tenth year, a cousin, the son of one of my mother's sisters, arrived in London from Przemysl on his way to the New World. His name was Joseph Hefter and he was, I suppose, in his early twenties at the time. Unlike every other member of my family I had met until then, he was both not orthodox and had received a well-rounded secular education. Joseph was cultivated in a way which was new to me, speaking several languages and being very well read. Most impressively, he played the violin which he had brought with him. He remained in London for some months while he was earning enough to pay for his passage to America.

After he had left, Joseph kept in touch with me, infrequently at first, but more often after he had formed a Jewish group the object of which was to create a territorial settlement in Southern California for Jewish refugees from Hitlerism. That was of particular interest to me for, at that time, I was engaged in a lengthy correspondence with Joseph Leftwich, a well-regarded Jewish writer, who was keen to have me join his group, the Jewish Territorial Association, which was supporting Jewish re-settlement elsewhere than in Palestine (I did nothing about that). But what impressed me even more than Hefter's association with the Jewish territorial movement, was the arrival of a bulky volume he had written called *Graphic Design* which was published by McGraw Hill.

Then, in the early days of the war, a long-playing record called 'Ballad for Americans' was released. It was treasured by almost everyone I knew in Cambridge who possessed a gramophone (which I did not). Featuring Paul Robeson, it presented an inspiring picture of the New World. That record encouraged the immature me to think of America as a nation of idealists pursuing the dream of a moral society in which all inhabitants possessed the inalienable rights of 'Life, Liberty and the pursuit of Happiness' and thus was planted the seed of what was to become a drive to visit the United States as soon as I could.

The opportunity came soon after the end of the war as a result of my association with the American Jewish Committee. Early in 1947 Simon Segal, who had succeeded Max Gottschalk as the Director of the Committee's Foreign Affairs Department, asked me whether I would like to talk to several of the AJC chapters about the post-war position of Jews in Europe and, of course, I accepted.

Timing was a problem since I could not afford to be away from my Bar practice during legal term time which in England started early in October. The lecture season among Jewish groups in America usually began after the Jewish high holydays and in 1947, Rosh Hashana would be celebrated on 24 September. But my friends at the AJC considered that such was the interest of their constituency in what I was to talk about and, in particular, what was happening to the Jewish community in Britain, that at least some chapters would be willing to invite me to talk even before Rosh Hashana. And so it turned out.

For months before my departure my excitement grew to the extent that I even now recall my vivid dreams of walking amid skyscrapers. My plan was to fly to New York because of my impatience to see America but to make a more leisurely return by ship on the Queen Elizabeth. I arranged it that way partly because I thought I should need some relaxation before returning to London and also because I expected to bring back food and clothing for my family and friends since severe rationing was still in force. Had I attempted to bring them back by air, it would have been an expensive proposition given the general practice at that time to charge for excess baggage.

So at 7.30 pm on 3 September I presented myself, with my inconsiderable luggage, at the KLM terminal in Sloane Street which was also used by American Overseas Airlines with which I had booked. The passengers were driven to what was then called London Airport and we took our seats on a large, propeller driven aircraft which left at about 11 pm for Shannon in Ireland where we disembarked for coffee and sandwiches while new passengers embarked. That flight left at 2 am for the long haul – after a brief stop at Keflavik in Iceland – to Gander, Newfoundland, then a bleak place seemingly on the edge of nowhere. But what was so remarkable about Gander was that it was indubitably in the New World of plenty because we were served with real orange juice, fresh fruit and real cream, and amazingly white bread – all virtually unavailable in rationed Britain since 1939.

Thus fortified, we boarded again for the last hop to New York which took eight hours. By the time we landed at La Guardia airfield at 2.30 pm, nineteen hours had passed since I had stepped into the London terminal. However, before we were able to disembark we had to wait until a doctor boarded the aircraft, fixed every passenger with what he must have imagined was a piercing look to ascertain whether they had any diseases which would bar them from entering the country and demanding to see everyone's vaccination certificate – a little unnecessary since this certificate had to be presented before embarkation. As I eventually walked down the steps from the plane, the air hit me, literally, as though I had been struck by a wet, hot towel. The customs formalities were leisurely, without any regard for the comfort of the drooping passengers, but eventually, when all was completed, my weariness was momentarily forgotten at the sight of two American friends from the New York AJC staff who had come to greet me.

Some disenchantment returned as I was driven from La Guardia to the Pennsylvania Hotel in Manhattan; the sky-scrapers did not seem all that tall and the streets through which we passed were dirty and unremarkable. What did impress me, though, was Lindy's restaurant where my friends took me to dinner after I had checked in at the hotel, showered and changed. As a keen Damon Runyon fan, Lindy's (which to him was Mindy's) was a must for me and I was not disappointed. The waiters were as disagreeable and dictatorial as I had imagined and the customers looked as though they had stepped out of Runyon's pages. But the food was the thing. After years of austerity and rationing, the quantities of food heaped on the plates, the pickled cucumbers and other crudités freely available on the tables, the varieties of bread and bagels, the sheer profligacy of it all made me gasp. The dinner was delicious and though I left half the food on my plate, I had eaten enough to make me feel extremely bilious for the next couple of days. It took about a week of discomfort before my nerves and stomach eventually recovered from the initiation excesses of the Big Apple.

A day or two after my arrival in New York, John Slawson, the dynamic professional head of the AJC, invited me to meet senior members of the staff and talk to them about some of the present concerns of the Jews of Europe. Of course I did but, in the course of my observations I said something which aroused John's ire and he made some caustic remarks which caused me some discomfort. The following day John called me at my hotel, apologised for his unnecessarily sharp comments and asked me if I would care to join him and his wife Ada on a visit to the Roosevelt home at Hyde Park. I did. We had a most enjoyable day together and that was the beginning of a beautiful lifetime friendship. I had a few free days before my first lecture engagement at Syracuse (I initially incited hilarity by pronouncing it Sigh-racuse instead of Sirra-cuse) so had time to take a train to Trenton, the historic capital of the state of New Jersey, to visit my friend Phillip Forman, a Federal Judge.

The grandeur of New York's Pennsylvania Station was startling to one accustomed only to the generally grimy and commonplace railway stations of Britain. The train, too, was a cut above those of the London and North-Eastern or the Great Western Railways. The carriages were long and intercommunicating and the seats faced the same way. At that time British trains consisted of small compartments in which passengers sat facing each other, four or five aside in closer proximity than most would have cared for. But what was most cheering about my first train ride in the United States was the shining face of the black refreshment dispenser as he wheeled his trolley along the gangway announcing, 'Hoyshey bars, coconut mounds, al-mond (pronounced al-mond) joys'.

Phil was waiting for me at Trenton Station and outside was his car driven by his black law clerk who was always addressed as Mister Moore. Phil was so unassuming an individual that it was something of a surprise that his car was a large Pontiac, but then all American cars were huge by British standards and, as he pointed out when I made a remark on the subject, this was not a particularly fancy model. I was beginning my education in American mores.

I was even more surprised when, after lunch, I visited the Federal Court which was in the Post Office building, a large and somewhat Stalinesque pile in the centre of the city. The Court had its own entrance, distinct from the post office, and there was also a private entrance for the judges. I had not expected the spaciousness and elegance that greeted me accustomed as I was to the generally small and poky rooms occupied by High Court judges in London. Phil's blue carpeted and richly furnished chambers consisted of a suite of large and lofty offices for his staff of secretaries and law clerks. His own room was impressively grand. In London, where we had spent a good deal of time together the previous year, he had given me no hint that his professional environment was so sumptuous.

We then went to his house which reminded me of the staple American homes I had often seen in movies involving small town living – a porch with rockers, lots of white paint, spacious rooms simply but comfortably furnished. His wife Pearl was waiting to greet me. Of Swedish origin, she was open-faced and open-hearted, honest, straightforward and completely un-affected. I took to her instantly while she, considering me a temporary refugee from the privations of post-war Europe, plied me with food and drink. She was an excellent cook and the dinner I had that night remains in my memory. I had never tasted such roast beef and it was kosher in deference to Phil's mother, Tilly, who was living with them. She was born in London, had been in the United States some sixty years but was at pains to preserve her English accent. Tilly was not easy, but her son and daughter-in-law dealt with her so patiently and so kindly that they grew even higher in my estimation. For many years, until their deaths, the Formans were my family in America and Trenton was my hometown. I would go there as soon as possible after my arrival in the States, spend at least a weekend with them which, more often than not, included a stay at their cottage on the bank of the Delaware River just outside the town of New Hope in Pennsylvania.

After dinner that first night, the combination of Scotch, ample food and fatigue had their effect on my endurance. Pearl and Phil had planned to show me a supermarket, a uniquely American experience, but I was in a daze. Still, I was anxious to see everything the New World had to offer and, moving on automatic pilot, I was driven to Food Fair where I observed

American shopping for the first time. The contrast with Britain was startling. Familiar now to all those accustomed to supermarkets, the sight, in 1947, of abundant shelves displaying huge quantities of every known food, unrationed and even inexpensive, was dazzling.

However, the highlight of my visit came on the second day when Pearl and Phil drove me to see the university at Princeton. It was not like the quadrangled, enclosed colleges of Oxford or Cambridge. The campus at Princeton was open and the dramatic autumnal colours of the abundant foliage enhanced the attractive, if studiedly old-fashioned and conventional, architectural style

Solicitous that I should not be deprived of my afternoon tea, Phil told me that he had made arrangements for me to partake of that refreshment at the home of a friend. Promptly at 4.30, he rang the bell of a pleasing but unpretentious detached house in a side street close to the university centre. Almost immediately, the door was opened by a stocky man wearing a sweater, baggy slacks, slippers over his bare feet and an unruly halo of white hair which crowned the gentle, beaming face of Albert Einstein. He later told me that he never wore socks; they were 'useless garments'.

He greeted my hosts affectionately and when we had been introduced shook my hand firmly and lengthily with warm words of welcome, ushering us into his living room/study where tea and cookies were waiting. My friends had not previously told me the identity of my teatime host and, when I mentioned this to Einstein, he responded by telling me that Judge Forman had sworn him in as an American citizen in the Federal Court at Trenton and that their friendship had then begun.

Phil Forman later gave me a photograph, which I believe to be unique, showing him presenting Einstein with his naturalisation papers in Court on 1 October 1940. In his speech Judge

Forman said, 'Because of his race, his writings were burned and he was forced to flee from his native land. I, too, am the son of immigrant parents of his race. I resort to the personal only in a spirit of humble gratitude because I am deeply cognisant that only in America would it be possible for me to occupy the position which I do as the representative of my country before you today.'

It took me a while to overcome my bewilderment at thus meeting the legendary figure of Einstein and then I began to take notice. The room was simply furnished, books occupied most of the wall space and a desk was uncluttered. The four of us, Phil, Pearl, Einstein and I, sat round a low table on which rested some magazines and the tea things. I looked more closely at our host and my first and lasting impression was of the gentleness and the kindliness reflected in his eyes and his facial expression. Whenever I now see Epstein's bust of Einstein at the Tate Gallery, I marvel at the way the sculptor has preserved the look of sheer goodness which so impressed me. The other outstanding impression I retained was my surprise that he spoke with a thick German accent. I imagine that, because of his fame as an international figure, it had not occurred to me that he would possess anything as commonplace as a foreign accent.

He talked volubly and entertainingly in heavy, guttural English, frequently interspersed with hearty rolls of laughter. That was emphatically the case when he recounted an incident which had occurred the previous day. He had had a dinner appointment at 7 and at about 6.45 his devoted secretary, Miss Helen Dukas, came in to say that it was time to leave. With him at the time, he told us, was David Mitrany, a friend who was then a visiting academic at Princeton and they immediately left together, continuing their conversation as they walked.

At about 7.30, said Professor Einstein almost doubled up with chortling, Mitrany reminded him of his dinner appointment. 'Of course,' said Einstein, 'but I've forgotten where it is.'

They agreed that the only thing to do was to telephone Miss Dukas and ask for the address. So they rang the bell at the first house they passed to ask if they could use the phone. A lady answered the door and, 'Can you imagine, she recognised me and invited me in by name!'

With more rumbles of delighted laughter at his own ineptitude and absent-mindedness, Einstein became almost helpless when he recounted how, standing at the telephone, Mitrany and he looked at each other in bewilderment for both had forgotten his unlisted number. Eventually, the genius remembered the name of a friend who knew the number, looked him up in the telephone directory, called him, got his own number and then phoned the good Miss Dukas for the address of his dinner hosts. By then he was about an hour late and since his secretary had no confidence that he would find his way, insisted that he wait while she took a taxi to collect and deliver him.

After this rare entertainment, we talked about the situation in Palestine – this was some months before the State of Israel came into existence. Einstein was passionate in his denunciation of the Irgun and the Stern Gang even though he conceded that its militant activities could possibly advance the creation of the Jewish state which was, in his opinion, both desirable and inevitable. I told him that it had been rumoured that he had been asked to become the first president of the Jewish state. He neither denied nor confirmed the rumour but did indicate that he would not hear of it.

He told me of his appearance, a few months previously, before the Anglo-American Committee of Enquiry on Palestine. The members of the Committee had impressed him, in particular Britain's Richard Crossman who had nodded his agreement as Einstein expressed his strong support for a national home for the Jewish people.

There can be few, in the Western world at any rate, who have not heard the name of Einstein, a genius who changed the intellectual face of the modern world. But he will always remain in my memory as the modest, self-deprecating individual I encountered over a cup of tea in a simple house in Princeton, New Jersey.

*

Phil and Pearl Forman were the first of the close friends I made in the United States. Although I have been fortunate enough to have made many friends, those I consider as close are extremely limited in number. The Formans were certainly in that category and I thought of them as substitute parents and, as Phil once wrote to me at the stressful time of my divorce, they considered me an adopted son. On later visits to the United States I acquired two other intimate friends, both rabbis. One was Wolfe Kelman who was the professional head of the Rabbinical Assembly, the association of Conservative rabbis. For some forty years we corresponded almost weekly – I telephoned or wrote to him about all my problems, personal and professional, and he was always understanding and helpful – our correspondence only ceasing when we were together either in the States, London or Israel.

The other rabbinical intimate was a non-practising reform cleric who had given up the profession when he made a huge success as a novelist. *The Conversion of Chaplain Cohen* was Herbert Tarr's first novel and it became a best seller. From that time on he wrote and lectured – and wrote to me. His letters were always a delight, always expressed with the humour which came naturally to him and which had made him a celebrity. The following paragraph in a letter dated 5 November 1969 is a sample:

'But here's the really big news, stop-the-press scoop for you. GOLDA MEIR AND I ARE ENGAGED. That's right. At the Golda Meir meeting with Jewish-American "intellectuals" (I was there as an observer). I popped the question to her brazenly: "Will you marry me?" Before I could even list what I had to offer (a color telly and American citizenship), Goldale replied: "And what would you say if I said yes?" (You know how these Jews are, always answering a question with a question). So that means we're engaged, no? Already my parents are practising saying "Our daughter-in-law the Prime Minister". And I'm looking around for a catering hall. I prefer a small wedding myself, just Jewish heads of state and a *JC* editor. But Goldale, I hear, is obliged to invite the presidents of every Jewish organisation. In which case we shall have to hire Switzerland.'

On one occasion, in conversation with Herbert, he made what I took to be an excessively complimentary remark about something I had done and I responded with an emphatic dissent. He then told me that when Sigmund Freud had come to New York he was visited by Rabbi Stephen Wise, then one of the most prominent Jewish leaders in the United States. Wise greeted Freud by saying how privileged he was to meet one of the three greatest Jews of modern times – Einstein, Marx and Freud himself. Freud returned the compliment with the observation that Wise himself should be added to that number to which Wise responded, 'Me? No, no, no!' Freud sternly replied, 'One no would have been enough.'

13

The Jewish Chronicle

During my second lecture tour for the American Jewish Committee in 1949, I was invited to a meeting of the organisation's Foreign Affairs Committee which was held over dinner at the Harmonie Club in New York. Founded early in the twentieth century by wealthy German Jews, the club occupied an extremely opulent building off Fifth Avenue not far from the Plaza Hotel. On that occasion, there was another English guest in the person of David Kessler whom I had not previously met but who I knew to be the Managing Director of *The Jewish Chronicle*, a weekly newspaper of which I, like practically every member of the Anglo-Jewish community, was a regular reader. It was the bible for anyone at all involved in Jewish life in Britain. The oldest Jewish newspaper in the world, it could, and did, justifiably claim to be the most influential. David appeared to be as happy about our meeting as I was, promised to get in touch with me after my return to London and thereafter we met regularly.

We got on well despite the differences between our backgrounds and life-styles. He was every bit the ex-Army officer living a country gentleman's life on a farm in Buckinghamshire. On the face of it he was an incongruous figure to be head of *The Jewish Chronicle* but, as I learned later, he was totally devoted to its purposes and was doing an excellent job. David told me that when the paper ceased to be privately owned it was formed into a company in 1906 by none other than solicitor David Lloyd George. His father, Leopold Kessler, was one of the original shareholders and, in the course of time, the Kessler family holding became the dominant one. That brought David into a controlling position on the paper first as its Managing Director and later as Chairman of the Board.

At one of our lunches in 1954, David took me by surprise by asking if I would be interested in the job of General Manager of the paper. I had had some previous dealings with the *Chronicle* as an occasional contributor and I knew slightly its then Editor, a former *Manchester Guardian* journalist named John Shaftesley, but it had never occurred to me that I might work for the newspaper. My practice at the Bar was reasonably good and I loved the life. I was cheered every time I arrived at the Temple, enjoyed the companionship of colleagues and was exhilarated by the work. Had the offer not come from Kessler, I would have happily continued at the Bar for I would never have taken the initiative to seek something else. But David's invitation had its attractions. First and most important to me, it offered financial security. I was then making a reasonable living at the Bar and the retainer I was receiving from the American Jewish Committee usefully augmented my income. But I was acutely aware of the hazards inseparable from the occupation of a practising barrister. There were, and are, no partnerships, and every barrister is an independent operator dependent on the goodwill and support of solicitors and on maintaining good health. Nor were there at that time any pension schemes available short of endowment insurance which would have made too great a demand on my resources. Kessler's offer, on the other hand, promised a good salary, useful fringe benefits and a pension. And I was also attracted by the idea of working on a newspaper for which I had great respect and admiration.

I mulled for days and, disturbingly, for nights. I positively did not want to leave the Bar but I was mindful of the fact that, with two young children to bring up and educate, Anne then aged eight and John who was six, the security offered by the job would be infinitely preferable to the uncertainties and hazards inseparable at that time from the life of a young barrister. While I was pondering, I received a call at my chambers from Barnett Janner, a good friend and an important instructing solicitor. Barney was kindness and decency itself and we enjoyed a close relationship but his voice on this occasion conveyed to me a hint of embarrassment. He reminded me that I had been briefed by his firm in a certain county court action which we had lost and had decided to take to the Court of Appeal. The case had now appeared in the Court List and would shortly be heard. In the normal course, the brief would have come to me and the point of the call was that Barney wanted to tell me that his son Greville, who had recently been called to the Bar, had not yet had the experience of appearing before the Court of Appeal and Barney asked whether I would mind if he was given the brief in this case. Of course I did not object. I really did understand and might well have done the same myself in his situation. But it was a telling reminder of the instability and impermanence of a Bar practice. Other solicitor clients could have sons or daughters coming to the Bar or cousins or in-laws. That decided me; the Bar was too insecure and unreliable for someone like myself who had no other financial resources. The following day, I telephoned David Kessler and told him that I would accept the offer.

In February 1955 I took up my new job. *The Jewish Chronicle* then occupied a converted Georgian house in Furnival Street, just a few minutes walk from the Temple. The quarters were cramped. On the ground floor a front office close to the house entrance served both to receive visitors and take advertisements. Occupying the rest of that floor, at the rear of the building, was the composing room with its bank of linotype machines. In the centre of the composing room stood a large table called 'the stone' on which the pages were made up from the trays of linotype which the compositors fitted into a frame the size of the page and added the headlines provided by the sub-editors. When these pages were made up, the frame would be securely locked and then despatched by lorry to the printers to be made into plates which were then fixed on the rotary printing machines.

On the upper floors, a warren of rooms housed the Editor, senior editorial staff, sub-editors, readers and editorial secretaries together with the administrative staff, general manager, accountant, advertisement manager and his staff and, surmounting them all, the comparatively sizeable office of the Managing Director which excited the envy of the other employees primarily because it had its own loo. A narrow staircase provided the only access to the upper floors – there was no lift – and the constant traffic brought to my mind Jacob's dream of angels going up the ladder and some coming down, only in the case of Furnival Street most of the ascenders and descenders were far from being angels.

I shared an office on the first floor with the Advertisement Manager, George Mandelson who was called George only by Kessler; to the rest of us he was Tony. Tony Mandelson added gaiety to my life at the office, all the more welcome because the job of General Manager, I discovered, offered nothing like the interest and variety of my previous occupation. Tony had come to the *JC* following in the footsteps of his father who had been a rather superior advertisement salesman at the paper well before my time. Tony loved selling and nothing pleased him more than to have attended a company meeting and come away with an ad. He was good looking, well dressed, gregarious and possessed of a delicious sense of humour. He had little to do with the Jewish community (his wife was the only daughter of Herbert Morrison, a stalwart of the Labour Party, later Lord Morrison) but was devoted to the paper and, with his connections both in the newspaper industry and the City, made a considerable contribution to its fortunes.

My job was, in brief, to ensure that the paper was as profitable as possible. To that end I had to deal with the two unions involved, that of the printers (by far the stronger) and the journalists. One of the weekly routines was to fix the number of pages in the current week's issue based on the volume of advertising, and then determine what proportions of the available column inches were to be allotted to news and to advertisements. I also had to keep a watching brief over the activities of the advertising staff, the most interesting and colourful of whom were the salesmen. They would not describe themselves as such – they were representatives, executives or the like. The *JC* was something of a paternalistic organisation; we paid our staff reasonably well, had a good, non-contributory pension scheme and took a personal interest in all employees, some of whom had been with the paper for many decades. As a result there was, when I arrived at the paper, an excellent relationship between management and staff which made that aspect of my job relatively simple.

Second only to Tony Mandelson in the ranking of my closest associates during my early years with the paper was the acknowledged star of the advertisement salesmen, the dignified Adolph Steinhart. Portly, lordly, well-dressed and rarely seen without his cigar, there was never any reason for anyone to ask why he was known throughout the paper (and possibly outside) as 'the Baron'. The Baron was a race-goer and, in the cartoon of the leading *JC* figures drawn by the distinguished caricaturist Ralph Sallon for inclusion in the *JC*'s 120th anniversary edition in 1961, he is depicted, puffing at his cigar, in grey topper and with binoculars slung over his shoulder.

He would generally put his head into my office when he had finished his work for the day and, if I were free, would treat me to a recital of his successes. How he had met Freddie Laker at the racecourse and had booked him for a series of ads for his airline or his chat with Lord King which would produce some healthy advertising from British Airways. He appeared to by-pass all the underlings who might work in advertising departments and dealt only with the chairmen of important companies of whom he invariably spoke as friends and intimates. He was always wheeling and dealing. One of his triumphs was a deal between his (and my) friend Abraham Wix who at that time owned, among other cigarette brands, Benson & Hedges. Steinhart had negotiated a deal with Lord King ensuring that these cigarettes would be available on BA flights in return for which Abe Wix would be taking a series of ads in the *JC* for one of his enterprises. As well as talking to me about his professional triumphs, the Baron was also the recipient of financial information from his high-placed friends which he applied to his stock-market dealings. Some of these tips he imparted to me and that led to my first dealings in shares; they were generally for trivial amounts but I found the activity interesting and have never given it up.

My predecessor as General Manager was A.B. Guthrie, non-Jewish, small in stature, well known in Fleet Street, a serious drinker – there was probably a relationship between these attributes – and casual in manner. I suspect this was also characteristic of his style of administration which seemed to me haphazard and I set about a reorganisation in which I was strongly supported by David Kessler. It became the regular practice for us to lunch together once a week, usually Thursday or Friday, the less busy days after the paper had 'gone to bed' and during those lunches we discussed many subjects other than management, in particular the editing of the paper about which neither of us was enthusiastic.

John Shaftesley had been Editor since 1946 and he was not particularly popular with his staff nor, for that matter, with the Board of Directors. A capable journalist, he was a dour man with little imagination and no sign of possessing a sense of mission for this unique newspaper. The paper reflected his weaknesses: it was dull in presentation and pedestrian in content though, because of its comprehensive news coverage, still an indispensable read for the majority of the Jewish community as well as for Jewish leaders throughout the world.

David Kessler was well aware of all this and we had talked about and around the subject. I think he would have acted sooner to replace John but there was no obvious successor among the staff and David was not sufficiently familiar with the wider Jewish community to know of any editorial talent it may have harboured. In any case, it was neither easy nor desirable to dismiss an Editor. David must also have been troubled by his role in the dismissal of Shaftesley's predecessor, Ivan Rich, who had alienated the Board through his support of Zionist revisionism. While one editorial dismissal might be regarded as unfortunate, a fairly immediate repeat would be seen as more reprehensible than careless. So he suffered and desisted from any action apart from a few, generally ineffectual, efforts to persuade John to change his ways.

After more than three years as General Manager, I was becoming rather bored with the job. It had little excitement and had become routine. I was beginning to think seriously of returning to the Bar and was weighing up the pros and cons. I discussed this concern regularly with Tony Mandelson who, though he understood my point of view, urged me to give it more time and he seemed genuinely reluctant to see me go. During this period of reflection I continued doing my work as efficiently as I could and part of the routine was my weekly lunch with Kessler. It usually took place in a basement dining room at Clifford's Inn, an office block in Fetter Lane, which was the favoured luncheon resort of some of the top people at the *New Statesman and Nation* whose office was also in the vicinity. We joined them at their table on a number of occasions which gave me the opportunity, as a novice in the profession of journalism, to learn more and to hear gossip about politicians and Fleet Street hacks. The conversation was much better than the fare.

One Thursday in the autumn of 1958, as we left the office to walk to lunch, David Kessler told me that we would be going to the Waldorf Hotel, a far better and more expensive restaurant than that at Clifford's Inn. I asked him if we were meeting anyone else there for, on occasion, we had entertained at the Waldorf, but he said no – it was to be just the two of us. I mused on this briefly because it was a departure from our regular practice and because I knew that David was not a happy spender, neither of the firm's money nor his own. That thought flashed momentarily through my mind and disappeared as our conversation meandered on.

We were shown to a table, sipped a glass of sherry while awaiting our first course and began to talk about some current issues connected with the paper. I could see that David was not really focussed on whatever the subject was that we were discussing and began to feel that he had something else on his mind. When the soup was on the table and the waiter had gone, David asked me, almost casually, whether I would like to become the Editor of the paper. I was struck dumb. For the first time in my life, and so far the only time, no words came to my mind or mouth. With or without my mouth open, I looked at him in silence for what seemed to me a long time though it was probably only seconds. I had never considered the possibility and had not the slightest inkling beforehand that anyone else had.

With the return of my composure, I asked him what he intended to do about John. He told me that he would ask him to take charge of a Jewish newspaper we had recently bought in Manchester and, as a sweetener also intended to save his face in public, would offer him membership of the Board of Directors of the *Chronicle*, an office to which he had long aspired. I had had a reasonably friendly relationship with John and was uncomfortable with the thought that he might consider that I had plotted his downfall with David Kessler.

We did not, at that time, discuss any terms because I had no thoughts about them. I was excited by the prospect of becoming the Editor, at the opportunities it would give me to advance ideas in the most influential platform of the Anglo-Jewish community and to promote the paper internationally. I concluded by saying that, yes, I loved the idea in principle but that I would not respond until I had a little time for thought and also talked about it with John Shaftesley.

David did not like that idea which would mean that John would first learn from me about his dismissal. Nor was David willing to break the news to John until he knew that I was in the bag. I appreciated the weight of this argument and, after a little further reflection, I accepted his offer and said that I would talk to John immediately after he had spoken to him.

David did not waste any time before talking to John and I think it caused him little perturbation as he was not averse to demonstrating his power when he had the opportunity. In any event, he was not particularly fond of Shaftesley who I went in to see immediately afterwards. To my surprise, John's face and body language showed no signs that he was as shattered as he must have been, but then he rarely displayed any emotion. I told him that I wanted to assure him that I had had no inkling of David's intentions and that I had neither suggested that I be appointed or indeed entertained any thought of it. He was gracious enough to respond that he accepted my assurances though I have never been quite sure whether he did for I had no conversation with him, other than the most formal, after that meeting. I can only add that, when the staff was informed of John's departure, there was jubilation. As for me, I thought that he had responded with considerable dignity to his downfall.

I was suddenly projected into an influential position for which I was completely unprepared – and I was acutely aware of that. So the weekend before I was to occupy the privileged chair, I decided to dash over to Paris to chew over this unexpected transformation of my career with Zack Shuster who was then running the European office of the American Jewish Committee. He was the obvious friend to talk to about my ambitions and anxieties, a former journalist in the American Yiddish press, a man of sound judgment and with a comprehensive experience of Jewish affairs. We talked the whole weekend only stopping for sleep and meals and I returned to London in a more settled frame of mind.

I would try to make the *JC* both a stimulant for and an accurate mirror of Jewish life. It seemed to me that our cultural and religious institutions (as distinct from the political and philanthropic) were, either from ignorance or fanaticism, reluctant to move with the times. The diaspora Jewish press with which I was familiar was no less culpable in failing to take issue with the backward-looking organisations and tended to fill its columns with self-congratulatory reports supplied by these bodies and such 'news' reports as glorified their leaders. Organised religious life was largely stuck in a rut. Synagogue affiliation in Anglo-Jewry was high but in many cases, if not most, that was attributable more to the desire to be buried in the cemeteries owned by the major denominations than to sincere acceptance of the beliefs and practices they advocated.

It must have been clear in the very first few months of my editorship that I had strong views about the need to make Judaism more comprehensible to an educated constituency and therefore more relevant to their lives. That called for change, a word that was anathema to the most authoritative orthodox Jewish religious leaders of the day, and orthodoxy was, by far, the largest and most important section of Anglo-Jewry. As early as June 1959, only eight months after I became Editor, Dayan

1

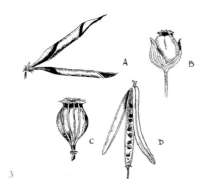

3

1] My parents (Father extreme right and Mother 2nd from right) with Mother's sister, Esther (front) in the Tym factory near Petticoat Lane soon after my parents' arrival in England.

2] Berner Street School, 1925. (I am 3rd from right, back row.)

3] Drawings from my biology exercise book at the Regent Street Poly.

4] My brother Benjamin's barmitzvah with the family, 1928. (I am on the right.)

4

2

5] Regent Street Poly sixth form, 1933.
(I am 2nd left, back row.)

6] The wedding of my first cousins in
Przemysl, Poland 1930s.

7] Genek, the son of my cousins. Both he
and his parents perished in the Holocaust.

8] My father in retirement, 1969.

9] A Young Sinaist group in 1934 – Sammy Segal (2nd left), Abie Baum (4th left), Monty Richardson (back row right).

10] Cambridge 1941: Chaim Herzog is on my right.

11] In front of King's College Chapel in 1942.

12] After being called to the Bar in 1944.

13

14

13] Outside Chambers, 1946.

14] Representing the Board of Deputies at a UN meeting in London addressed by Eleanor Roosevelt in 1945.

15] With Judge Phillip Forman in New Hope, PA, in 1947.

16] Albert Einstein receiving US citizenship from Judge Phillip Forman in 1940.

15

16

17

18

19

20

17] Addressing a meeting of the World
Union of Jewish Journalists in Jerusalem
with Prime Minister Levi Eshkol.

18] With Arthur Goldberg, US Ambassador
to the UN.

19] With Abba Eban in the 1960s.

20] At my retirement party at Stationers' Hall
in 1977, with 2nd from left, Bernard
Levin, Gerald Kaufman and David Kessler.

21] With Prime Minister
    Indira Gandhi in New
    Delhi in 1977.

22] The first meeting of
    the Jewish Chronicle
    Trust on 21 November
    1969.

23] At dinner for the
    British Friends of the
    Diaspora Museum,
    Tel Aviv, 1982.
    With Willy Brandt,
    June Jacobs and
    Harold Macmillan.

24] Claire arriving for our wedding in Baltimore on 16 December 1973.

25] At my 80th birthday party given by the JPR at the Savoy. With Isaiah Berlin (left) and Chaim Herzog.

26] Also at my 80th party, with Peter Levy (left) and Jacob Rothschild (centre).

24

25

26

27] Receiving an award from Lord Woolf, Lord Chief Justice, at a dinner in my honour given by the JPR at the Savoy in 2003.

28] In the Caribbean with Claire.

Swift, the strongest personality on the London Beth Din, the religious court which was presided over by Chief Rabbi Brodie, characterised the *JC* in a public lecture as 'one of the most powerful influences in the Anglo-Jewish community and also, of late, one of the most dangerous'. His reason for this conclusion was that recent leading articles in the paper advocated 'change, variety and enterprise' in matters of religion and that 'no lay editor has any right to propagate those particular religious concepts'.

Most Jewish newspapers and journals in the English-speaking world tended to be funded by institutions, religious, political or charitable, and could by no means be considered as independent. The *JC*, by contrast, was financially successful and, in the newspaper world at any rate, prosperity is the condition of independence. That issue came to the fore years later when I was approached by members of the United States' Conference of Presidents of Jewish Organisations (US Jewry does not have a single representative organisation like the Board of Deputies of British Jews) to discuss the possibility of collaborating with them in the production of a national Jewish newspaper. There were, and are, dozens, if not hundreds, of local papers in America but the Jewish scene in this respect followed that of the United States generally where there are no more than a handful of truly national newspapers.

After several lengthy meetings with lay and professional leaders, I came to the conclusion that, desirable though it would be to create a national Jewish newspaper, for the *JC* to join such an enterprise in conjunction with the organisations was bound to lead to discord. The organisations involved would, I told their representatives, expect the newspaper to be supportive of their own interests while the newspaper in which I would be interested would tend to publicise precisely what they would prefer to keep to themselves.

I made some of these points in a speech I was invited to

deliver at a session attended by Israel's Prime Minister, Mr Levi Eshkol, of the World Conference of Jewish Journalists which took place in Jerusalem in March 1968. My theme was the role of the Jewish press in the efforts to ensure Jewish survival in the Diaspora. In an article in the *JC* soon after the establishment of the State of Israel, Arthur Koestler had argued that, now that the survival of the Jewish people was assured, the Jews of the Diaspora who wanted to adhere to Judaism could do so by emigrating to the Jewish state and the rest should feel no compunction or guilt in assimilating to the mores of the countries in which they lived. Of course, this prescription was far too simplistic. I was one of the many who were strongly in favour of Jewish continuity in the Diaspora but I argued that this would only be desirable if it was based on the maintenance and development of positive Jewish religious and cultural values. Or, as I then put it, 'are our children going to remain Jewish because they want to be members of a Jewish golf club?' The problem of Jewish survival in the Diaspora was, I asserted, a religious one for 'if Judaism means nothing to our children they will not remain Jews ... and (Judaism) will mean nothing if it is shackled to concepts ...which are either irrelevant or call for the suspension of reason'.

This was at a time when the reverberations of the 'Jacobs Affairs' (see Chapter 14) were still rumbling in Anglo-Jewry and I thought it useful to raise the same fundamental issue on an international platform at the Jerusalem conference. There was, and still is, no evidence that I have been able to discover that my efforts were in any way rewarded. During the Jacobs Affairs, because of my perhaps too forceful support of Rabbi Jacobs, I became highly unpopular with the extreme orthodox section of the Jewish community who purported to know precisely what I had in mind even though they ostentatiously boycotted the *JC* and would not admit to reading it. There were even a few who announced they would no longer advertise in the paper. It might have been assumed that the directors of the paper (I had been invited to join the Board not long after my appointment as Editor) would have been, at least, perturbed. But although my handling of the subject was discussed exhaustively and sometimes critically at Board meetings, I was always fortified by their consistent recognition of editorial independence.

There had only been one occasion when it appeared to me that my authority was being challenged. Before my first visit to the United States after my appointment as Editor, I had left a leading article for use in the next issue of the paper. When a copy reached me in New York, I was surprised to see that the leader had not been published and, when I returned to London, my deputy informed me that David Kessler had read the galley proof and had asked for the leader to be held over until my return since he wanted to discuss it with me. I went to see David and told him that this was an encroachment on my authority which I was sure my staff would see in that light. I asked for a note from him regretting his action and assuring me of my editorial independence. If he did not feel he could do that he would have my resignation. He accepted the situation and sent me the required note which I showed my senior staff. There was never a repetition.

Throughout my editorship, David was Chairman of the Board and I cannot speak too highly of his devotion to the paper. His deputy was Ellis Birk, a successful City solicitor who was influential in the *Daily Mirror* and actively involved in a number of respected communal organisations. The oldest member was Leonard Stein, a barrister who was formerly a highly regarded adviser to top Zionist leaders, President of the Anglo-Jewish Association and, later, the author of the definitive book on the Balfour Declaration. Leonard, at the request of David Kessler, wrote a weekly critique of the contents of the *JC* which was passed on to me. His comments were invariably meaningful and I gained a great deal from them. He was, however, somewhat out of date when it came to popular talk and it once gave me considerable amusement when one of his comments read 'Who *is* Dr Spock?' – a medical commentator on child-rearing whose name was then a household word but clearly not in the Stein household. The other directors were Philip Zec, formerly an eminent cartoonist and the Hon. Edwin Samuel, son of Viscount Samuel, who lived in Israel and attended few Board meetings.

My ambition and hope was to consolidate the status of the *JC* as the outstanding world Jewish newspaper. Throughout the nineteen years of my editorship, the lead stories on the front page were predominantly those of international interest, particularly of significant developments in Israel. The *JC* was not to be a merely parochial paper – there were local Jewish newspapers which covered that area of journalism and, while we obviously published reports and features on domestic events, it was always at the forefront of my mind that we had to retain the interest and respond to the needs of Jewish leaders throughout the world.

I had also to come to grips with a subject that had, for decades, been floating in my mind but had always been supplanted by other more urgent – and more mundane – concerns. Now, with the responsibility of commenting on religious affairs, I had to define to myself my own approach to Judaism.

My upbringing had been to accept my religion unquestioningly as a series of beliefs and observances which did not require to be thought about, only practised. It was a time when orthodoxy was all-embracing and easy-going; in a way it was fun. But now, in 1958, orthodox leadership was changing, moving steadily and successfully in the direction of greater assertiveness and dogmatism in an endeavour to have its views regarded as the only acceptable face of Judaism. The leaders had no problem in their own adherence to the strict orthodox lifestyle because they had removed themselves, as far as humanly possible, from the questioning and doubts of the twentieth century by living in physical and intellectual ghettoes. But this was an attitude which most members of the Jewish community were highly unlikely to follow, nor was it likely that many would accept the other extreme by opting out of the community. I believed, and still believe, that most Jews entertain some deep-rooted desire to adhere to their inherited culture and faith, and that this feeling comes to the surface either as the result of some personal experience, a major historical event like the Holocaust or a threat to the security of the State of Israel.

I was convinced that a path should, and could, be found between the extremes of ghettoisation and assimilation and that it had to be one which was intellectually acceptable. There is a Yiddish saying which I had often heard in my youth that people walk on the pavements and only horses walk in the middle. It was a good line, but not persuasive. One of my far-fetched hopes was that I could help to find a middle-of-the-road compromise, that the term was not pejorative but expressed an attitude of considerable virtue.

14

In the Editorial Chair

On 10 November 1958 I moved into the Editor's room on the first floor of the *JC*'s offices in Furnival Street. I decided that it would be too disruptive to make any immediate changes in personnel though I was far from satisfied with both the news content and its presentation. The senior member of the editorial staff, the Foreign Editor, was Joel Cang, a veteran journalist who had been the *JC* correspondent in Poland when he made his escape to England before the war. Courteous, cultivated and professional, he had, or so it seemed to me, a somewhat condescending attitude towards the new Editor who, it was true, had absolutely no journalistic experience. Early on I asked him for a list of our foreign correspondents and after several reminders, it appeared. I was taken aback by both the length of the list and the number in receipt of retainers from whom we had not heard for years. I suggested he prune the list, to which he nodded a somewhat grudging assent but took no action. He was right and it was a lesson for me. Soon afterwards, the Congo was invaded and our man in Rhodesia, from whom we had not heard for three or four years, was the only journalist to travel there and report to us exclusively on the situation of the Jewish community in Elizabethville. Joel retired four years after I became Editor; he had always been friendly and I learned to respect his judgement but I could never shake the belief that he rather resented my being his boss.

It was easier to deal with presentation than content and the first major change I made was a re-design, for the paper looked stodgy, lacking sparkle or elegance. I commissioned Allen Hutt, a senior member of the staff of the communist *Daily Worker* and an authority on newspaper design. Another re-resign was made some years later by Terence Conran. With the paper looking better and with the encouragement of David Kessler, I next turned my attention to the features. Under my predecessor only rarely were articles commissioned and most of those printed were submissions, in the main from rabbis who sought a wider audience than the one they could reach from their pulpits.

At the end of my first week, I took home some twenty or thirty of these submitted pieces. Reading them was a depressing experience and it was only when I reached a non-rabbinical submission from a Glaswegian named C.I. Bermant that my spirits were lifted. His light-hearted but well-informed article on Jewish life in Glasgow stood out from its mediocre companions for Bermant possessed a captivating and finely honed writing style. On returning to the office the following Monday, I asked my secretary to reject all the submissions other than that from Bermant. To him I wrote accepting the article and I did not waste any time in using it – it appeared in the following week's issue. In my letter I invited him to come to London because I wanted to talk to him and he promptly accepted the invitation.

We lunched together and I was impressed both by his Jewish knowledge and by his perceptive, critical and wittily irreverent approach to contemporary Jewish issues. Chaim told me that when he was nine years old, he had accompanied his parents when they emigrated from Vilna to Scotland and that his father was an orthodox Lithuanian Jew who held a non-rabbinical, religious position in the Glasgow Jewish community. He was, as far as I could gather, religiously observant but was ready, willing and indeed eager to challenge religious authority when its rigidity opened it to criticism. My only problem with him was following his speech which was a mixture of heavy Glaswegian and Lithuanian accents made even more difficult to comprehend by the speed of his delivery. I offered him a full time job as a feature writer and he accepted, becoming the paper's columnist, first under the nom-de-plume of Ben Zakkai and later under his own name. In addition he was also a leader writer (responsible during the Jacobs Affairs for most of the powerful editorials on the subject) and feature writer. His strength was the maintenance, throughout his life, of his sceptical attitude towards authority (and that included me) and he became the most valuable editorial asset of the *JC* for more than three decades until his untimely death.

A short while before I moved into the Editor's office, a first novel by Brian Glanville entitled *The Bankrupts* engendered some controversy in the Anglo-Jewish community. The bankrupts in the story lived in an affluent north-west London suburb popular among other upwardly mobile Jews and the novel dealt with the lives of these largely materialistic and uncultivated people. Some Jews saw it as anti-Semitic – the review in the *Observer* described the setting as one of 'spiritual squalor' – but others thought it an honest portrayal of a section of the community. I was among the latter and so I telephoned Glanville and invited him to come to the office for a chat. This was at a time when a wealth of young Jewish talent had suddenly erupted on the British literary scene. Playwrights like Harold Pinter, Arnold Wesker, Wolf Mankowitz and Peter Shaffer were being enthusiastically received. There were also new novelists like Alexander Baron, Freddie Raphael, Bernice Rubens and Gerda Charles. They were nearly all first-generation British Jews but most had no involvement in specifically Jewish concerns, religious, Zionist or philanthropic. I regarded them as the articulate representatives of the rising generation of British Jews and being keen to know why they were so remote from Jewish affairs and, anxious to bring them closer to the Jewish community, I sought to offer them a platform in the *JC*. So my suggestion to Brian Glanville at that meeting was that we should begin with his interviewing some of the rising stars to ascertain what being Jewish meant to them. He interviewed six of them – Dannie Abse, Alexander Baron, Bernard Kops, Wolf Mankowitz, Peter Shaffer and Arnold Wesker – and his articles were published in successive issues of the paper in December 1958 and January 1959 under the general title of 'The Man Behind the Pen'. Some evasively, but most forthrightly, were either indifferent or hostile to things Jewish and to the Anglo-Jewish community.

Mankowitz was probably the most outspoken: 'I don't play any part in Jewish communal affairs . . . I don't know what the Anglo-Jewish community is doing. Its concept of religion is not mine. It's social life is of no interest to me,' while Peter Shaffer declared that although he was a religious person, he saw nothing positive in the kind of Judaism practised in this country. 'When people talk about Judaism, they're simply talking about *Yiddishkeit* really and I'm sick and tired of *Yiddishkeit*.'

The series attracted an unusually heavy correspondence, most of the letters not only attacking the young writers but also the *JC* for providing space for what many correspondents considered ill-informed and egocentric opinions damaging to the community. Reading all these letters week by week became an increasingly depressing experience and to abbreviate the agony, I published the last two interviews in the same issue. The controversy over the Glanville series continued to stimulate correspondence and I was regularly accused of giving my support and encouragement to negative elements in the community. The dissemination of their views, I was reproachfully advised, would damage religious institutions and, chiefly, the rabbinate. In a leading article I expressed the view that I was rendering a service in publishing the opinions of some of the most prominent representatives of the rising generation. The fact that they were, almost unanimously, unobservant, regarding their ancestral religion as irrelevant in their lives was, I wrote, an indictment of their parents, teachers and the religious leadership. The 'Man Behind the Pen' series, I wrote and thought, should be regarded as a red light, warning those who hold Judaism dear that we were in danger of losing the best of the next generation. The leadership, I urged, should be considering what was to be done to improve the situation rather than hurling bricks at the warning light.

Controversy over what came to be known as the Jewish 'angry young men' continued for many months after the series had appeared and extended even to South Africa where almost a year later an article in a local Jewish newspaper concluded, wryly, with the observation that 'the trouble with our young men is that they aren't even angry'. One of the benefits it brought to the *JC* was that the capable and professional Brian Glanville became a regular contributor to the columns of the paper interviewing celebrities like Sophie Tucker, Harold Pinter and the boxing promoter Jack Solomons.

The Anglo-Jewish community which, during the early years of my editorship numbered some 400,000 (an estimate only – there has never been an accurate census of professing Jews in Britain), was overwhelmingly orthodox in religious affiliation. This did not mean that all members of an orthodox synagogue punctiliously observed the practices of their faith or were even believers. Synagogue membership was a declaration of Jewishness, of a desire to maintain some affiliation and, most important, to be buried in a Jewish cemetery. Synagogue groups owned the Jewish cemeteries and individuals, preferring to be buried with their families, remained members of the same synagogue almost irrespective of their religious attitudes. It did not matter to them which synagogue they did not attend.

By far the most important of the synagogue organisations

was, and is, the United Synagogue which was founded early in the nineteenth century. It was the anglicised group as distinct from the hundreds of smaller and far less decorous synagogues founded by later, predominantly East European, immigrants. The Rothschilds had been prominently connected with the United during the nineteenth century and it was in conscious, or unconscious, emulation of the hierarchy of the Anglican Church that they introduced the concept of a Chief Rabbi which was alien to the Jewish tradition in which each rabbi is the sole authority in his own congregation. With a Chief Rabbi solely responsible for making the decisions, the rabbis of the United (at the time I became Editor, they were generally described as ministers) became little more than functionaries.

Ambitious to extend its authority and that of its Chief Rabbi over the whole community, the United Synagogue constituted a religious court, a Beth Din (House of Judgment) to decide the law on religious controversies or disputes between Jews which for one reason or another it would be undesirable to refer to the national court system. Until the end of the Second World War, the religious position of the United had been described as 'progressive conservatism'. At that time, the Chief Rabbi, Dr J.H. Hertz, was a moderate 'middle-of-the-roader', avoiding the extremes in practice and beliefs of the ultra-orthodox who, in any event, would never accept the authority of the Chief Rabbi or his Beth Din, but at that time they did not matter.

In the mid-1950s, the more zealous and meticulously observant Anglo-Jews, supported by ultra-orthodox immigrants from Europe, began to display their muscle, working assiduously to move the United Synagogue establishment to the right and they were exceedingly successful. The majority of members did not care enough to make a fight of it and, during a comparatively short period, the United Synagogue and its Beth Din began to display less flexibility in the application of Jewish religious law while, at the same time, the traditional, decorous Anglo-Jewish style of the United Synagogue was also transformed. Ministers (now all rabbis) were no longer garbed in dignified canonicals at services, women were barred from synagogue choirs and no change, however superficial, was permitted in the forms of service.

When I joined the *JC* in 1955 as General Manager, I was a Warden of the New West End Synagogue, possibly the jewel in the crown of the United Synagogue, and I gained some practical experience of the operating procedures of that well-organised institution. I rather liked the New West End, its dignified services and gentility, its Englishness, a far cry from the cheerfully haphazard Jewishness of my East End cradle. Its members, as well as the Rev. Ephraim Levine who was then its minister, represented to me a new and agreeable brand of Anglo-Jew, integrated, cultivated yet deeply involved in Jewish affairs, religious, cultural and philanthropic.

They recognised that there were more devout Jews than themselves and wished them well, provided that they did not try to impose their standards on others. It was when the 'counter-reformation' of Anglo-Jewry began in the 1950s (ironic since it had not been preceded by any recognisable reformation) that I, like other members of the New West End, began to experience some unease.

It first expressed itself in my *JC* editorial capacity when, early in December 1960 I read a news report that had come into the office from our local correspondent concerning a visit by some orthodox London rabbis to the Jewish community in Leeds. It was not a long report, but what affected me when I read the galley proof was that the purpose of their visit was the denunciation of a dance which was to take place in the hall of a local orthodox synagogue. It was, declared the rabbis, a licentious event since it was immoral for married men and women to dance with anyone but their partners. Mixed dancing, declared one of them, 'desecrated one of the fundamental principles of

Judaism' and should not be permitted in any orthodox environment, let alone a synagogue.

I read it with a mixture of amusement and irritation and it
was one of the very rare occasions when I took pen in hand and
dashed off a 'leaderette' intended to be more or less gently
mocking. Readers of the report in the news pages, I wrote,
who might have been wondering 'whether Leeds Jewry had
been emulating Babylon or the Cities of the Plain ... will be
relieved to hear that the sins involved amount to nothing more
than men and women dancing together'. I attributed 'outbursts
of this kind in part, at least, to the wave of reaction and
contentiousness which have afflicted orthodoxy in the country
in recent years'. And I could not avoid commenting that 'it
arouses doubts as to the emotional stability and mental hygiene
of those who can project sin and licentiousness into a synagogue
dance'.

It was that sentence which produced an outraged response
from the rabbis. The Monday after publication I received a
letter from solicitors acting for them claiming that they had
been defamed and requesting a retraction, an apology and
substantial damages. I had begun to think by then that I had
been unkind to the rabbis and, on receipt of the letter, my first
inclination was to agree to a suitably worded retraction and
apology for any implication that they were psychologically
challenged, and I would have done so had it not been for the
claim for damages. I replied giving the name and address of the
JC solicitors who would act for us in any proceedings they
were minded to institute.

I heard no more from the rabbis' solicitors but instead
received a summons to attend the Beth Din, the United
Synagogue's ecclesiastical court under the Chief Rabbi, to hear
their complaint. I did not, for a moment, consider accepting
the jurisdiction of this tribunal for that would have been
tantamount to relinquishing my editorial independence. But I

did regard it as proper and courteous to appear and personally explain my inability to abide by the Beth Din's decision on this matter.

So I attended on the day of the hearing accompanied by the *JC*'s (non-Jewish) solicitor wearing his professional black jacket and striped trousers, his clerk similarly attired, and one of our reporters capable of taking a verbatim note of the proceedings. We took our seats while, on the other side of the courtroom sat the aggrieved rabbis and their representatives. The *Dayanim* (rabbinical judges) forming the tribunal entered from behind the dais led by Chief Rabbi Brodie who, so it seemed to me, looked somewhat uncomfortable As soon as they were seated I rose to say that I was there as a mark of respect to the learned judges but that I could not possibly accept their jurisdiction which would have the effect of making them editors of the *JC*, a situation I could not possibly be expected to entertain. I then made to leave. Rabbi Brodie, however, stopped me, requesting me to wait while the bench adjourned to consider my submission.

I sat down with my group and, while the learned judges were, I assumed, having a cup of coffee, one of the plaintiff rabbis who knew my father came over for a chat. He asked me why I had not apologised and I told him that I would have done so, had it not been for his concurrent request for substantial damages. 'How much did you expect to get?' I asked. 'Well,' he replied, 'the *Chronicle*'s a rich paper and we thought that ten thousand would be about right.' I indicated my amusement and we parted amicably after the Chief Rabbi had returned to inform us that the matter would be adjourned to an unspecified future date.

Some time afterwards the issue was drawn to the attention of a leading authority on Jewish law, Rabbi Isaac Jacob Weiss of Manchester. In a volume of his *Responsa* published in 1962 entitled 'Minchat Yitzhak', his Hebrew responsum No. 112

was a reply to the following question (abbreviated in the translation from Hebrew). 'In the matter of the editor of a Jewish newspaper who was impertinent to famous rabbis who had rebuked the people for great licentiousness ... even among synagogues described as "orthodox" in that they arrange dances of young men with virgins and men with women, God forfend us. This editor ... opened his mouth wide in a leading article ... to speak revolt against the rabbis ...' Answer: 'He who insults a rabbi even of the lowest degree has no share in the world to come ....To shame a rabbi because he publicly rebukes the people is akin to sexual immorality. The punishment for such a deed is the severest degree of excommunication ... Such a man must, of course, be driven out of the synagogue and his son must not be circumcised until he makes great amends in public and pays a fine of 35 golden dinarim.' The responsum concluded with a discussion of the current value of a dinar and came to the conclusion that it was worth a pound of gold. The calculation was too intricate for my comprehension, but I assumed that the value of a pound of gold was probably £10,000.

*

I have always been a voracious reader of novels as well as the non-fiction books in my areas of interest and one of the contemporary novelists I most enjoyed was C.P. Snow. His series dealing with the 'corridors of power', a phrase he coined, concluded with a novel entitled *The Conscience of the Rich*. I read it with more than usual avidity because not only was it a story well told, as usual, but also its central characters were members of a cultivated and wealthy Jewish family. Intrigued by this, I communicated with Snow and asked him to lunch.

He accepted and I spent an enjoyable few hours with him at my club. My first question, of course, was to ask him if he was free to reveal to me the identity of the Jewish family and he readily responded. It was the Waley Cohen family with which he was familiar and, so he led me to believe, he was particularly close to Sir Robert whom he knew as the Chairman of the Shell Transport & Trading Company. I knew him as President of the United Synagogue and, at that time, the outstanding leader of the Anglo-Jewish community.

As we parted, I told my guest that I would be delighted if, whenever he thought of a subject of particular Jewish interest he would write about it for the *JC* and he promised he would. Some months later he sent me an article which began with the proposition that while Jews constituted a minute fraction of the world's population they had been awarded well above ten per cent of the Nobel prizes. His well argued and expertly written conclusion from this disparity was that Jews possessed superior intellectual genes.

I was somewhat troubled by this and reluctant to publish a claim of genetic superiority reminiscent of the Nazi claims of Aryan superiority, unless it was supported by authoritative scientific evidence. I decided to consult Sir Ernst Chain, an eminent geneticist and himself a Nobel laureate with whom I was acquainted.

We met in his room at Imperial College in South Kensington where he slowly and carefully read the Snow manuscript, lifted his head and emphatically commented that there was not a scintilla of scientific evidence to support its thesis. I wrote to Snow, returning his piece and hoping he would understand my reluctance to publish it. He responded understandingly – but I never received another article from him. Some time later, when Snow received an honorary degree in New York, he used the Nobel Prize argument in his acceptance speech and I was told that it was received with applause.

It was disappointing for, as a member of the editorial staff informed me, it could have been a scoop for the *JC*. But another opportunity to publish a literary eminence occurred soon after. At a cocktail party in Bloomsbury, I was introduced to Robert Graves, poet and novelist, whose Claudius novels had recently been made into a highly successful television series.

He was very interested to learn something more about the *JC* for which he said he had a high regard and, as our conversation developed, he took me by the arm and led me to a quiet corner of the room where we could continue our talk. After a while, he asked whether I would care to go out for a walk with him. I chided him for the thought since he was the guest of honour at the party, but he insisted that he was uncomfortable and needed some fresh air. So out we went. I relished the prospect of a conversation with the great man about his poetry and his novels but he preferred to talk about the tax advantages of his residence in Majorca.

That led him to turn to what was to me a more interesting aspect of his sojourn on the Mediterranean island. There was, he said, a group, known as the Xuetas, living in the centre of Palma, the capital of Majorca, who were of unmixed Jewish stock but strict Catholics. Its founders had converted to avoid the slaughter of the Spanish Inquisition and Graves imparted to me some fascinating aspects of their history and current situation which he later elaborated in a series of three articles in the *JC*.

I had another encounter with Catholicism in 1964. The meeting that year of the Vatican Ecumenical Council was followed with interest by Jewish leaders all over the world and, of course, by the *JC*, because its main purpose was to consider the publication of a declaration by the Roman Catholic Church on its attitude to the Jews. In November of that year, what became known as the 'Jewish Chapter' of a Declaration on Non-Christians was adopted by an overwhelming majority of the Council. Its most important decision was a repudiation of the teaching that the Jews bore lasting responsibility for the crucifixion of Jesus.

The driving force behind this Declaration was, ironically, a German-born Jesuit, Cardinal Bea. One of his closest Jewish advisers throughout the long process of drafting and re-drafting to meet objections from some Vatican sources was my friend Zack Shuster, then the Director of the Paris office of the American Jewish Committee. At Zack's suggestion, Father Malachi, an assistant to Cardinal Bea, telephoned me regularly while the Vatican Council was in session to report what was going on with the 'Jewish Chapter'. He had a dual purpose, one, of course, being to keep the *JC* informed. But, more importantly from the Cardinal's point of view, the prior publication of proposals likely to be controversial would, he envisaged, forestall the opposition from conservative elements in the church which preferred to operate in their private cabals.

It all ended well and so did my contact with Father Malachi who, I learned subsequently, had put a foot wrong somewhere and, as a result, had left the Vatican. Some time later I was in New York and was invited to a reception at the home of a member of the Israeli delegation to the United Nations. There were some twenty or so other guests, all strangers to me, and my host performed his duty and introduced me to them.

The liveliest group consisted of three or four attractive young ladies surrounding a youngish man by whom they were clearly captivated. I was introduced to the ladies and then to the man whose name was Dr Malachi Martin. When he heard my name he embraced me saying that he had long wanted to meet me and that he was Father Malachi. We saw a good deal of each other during my stay in New York and we renewed our friendship when he visited London later in the year. Dr Martin, who had by then written a well-received book on the subject of the Catholic church, was every bit as cordial and engaging as he had been during our Vatican telephone conversations.

*

One of the interests to which the *JC* catered was the almost universal curiosity among Jewish people in ascertaining who else was Jewish and what they were doing if of general interest. We therefore always listed the names of the Jewish candidates before a general election and then followed with a list of those who had been elected to Parliament. Only on one occasion did I receive a complaint from one of the names included in the list of Jewish MPs after the 1964 general election. On the Monday after the issue in which it was published, Robert Maxwell telephoned to inform me that he was not a Jew and would I please publish a correction. I did so and the issue of 30 October contained the following: 'Captain I.R. Maxwell, the new Labour MP for Buckingham, has informed *The Jewish Chronicle* that he is now a member of the Church of England.'

Maxwell was, of course, an immigrant Jew who had been phenomenally successful as a newspaper tycoon. He later became the subject of a financial scandal which was followed by his death (it is still not known whether it was suicide) and his burial took place in the graveyard at the Mount of Olives at which a eulogy was delivered by the then President of Israel, Chaim Herzog. Why Maxwell was so anxious at that time to deny his Jewishness I doubt that I shall ever know.

*

Among the mail I received at the office one morning was a letter, dated 8 June 1966 and marked 'Private'. The sender was Sir Oswald Mosley who had moved from the Conservative to the Labour Party and then, in the 1930s, had founded his own party, the British Union of Fascists (BUF), in emulation, first, of Mussolini and then of Hitler. 'The Leader', as he liked to be known, had adopted the Hitlerian doctrine of attributing all the miseries of the world to the malign influence of the Jews.

I was well aware of Mosley's views and career, as was every Jew in the East End where he had concentrated the efforts of the BUF, presumably because the violent opposition of the large Jewish community would give him the publicity he courted. I was nineteen when the 'Battle of Cable Street' took place. A mass of some 100,000 anti-fascists, among whom Jews were prominent, had blocked an intended march by 2000 'blackshirts', as the fascists were known. I was not one of the militants but I did learn a good deal about the event through some of my friends who were communists. So, I was both chilled and intrigued to receive a letter from the man long regarded as British Jewry's arch enemy.

Mosley had been prompted to write by a comment in the *JC* on a correspondence which had recently appeared in the *Observer* and to which he had contributed a letter dealing with his attitude to the Jews. He sent me a copy of that letter in which, as he put it to me, he '... explained the reason for a certain quarrel before the war. I reiterate this quarrel is now over. It does not seem to be in accord with the traditional wisdom of your people to turn a past quarrel into a personal feud.'

In my reply, I disclaimed the notion of a 'personal feud' but added that 'Jews cannot be expected to have any great affection for one who is known to have held opinions to which you gave expression in the past, unless it was patent that there had been a sincere change of attitude'.

Mosley took almost a month to reply and, when he did, claimed that a change of attitude did not enter the question 'because I have never been an anti-Semite ... I had before the war a quarrel with some Jews who in my view desired a war between Britain and Germany for the very intelligible reason that Jews were being persecuted in that country. The reason for that quarrel is clearly now over.'

To that argument, my response was that 'there were, in fact, many Englishmen of all religious denominations who shared hostile views about Hitler, contrary to those you held at that time, and to single out "some Jews" appears to me evidence . . . of anti-Semitism'.

Another month passed before I received a lengthy, hand-written reply from Mosley's home in France in which he agreed that many Englishmen had, indeed, shared the Jewish antipathy towards Hitler but, he assured me, he had 'attacked them at least as vehemently as the Jews in question . . . Also I stood throughout my life for a national home for the Jews who would go there, which would have solved the question of German Jewish refugees.' He concluded, 'it seems to me a considerable folly to fight each other on account of a quarrel years back which no longer exists' and went on to suggest a personal meeting.

Some time that autumn Mosley telephoned me and we arranged to meet at my club on 3 November. I told nobody about this arrangement. Mosley arrived punctually, was self-assured and extremely courteous though somewhat loquacious and perhaps a little over-anxious to appear friendly. He began by expressing his gratitude for the opportunity of a frank discussion about an issue that was troubling him and he seemed almost fervent in his desire to make his peace with the Jews. He was wrong, he told me, to have singled out Jews for trying to involve Britain in a war with Germany. He also accepted that he had been at fault in failing to recognise that Jews could legitimately feel both a Jewish loyalty and a British loyalty – he himself now affirmed loyalty to Europe as well as to his own country.

Of his earlier utterances on this subject, Mosley's plea in mitigation was that, in the course of a fight, it was natural to use any weapons against the perceived enemy. He repeatedly urged that the old quarrel be left to the historians, arguing that, as an Englishman, he had always believed that, when a fight was over, the contestants should accept the bona fides of opponents and try to establish good relations. He clearly had no concept of the depth of Jewish grief over the Holocaust and it seemed obvious to me, as he later conceded, that he had not talked to any Jews on this subject.

I tried to convey to him some idea of the still-bleeding wound the Holocaust had inflicted on every Jew. He appeared shaken by what I was saying and, hesitantly, indicated that it would probably be unrealistic, in the light of what he had just heard, to expect Jews to welcome his offer of reconciliation.

Before he left, Mosley asked me what I thought it would be necessary for him to do to clear his name in Jewish eyes. I responded that I thought it was quite likely that nothing would but, whether or not it would have the effect he desired, he might consider making some public expression of his remorse together with a statement of his present attitude to the Jews. However, I continued, since words were cheap, many Jews would dismiss his contrition if it were not accompanied by some evidence of sincerity. When he asked what that could be, I offered the example of the restitution that was being made by Germany and floated the idea that Mosley might consider making a substantial contribution to an appropriate Jewish cause.

Mosley pondered in silence for some time. He would, he said, think very hard about our conversation though it was difficult for a politician to don sackcloth and ashes. I replied that, from the Jewish perspective, the enormity of the offence was such that nothing less than sackcloth and ashes would suffice. I did not hear from him again.

*

During that same year of 1966 I received a letter from Moshe Menuhin in California submitting an article for publication. I was, of course, familiar with the name of my correspondent as that of the father of the celebrated violinist and, knowing something of his eccentric views, I was not surprised that the article was a tirade against Israel. It lacked any semblance of balance and, moreover, it was so poorly written that I had no hesitation in asking my secretary to return it with the usual rejection slip.

Soon afterwards, it may even have been later the same day, I received a telephone call from Yehudi Menuhin. His father must have sent him a copy of the article and Yehudi was calling to ask me not to publish it since that would be a considerable embarrassment for him. We talked for a while and he told me that he did not, in any way, share his father's opinions about the Jewish state and that, although he was not closely involved with the Jewish community in Britain, he was positive about his Jewish identity and had considerable respect for *The Jewish Chronicle*. The conversation concluded with an invitation to visit him at his house in Highgate and some weeks later I had tea with him and with his wife Diana.

We got on well for, though I had never met him before, I was a great admirer of his virtuosity and had heard a great deal about him from Diana's sister Griselda who was married to Louis Kentner, a greatly admired pianist. The Kentners were a delightful couple. Louis was of Hungarian-Jewish origin and had, I believe, been baptised by his parents as a child but when I knew him he considered himself a Jew and Griselda heartily endorsed it. Claire and I saw a good deal of the Kentners and, after the death of Louis, kept in touch with Griselda, who had retired to Tunbridge Wells, maintaining our friendly relationship by correspondence. Griselda, bright and good-natured, also possessed a sharp and caustic wit, never illustrated better than in a doggerel about her brother-in-law which she sent me early in 1991. Now that all those most closely concerned have passed on, I feel free to record it here:

I am the man the world applauds
covered with medals, knee deep in awards

of Universal Fame
what more can I add to my name?
The realisation of canonisation
is well within my scope
(I've had a word with the Pope)
My ego would be gratified
were I to be beatified;
I am immortal so they say
so I should see that happy day.
But still a nagging doubt arises.
There are some more prestigious prizes
the Nobel *inter alia*;
To miss that might spell failure.
And as I'm rather short of cash
perhaps I'd better have a bash
and let the credit go.
But if I should stay down below
perhaps I really ought to wait,
Decide to re-arrange my fate
By going to the House of Lords
along with all the other old frauds.

There was no love lost between the sisters and when Griselda died, Claire and I were invited by Yehudi's son, who was very close to Griselda, to be present at her funeral in her local churchyard in Tunbridge Wells. As we left the church, Yehudi and Diana bade farewell to the visitors and, when I offered my condolences to Diana, adding the customary Jewish salutation on these occasions 'I wish you long life' Diana immediately responded, pointing to the new grave, 'She didn't.'

*

Some years after my first meeting with Yehudi I was approached by a friend, the composer Wilfred Joseph, who had written a

Requiem for the Six Million which had been performed once and of which he had a tape. He knew that *The Jewish Chronicle* had, many years before, sponsored the recording of Bloch's *Sacred Service*, and he asked me whether the paper might do the same for his work. He let me have the tape and, since I had no particular expertise on, or, for that matter, love of contemporary music, I asked Yehudi if he would come to my house, hear the recording and give me his opinion which he did. My mother-in-law, Dorothy, was staying with us at the time. After hearing the tape and commending it, he joined us for tea where he was his usual engagingly outgoing self. At one point Dorothy told him that when she was a child and learning the violin she was taken to the railway station in Dallas, Texas, where she lived, to be among the welcoming party to greet Yehudi. He responded graciously and the conversation moved on to other things.

After he had left, Claire and I both turned on Dorothy. She was many years older than Yehudi and, when she was a child in Dallas, Yehudi would not have been born. We had no doubt that Yehudi had immediately recognised the absurdity of her recollection. Dorothy now recognised it too and was aghast at her *faux pas*. 'Yes,' she said, 'you're quite right. It was Jascha Heifetz.' Menuhin's diplomacy in handling the situation was delightful.

15

The Six Day War and
'Britain and Israel'

Excitement was never lacking in the course of producing almost every issue of the *JC*. I was always conscious of the necessity of maintaining the paper's status not merely as 'The Organ of British Jewry' as it proudly described itself on its masthead, but also as a journal of record. Never was this latter responsibility more in the forefront of my mind than during the weeks up to and concluding with the Six Day War in 1967. Before Israel's decisive attack on the massed forces of its Arab enemies, I discussed endlessly with the senior editorial staff how best to cover the war which we were all sure would follow the threat from the Egyptian and Jordanian forces.

This was clearly to be a life or death event in Israel's short history and I was determined that the *JC* coverage would be comprehensive and authoritative. Our correspondents through-out the world were alerted to our intentions and, to supplement their coverage, we decided to recruit the best commentators we could get on every aspect of the situation. First, of course, was a military authority in Israel and there could be no one better than my old friend Chaim Herzog, by then a brigadier in the Israeli army and a highly regarded radio commentator on military affairs in his own country. Herzog accepted the assign-ment with the qualification that, if Jordan decided to take part in the fighting, he would be unable to write for us since he would then assume a post of responsibility for the government of the West Bank which was likely to become occupied territory. But, he added, he could not believe that the Jordanians would be so crazy. In the event, the Jordanians were crazy and all Herzog produced for us was one report which appeared in our issue of 2 June.

We hurriedly found a replacement as well as a first-class group of authorities in military, naval and air warfare and in the diplomatic and Jewish communal areas. For reports from the home front in Israel we relied on our staff correspondent whose coverage was to be augmented by regular features from Meyer Levin, the well-known American writer who was then living in Israel. They turned out to be memorable. We also commissioned feature articles, world-wide. Major coverage of the events began early in May with a front page report from Israel of an 'almost unavoidable clash with Syria unless outside influences persuade Damascus to end its terror raids'. From then until the end of June, every issue of the *JC* contained many pages of reports and analysis, sometimes extending to half the paper's total news content. Israel's 'blitzkrieg' started on Monday 5 June and our previous issue, that of Friday 2 June, headed its lead story 'Israel Ready to Act Alone'.

The following Thursday, as usual, the paper was 'going to bed' but standing with my senior colleagues 'at the stone' making up the front page we were faced with the problem that, though it was clear Israel was about to achieve an almost miraculous victory, that event had not yet occurred. One of my rare headline contributions to the paper then flashed through my mind and we used it. In our largest type the front page headline read 'Israel Sweeps to Victory'.

During this period, my colleagues and I, like all our readers, experienced the gamut of emotions from the depth of anxiety to jubilation. The spirit among Jews in Britain in rallying to the cause of Israel was unlike anything I have, before or since, experienced – and it was not limited to Jews. Even Vanessa

Redgrave, who later became a staunch pro-Palestinian, signed a petition of solidarity with Israel. The *JC* office, and doubtless Jewish institutions throughout the country, was overwhelmed with enquiries. 'What can I do?' they all wanted to know and were willing to do whatever was asked of them. At a meeting convened by the Anglo-Jewish community's leadership, the then astronomical sum of £11,000,000 was raised to be sent to Israel. Even the largely uninvolved 'angry young men' rallied to the cause. A mass meeting of solidarity with Israel at the Royal Albert Hall attracted a capacity audience with hundreds more standing or waiting outside. Alas, the spirit did not endure for very long.

A few weeks after the war's end, I reprinted an article by Michael Frayn whose first journalistic assignment, he once told me, was interviewing me for the *Manchester Guardian* soon after he had joined its staff. It was a letter addressed to 'My Dear Israel' and signed by 'Your affectionate great-aunt Britain'. Its delightful irony was revealed in one of its early paragraphs. 'Of course, we all realise that you were provoked – strongly provoked. We could have overlooked your having become involved in a war; it happens to the best of us at times. What we cannot so easily forgive is your insistence on *winning* the war – particularly in such a brash and violent fashion' and the piece concluded 'Now, *how are you going to make amends?* ... undoubtedly you must go to your neighbours without delay and *hand back* every one of the territories which you inadvertently occupied during the fighting' – a prophetic forecast of later developments! The italics are his.

Soon after the Six Day War I received a telephone call at the office from Dorothy de Rothschild. We had never met but I knew her to be the widow of James de Rothschild, the son of the French Baron Edmond de Rothschild. James had become a naturalised British citizen when he had inherited the fabulous Waddesdon estate and later became the Liberal MP for the Isle of Ely. After his death in 1957, Dorothy assumed his extensive philanthropic responsibilities and, by the time I got to know her, she had become the matriarch of the legendary family into which she had married.

She had called me to express her anxiety about the strong swing in public opinion and the critical press Israel was receiving following its overwhelming and dramatically swift victory. Israel was now regularly presented as the arrogant oppressor of the vanquished Arabs (at that time they were not known as Palestinians). Dorothy, who soon became Dollie to me, asked if I would attend a meeting at her house to discuss whether anything should, or could, be done to improve this situation. Of course I said I would and, on the appointed day, some dozen guests, most of them eminent figures, were seated round the dining table of her house in St James's Place.

We all agreed that the Israeli case was not being adequately presented to the British public. The government of Israel had never thought it necessary to set up any sort of Ministry of Information, nor did its Embassy in London have any staff members with experience in publicity or public relations. The unanimous view of the meeting was that we had to do something to try to counter the then pervasive anti-Israel sentiment in the media. As a result an office was established calling itself 'Britain & Israel' and we recruited Terence Prittie as its Director. Terence was a highly respected journalist, at that time the Diplomatic Correspondent of the *Guardian* newspaper and I had got to know him. As our friendship blossomed, he had told me of his discomfort in his job since the editorial policy of his paper was not at all sympathetic to Israel, a nation to which he was strongly drawn. Until his untimely death some few years later, Terence did a splendid job and Dollie was in almost daily touch with what he was doing.

For twenty-one years, until her death at the age of ninety-three in 1988, I met with her practically every week when I was in London, either for lunch or tea, initially to discuss the work of 'Britain & Israel'. But as our friendship grew, she talked to me of her other concerns and lent a sympathetic ear to my problems. I loved her dearly for, as Isaiah Berlin put it in the obituary he wrote for *The Times*, 'She combined an unsullied innocence, purity of heart, the sweetest of natures and, indeed, a saintliness of character, with overwhelming charm, great dignity, a very lively sense of humour, pleasure in the oddities of life, an unconquerable vitality and a kind of eternal youth and an eager responsiveness to all that passed – which lasted to her dying day.' There is not a word of exaggeration in that description.

She once told me that, when she was born, her father's immediate response was to take a long walk in Regent's Park where they lived. A neighbour, seeing his dispirited look, asked if mother and child were doing well. When he received a positive response, the neighbour commented, 'Then that's fine, congratulations.' 'Thank you,' said father Pinto, 'but it's only a girl.'

Dorothy was extremely fond of her father-in-law, Baron Edmond, who, she said, the rest of the family thought crazy for his devotion to the idea of helping Jews to settle in Palestine. Baron Edmond, who lived to the age of eighty-nine, was, and still is, known in Israel as '*Hanadiv*', the benefactor, and as one of the founders of the Jewish state. Ben-Gurion had told Dollie that on one occasion when he was on good terms with General de Gaulle, the name of Baron Edmond had come up in conversation. 'But he wasn't French,' said de Gaulle, 'he was German.' Dollie replied to Ben-Gurion, who had believed de Gaulle, by explaining that she knew her father-in-law very well, that he was thoroughly French and spoke no other language. 'But Ben-Gurion wouldn't have it,' she commented, 'de Gaulle said he was German so he had to be German.'

I once remarked to Dollie that, while I was always offered

delicious wine when I lunched with her, she always took a soft drink which inspired her to tell me why. She had only once gone to the Rothschild family's famous Château Lafite in Bordeaux. That visit came about towards the end of the First World War when her husband was in France with the British army and she went to see him, staying at her father-in-law's home in Paris. One night they were all awakened by a huge explosion. They hurried to the air raid shelter in the cellar and later learned that it was the sound of an exploding shell from the German cannon called Big Bertha. Dollie and a female cousin were thereupon despatched to Château Lafite where the sole retainer met them; all the others were serving in the forces. That evening, the two ladies were served dinner by the same retainer who first poured glasses of wine for them intended, no doubt, to stimulate their appetites. Dollie did not want any but her cousin gave her such a sharp look that she felt she had to drink the glass. With the food came more wine which she wanted to decline but, said her cousin in, as she put it, a no nonsense voice, 'It's a '75, you must taste it.' So they both drank and, when the meal was over, Dollie could not get up from her chair and had to be helped to her room. She had not touched a glass since.

Just a couple of months before her death, while I was lunching with Dollie, she was reminiscing about Herbert Samuel who was the first British High Commissioner for Palestine. In January 1921, she told me, Samuel hosted a house party over three or four days at Government House. She and her husband were invited and, among the other guests were the Winston Churchills and the grandfather of King Hussein of Jordan, King Abdullah, who, she said, was a 'very nice man'. James de Rothschild was already in Palestine and Dollie had travelled by ship to join him. James, who did not have a high opinion of Lady Samuels' cuisine, asked his wife to bring over a couple of Stiltons. This she did, but by the time she arrived at

Haifa the cheese which had been kept in her cabin 'smelled to high heaven'. Lady Samuel, who was known to be inexperienced in catering matters, received the gift very happily. 'Whenever I met Churchill afterwards,' Dollie told me, 'he made a point of mentioning that my cheese saved him from starvation.'

The first night there, the party had to wait for dinner because the Churchills were late coming down. It later transpired that, because the house was so cold, Churchill had asked for a heater. An oil heater was sent to their room but 'promptly went phut' covering them with smut which took some time to remove.

The Rothschilds habitually talk of each other as 'cousins' although the relationships are often far more remote. Dollie, however, always referred to them as the Rothschildren and, of the British members of the family, she always seemed closest to the young Jacob Rothschild who became her heir. During the time I knew her, she no longer lived at Waddesdon, which had been given to the National Trust after the death of her husband, but in a charming house in nearby Eythrope. On one occasion, when lunching there with Claire and her parents, Dollie astonished us all by lowering herself down on her knees to feed her two dogs out of the palm of her hand. She told us that they would not eat otherwise.

*

One of the many debts I owe Dollie was the burgeoning of my friendship with Isaiah Berlin. I had known of him for the whole of my adult life but met him for the first time when, during the early days of my editorship, I decided to publish a series of profiles of eminent figures in the Anglo-Jewish community to be illustrated with caricatures by Ralph Sallon, an eminent figure on the *Daily Mirror*. Naturally Isaiah was included in the list and one of our reporters, assigned to write the profile, telephoned him to request an interview. He declined and asked to speak to me. On the telephone he told me that he had a deep aversion to personal publicity, would not give us an interview and pleaded that he be omitted from the series. We had a lengthy telephone conversation, each of us adamant, and left it at that. But since I would be coming up to Oxford the following week, he suggested we continue the conversation then.

We met in his room at All Soul's and the upshot of the discussion was that in return for my compliance with his plea, he would, when next asked, write an article or book review for the *JC*. (We had, on several occasions, invited him to contribute to the paper but he had, until then, generally declined.) He did as he had promised.

Isaiah was one of my fellow guests at Dollie de Rothschild's house in St James's Place when we met in 1967 and decided to form 'Britain and Israel'. Isaiah's obituary of Dollie, from which I have quoted, illustrates the enormously high regard he had for her and it was no less deeply reciprocated. On everything to do with our efforts for Israel, Isaiah and I were, I believe, the two people she consulted more than any others. Isaiah and I got into the habit of lunching together, usually once a month but sometimes more frequently, to talk about 'Britain and Israel' and Jewish affairs generally. Gradually these conversations moved on to our personal concerns. He became my guru and there was no problem on which I did not seek, and gain, the invaluable benefit of his guidance.

Isaiah was then the Chairman of a Rothschild-funded charitable foundation devoted mainly to cultural projects in Israel. Early in the 1970s he asked me to join the board of trustees and I readily accepted. All the trustees worked together harmoniously until I introduced controversy by opposing a grant for a project which the foundation had long supported and to which its professionals were passionately dedicated. When the subject had first come up and I had raised some objections, it was suggested that I investigate the project and report to my fellow trustees. This I did and my report to the board was adverse. After an exhaustive discussion, the meeting was adjourned without a decision having been taken. I was disappointed that Isaiah had not supported me and I explained his silence to myself as being due to his desire as Chairman to remain non-partisan until a vote had to be taken. But after the meeting I received a letter from him which began 'Dear William, I'm a coward'. He agreed, he wrote, with every word of my report but was disinclined to enter into a confrontation with the professionals and so would not support me. He hoped I would understand. I did. Isaiah, I learned, hated raising his head above the parapet when there was an argument for he was always reluctant to become involved in a controversy. That was, as far as I was concerned, his only weakness.

16

The Jacobs Affairs

The 'Jacobs Affairs', there were two of them, were seminal events in the evolution of the Anglo-Jewish community. They also crystallized my own religious attitudes.

I have always had an emotional attachment to traditional Judaism stemming from the cosiness and warmth of my own religious background. But as I moved out of this comfortable womb, beginning when I first attended a school which did not have a preponderance of Jewish pupils, I recognised that some of the beliefs and practices of the faith in which I had been nurtured appeared to conflict with what I was learning and what was generally accepted among educated people. The Pentateuch, I had been taught at home, in the synagogue and in *heder*, was the actual word of God and therefore could not be challenged, including its account of the creation. But in school I had learned something about Darwin and evolution. Both could not be true.

However, there wasn't much I could do about it, nor was I so troubled by the problem as to feel an irresistible need for some action on my part. The old-fashioned rabbis with whom I was acquainted through the synagogues I attended with my father were insufficiently versed in secular studies to understand the questions let alone possess the ability to answer them. The more modern orthodox rabbis tended to take the line that beliefs were less important than the practice of a Jewish way of life and the performance of *mitzvot* (good deeds). At that time, my only acquaintance with what is now called progressive Judaism was the Liberal service conducted by Basil Henriques on Friday evenings at Berner Street School where he ran the Bernhard Baron Jewish Settlement after school hours. I attended once, and found the predominantly English service rather bizarre and more akin to the church rituals I had sometimes seen in the cinema than to the all-Hebrew prayers of the orthodox synagogues with which I was familiar.

My traditional loyalties remained paramount and, although my intelligence wasn't really satisfied by the observances I performed, I was too busy to be overly concerned with my growing perplexity. Religious beliefs and Bible criticism were not subjects for discussion in the environment of my youth. I suppose I became what David Daube, whom I met some years later in Cambridge, described as orthoprax rather than orthodox. But I could not escape the issue of tradition versus reason when I became involved with Rabbi Jacobs.

Louis Jacobs, the only son of working-class parents in Manchester, showed an early aptitude for rabbinic studies. He was the bright boy of the Manchester Yeshiva at which he became a full-time student and, at the instigation of his teachers, Louis' parents allowed him to undertake advanced rabbinical studies at the Kolel in Gateshead, the scholarly rabbinic centre of East European-type orthodoxy in England. At the same time, or soon after, he pursued secular studies at the University of London and gained both bachelor and doctoral degrees.

He became the darling of Anglo-Jewish orthodoxy and greatness was predicted for him. His rabbinic scholarship, wide reading, retentive memory and clarity of expression made him, while still in the very early years of his rabbinical career, talked about as a future Chief Rabbi.

In 1953 Rabbi Dr Louis Jacobs, then in his mid-thirties, accepted a 'call' to the pulpit of the New West End Synagogue in London and that came as a shock to the orthodox community, for the anglicised New West End was on the left wing of the United Synagogue, the most powerful orthodox synagogue association in Britain. This synagogue had a tradition of mild reform symbolised by its mixed choir – anathema to the strictly orthodox who accepted the rabbinic dictum that a woman's voice is lewd. The membership of the New West End Synagogue included such luminaries as Viscount Samuel, Lord (Simon) Marks of Marks & Spencer fame, Lord Swaythling and the President of the United Synagogue, the Hon Ewen Montagu, QC. I was a Board member and former Warden of the New West End when Jacobs arrived and, because of my activity in the synagogue, we saw a great deal of each other and became good friends. At the time of his appointment I was still practising at the Bar.

Very early in his new pulpit, Louis delivered a series of sermons on Jewish prayer which impressed me greatly. By that time I had become the General Manager of *The Jewish Chronicle* and I offered to publish them under the imprint of Jewish Chronicle Publications. He was happy about that and the booklet did rather well, particularly in the United States. It was his first publication and its success must have inspired him to undertake more writing.

A while later he gave me the manuscript of a book entitled *We Have Reason to Believe* which had emerged out of a discussion group he had led at the synagogue. It was intended as a modern kind of guide to the perplexed (though Jacobs himself never claimed it to be such) and his thesis was that true belief did not demand an abdication of reason. He took the position that although faith is above reason, those elements of religion which were capable of being tested should not be exempt from scholarly enquiry. As a result he concluded that Judaism had to accept the fact that the Bible was the work of human beings, albeit divinely inspired.

I read the manuscript and invited Louis to talk to me about

it. I told him that I thought it an important book and was sure that Vallentine Mitchell (the publishing subsidiary of *The Jewish Chronicle*) would publish it. But I advised against early publication the reason being that the retirement of Dr Israel Brodie, then Chief Rabbi, was expected in the next few years. I had no doubt that Louis would be a strong candidate to succeed him but I took the view that publication of the book now would provide ammunition to the right-wingers likely to oppose his appointment. Why not wait until after the event and publish then? Louis was adamant. He did not want to wait and if his views were likely to be controversial, he thought it right that they should be known before his name was considered rather than afterwards. I naturally deferred to his opinion and the book was duly published in 1957. I still believe that if publication had been delayed, Louis would, in all likelihood, have been appointed Chief Rabbi and the religious complexion of the Anglo-Jewish community would have differed profoundly from what it became.

In fact the book did not create an immediate stir and was well received by all sections of the community including the orthodox. The reviews were good and one that appeared in the organ of the Mizrachi, the religious Zionist party, enthused about it as the modern man's guide to Jewish orthodoxy. I was amused some years later, when the Jacobs Affairs Part 1 had begun, that the same journal refused to accept an advertisement for *We Have Reason to Believe* consisting exclusively of extracts from its own review.

My good friend Louis Finkelstein, Chancellor of the Jewish Theological Seminary of America (JTS), visited London every summer to work at the British Museum staying at an unpretentious hotel in that neighbourhood. I introduced him to Louis Jacobs who greatly impressed the American scholar and in 1959, the American Louis offered the British Louis a senior appointment on the academic staff of the JTS. (Ironically in the light of subsequent developments, the ethos of the JTS was created by its first Chancellor, Dr Solomon Schechter, who came from England and brought with him the concept of 'progressive conservatism', then the slogan of the United Synagogue which, later, rejected Louis Jacobs for propounding the same philosophy.) It was an extremely attractive invitation for the JTS faculty included some of the most illustrious names in Jewish scholarship among them Louis Ginzburg, Saul Lieberman, Abraham Joshua Heschel and Louis Finkelstein himself. To join that company was an irresistible temptation and Jacobs was strongly inclined to accept.

That saddened me. There was no other orthodox rabbi in Britain possessing Louis Jacobs' levels of Jewish and secular scholarship as well as the intellectual honesty which appealed to the thinking Jew. I thought it would be an irreparable loss to the Anglo-Jewish community if he left the country and I discussed the problem with Ewen Montagu, President of the United Synagogue, who was a Jacobs admirer and also saw him as the next Chief Rabbi. Ewen was in complete agreement that we should try to keep Jacobs in this country and we both thought that the best way of achieving that, as well as preparing him for the Chief Rabbinate, would be an appointment at Jews' College, the seminary for the training of the Anglo-Jewish Ministry. The Principal of the College at that time, Rabbi Dr Isidore Epstein, would reach the age of retirement in the next year or two and Jacobs would then be a natural successor. From the leadership of the College to the Chief Rabbinate would be an easy transition. Ewen agreed to put the proposal to Sir Alan Mocatta, a High Court judge, then President of the College and met with an immediate and positive response. Mocatta subsequently spoke to Chief Rabbi Israel Brodie who, under the constitution of the College, possessed a power of veto over its appointments. Brodie agreed to the appointment of Jacobs as Moral Tutor. I am not sure now whether the proposal to appoint him as Principal on Dr Epstein's retirement was put to him by Ewen Montagu at that time. But I did mention that aspect to Dr Solomon Gaon, the Haham of the Spanish and Portuguese community, also a spiritual authority at the College, who thought that Louis would be an excellent successor to Dr Epstein and then to Israel Brodie.

So, with little comment and no fuss, Louis Jacobs was appointed Moral Tutor at Jews' College and took up his duties in 1960. He resigned his post at the New West End Synagogue and was succeeded as Minister by the young and engaging Rev Dr Chaim Pearl whose theological views did not conflict with those Jacobs had propounded in his publications.

In 1961 Rabbi Dr Isidore Epstein retired as Principal of Jews' College. Sir Alan Mocatta and the other lay officers of the College proposed that Louis Jacobs be appointed his successor but, to widespread surprise, Chief Rabbi Brodie vetoed the appointment. After much procrastination, he gave as his reasons, first, his objections to Jacobs's 'published views' and, secondly, that Jacobs did not possess the 'outstanding scholarship and other qualifications' required for the principalship of the College. That was the beginning of the public controversy which constituted the Jacobs Affairs Part 1. The more intense Part 2 erupted three years later in 1964.

With the veto on his appointment as Principal, Louis resigned his post at the College and Sir Alan Mocatta and the other Honorary Officers resigned in sympathy. I had urged Louis to stay because I was convinced that, sooner or later, the appointment would come to him: there was no other obvious candidate and the College could not go on long without leadership. However, Louis felt that he had no other honourable course than resignation. A few 'Jacobites', led by former New West End congregant Ellis Franklin, formed the Society for the Study of Jewish Theology with Louis as its director.

That was intended as a stopgap arrangement while Louis and his supporters gave thought to a long-term strategy to advance the concept of tradition with change within the orthodox community.

In the meantime I remained a congregant and friend of Chaim Pearl at the New West End. He did not find his appointment fulfilling and considered the synagogue's membership staid and disinclined towards innovation. The elderly congregants gave few such opportunities to as energetic an individual as he and he occasionally confided his frustrations to me, comparing the New West End Synagogue unfavourably with the vigorous activity of the Conservative congregations of the United States with which he was familiar and to whose religious approach he was sympathetic. That gave me the thought of solving two problems at a stroke. If Chaim were to find a rewarding pulpit in America, he would be happier and it would also leave a vacancy at the New West End to which Louis could return. I spoke about this to my friend Rabbi Wolfe Kelman, the executive head of the American Conservative Rabbinical Assembly, and, as a result, a prestigious congregation just outside New York approached Chaim. He visited and preached and thereafter readily accepted a call to become its rabbi.

The Board of Management of the New West End then unanimously invited Louis Jacobs to return to his former pulpit. We were aware that the United Synagogue required the ministers of their constituent synagogues, before being appointed, to obtain a certificate from the Chief Rabbi stating that they were fit and proper persons for the job. Louis had received such a certificate on his original appointment to the New West End and I had no doubt at the time that he would not be called upon to obtain another certificate, not only because he already possessed one but also because an application for a new one would place the Chief Rabbi in another awkward situation I felt sure he would rather avoid. I was wrong. Officialdom at the United Synagogue decreed that a new certificate was required and it was intimated to the New West End officers that if Louis applied for one, it would not be granted. The New West End Synagogue Board of Management did not accept this ruling and formally appointed Jacobs to the post.

Of course the United Synagogue could not accept this mutiny and its Secretary wrote to the Wardens condemning the 'distinct flouting' of the Chief Rabbi's authority, calling on them to 'desist from taking any further action' and 'not permit Dr Jacobs to officiate at the services of the synagogue'. When the Synagogue Board ignored this prohibition it was summarily dismissed by resolution of the US authorities and replaced by four 'managers'. As a result, the dismissed Board and a substantial proportion of the New West End's congregants formed the New London Synagogue with Louis as its rabbi.

The tumult and shouting over the Jacobs Affairs, which deeply divided Anglo-Jewry in the 1960s, have long since died but that period will always remain in my memory as the most trying time of my editorship. Needless to say, I sided wholeheartedly with Louis Jacobs but, while giving him the fullest editorial support, I was acutely aware that, as a responsible newspaper, *The Jewish Chronicle* had to give the issue the most comprehensive and objective coverage. The only snag about presenting the case of those on the side of the Chief Rabbi was that it was extremely difficult to persuade any of them to write articles setting it out. Moreover, a substantial proportion of the correspondence on that side was either illiterate or simply vituperative. Of course, we were given no credit for our efforts at balanced reporting (as distinct from the editorials which were certainly partisan) and the paper and I were subject to much vilification with the refrain, constantly repeated, that our objective was solely to undermine orthodoxy.

I never thought that Brodie's heart was in the fight for I had not a moment's doubt that his views on revelation were no different from the thesis of *We Have Reason to Believe*. I was sure that his virtual excommunication of Jacobs was entirely due to his 'fear and trembling' of the orthodox right-wing, even though I was reliably informed later that the members of his court, the Beth Din, would have preferred to see Louis back at the New West End and under their control. Brodie would never have claimed to be an authority on Jewish law and, I believed, he had made the decision, albeit reluctantly, to defer to the militant faction of extreme orthodoxy for fear of being denounced by them. By that time Brodie had become somewhat paranoid. He could not believe that his critics could possibly have been motivated by an opinion honestly held, but frequently expressed the opinion to his supporters that there was a conspiracy against him.

For a long time Brodie avoided any reasoned justification of his objections to Louis but eventually it had to come and, on 5 May 1964, he convened a meeting attended by 134 rabbis and read a statement which included the following passage:

'The travesty of our traditional Judaism has been featured in our monopolistic Jewish press for some time. There has been a constant denigration of authentic Judaism and religious authority which has tended to create religious confusion and a spirit of divisiveness within our community and which, in no small measure, has contributed to the present situation. Whilst we believe in the freedom of the press, we should not allow this freedom to be abused and even turned into a tyranny as is attempted by *The Jewish Chronicle* which, in recent years, no doubt for reasons of its own, has not presented an objective picture of the Anglo-Jewish scene, nor has it reflected the tradition and sentiment of Anglo-Jewry.'

The Chief Rabbi read this *ex cathedra* statement – reported fully in the *JC* – and no discussion was permitted. It pointedly refrained from according Louis the appellation of Rabbi, a surprising discourtesy to a recipient of the Rabbinical Diploma from the heads of the Manchester Yeshiva and of the Manchester Beth Din, both institutions of unimpeachable orthodoxy. A voluminous postbag poured into the *JC* of which we printed a representative selection. In a strongly worded editorial I rebutted Dr Brodie's accusations. By that time, the controversy had become international news with frequent reports and features appearing in the British press as well as worldwide with particularly extensive reporting in the *New York Times*. *The Economist*, in a leader, made the point that 'by vetoing Dr Jacobs' appointment at the New West End Synagogue, Dr Brodie appears to be taking up the illogical position that, while Dr Jacobs is fit to train future rabbis, he is not fit to be a rabbi himself'.

To some, I was the villain of the piece, abusing my office as Editor to advance a personal cause and the career of a friend. But in fact, the *JC* had, long before my time, espoused the very cause which had constrained Chief Rabbi Brodie to denounce Louis Jacobs as a heretic. The issue of 5 March 1886 began with a leading article headed 'Judaism and Theology' which dealt with 'the position taken up by the old fashioned school of theologians', that every word of the Bible is of directly divine origin. It argued that this had proved to be untenable and concluded 'For if the religious and ethical ideas of the Jews are wonderful when regarded as the outcome of a direct communication from God to Man, they become still more marvellous viewed as the result of, so to speak, a partnership between the Deity and mortals.' Louis Jacobs could not have put it better.

Two rabbinical friends, one in the United States and the other in Israel, with whom I was in regular correspondence during this period, fortified me in my belligerence. The Israeli was Rabbi Dr Louis Rabinowitz, a forceful spiritual leader who had, for many years, been one of Anglo-Jewry's outstanding religious figures, and Minister of the Cricklewood Synagogue, one of the more important constituents of the United Synagogue. Settling in Israel after his retirement, he remained a devoted reader of the *JC* and frequently favoured me with his advice and opinions.

He was what is now termed 'modern orthodox' and would, in my opinion, have made an excellent Chief Rabbi after Brodie's retirement. But the hardliners ganged up on him and persuaded Sir Isaac Wolfson, then President of the United Synagogue, that he was too old to be considered. Rabinowitz was then fifty-eight – the age of Brodie when he became Chief Rabbi – and his appointment would certainly have halted the right-wing stranglehold on both the United Synagogue and the Chief Rabbinate, but that was not to be. The United Synagogue decided that the age limit this time was fifty-five!

During the second act of the Jacobs drama, Rabinowitz wrote to me from Jerusalem, 'The whole orthodox intelligentsia in Israel agrees with me that Louis Jacobs was shamefully and cruelly treated.' He continued, 'a spirit of fanatical obscurantism has seized the whole official [Anglo-Jewish] community.'

In this instance, the Chief Rabbi was following the precepts of the right-wing orthodox rabbis, but it was a disappointment to me that even those who professed to being modern orthodox, with a few honourable exceptions, lined up behind him or sought to keep out of the controversy. Rabbi Joseph Lookstein, a leader of modern orthodoxy in the United States, was a case in point. In a letter I received from him in April 1966 he wrote, 'Please tell Louis Jacobs that his book on the "Principles of the Jewish Faith" is an excellent and superb piece of work.' When I replied to Lookstein, asking whether his comment could be used in advertisements for the book, he hastily replied, 'Do not print any blurb of my opinion of Louis Jacobs' book ... I would rather remain quietly neutral.'

Ultimately, this was a battle for the soul of Anglo-Jewry

between those advocating a free spirit of enquiry as reinforcement to faith and tradition and those who shunned reason out of blinkered, diehard, fundamentalism. Like most battles of this nature it generated much vehemence and acrimony. But I believe that the controversy did achieve the positive result of freshening the dormant waters of the Anglo-Jewish community, encouraging at least some of its members to face the challenge of reconciling tradition with modern knowledge.

It was unreasonable to expect that the establishment would be defeated in the Jacobs Affairs Part 2 for it became clear that the Chief Rabbi could not be expected to rescind his veto. Sir Isaac Wolfson, then President of the United Synagogue and in a sense his employer, had, I had reason to believe, tried to persuade Dr Brodie that it would make sense to permit Louis Jacobs to return to the New West End Synagogue. But Brodie was not big enough to change direction and, in any case, was totally intimidated by the orthodox extremists. On one occasion during the height of the controversy, Sir Isaac invited me to his flat on Portland Place for a chat. We discussed every aspect of the affair and the possible outcomes and my host was clearly highly perturbed, torn between his duty to support the religious leader of the United Synagogue and his own inclination to compromise. As I was leaving, he put his arm around my shoulder and said, 'Why don't you come and work for me? I'll pay you twice what you get from *The Jewish Chronicle*.' I laughed it off and we parted good friends. A little later, I heard that he intended either to make a bid to take over my paper or to start another one in opposition to what Brodie had, in his only major statement on the Jacobs Affairs, referred to as 'the monopolistic Jewish press'. Nothing came of this but the thought that shareholders might be tempted to sell out to a high bidder led David Kessler to set up a trust which would make it extremely difficult, if not impossible, for a hostile bid to succeed.

I fought the battle because I believed I was serving the best interests of the Jewish community and that, even when it was clear that I could not win, I hoped it might prepare the ground for a 'progressive conservative' movement within traditional Anglo-Jewry, in a sense a return to the most successful era of the United Synagogue and that was, in fact, the result. Immediately after the management of the New West End Synagogue had been dismissed, its former wardens convened a meeting of congregants. A large number attended and a resolution was unanimously passed to form an independent traditional congregation with the name of New London Synagogue and with Louis Jacobs as its rabbi. Since we had no premises, I asked the rabbinic leader of the Spanish and Portuguese community, Haham Dr Solomon Gaon if we could use the hall of their Lauderdale Road Synagogue for Sabbath morning services. He was a good friend, a sophisticated and engaging Gibraltarian who, privately, was sympathetic to the Jacobite cause and he readily agreed. The first service of the new congregation took place before a packed and reverent assembly and I think that my father, who had always wanted me to be a cantor, would have been happy that I was asked to lead it although he would probably have disapproved of the New London's theology.

Our sojourn at Lauderdale Road was not of long duration. Dr Gaon had to go on a visit to the United States and, during his absence, the Acting Haham, Rabbi Solomon Sassoon, whom I had known in my childhood, objected to this heretical activity on the synagogue's premises. His opposition to the Jacobs congregation could not be ignored. Gaon was unhappy about having to withdraw his support but was unwilling to provoke a split in his own community which would undoubtedly have occurred had the arrangement continued. Of course I understood his predicament and when I communicated his message to the committee of the new synagogue, a hall in a Kensington hotel was rented for the New London's Sabbath services.

There we continued for some months while the leaders of the congregation scouted around for permanent premises. One Saturday evening, returning from the synagogue service, I received a telephone call at home from Alec Colman, a well-known and successful property man. He told me that some time ago, he had purchased the old building of the St John's Wood Synagogue in Abbey Road, a constituent of the United Synagogue, which was about to move to its new, spacious home. He had received planning permission to demolish the old building and replace it with a block of flats but, he told me, he felt very uncomfortable about pulling down a synagogue. Would we like to have it for the New London and, if so, he would sell it to us for the price he had paid. I told him that I was sure it would be of interest and would inform my friends. He only asked one thing and that was that his name should be kept out of it. He was a friend of Chief Rabbi Brodie, as well as of Sir Isaac Wolfson, and did not wish to have those relationships impaired. I assured him that his request would be honoured.

I passed on the proposition to David Franklin who had become the Treasurer of the new congregation and was a close personal friend. David was the eldest son of Ellis Franklin, the head of the distinguished Anglo-Jewish family, who had been one of Louis Jacobs most loyal supporters. Without hesitation, David told me that he was sure he could find the money. Then followed some negotiation with Colman who reiterated his insistence that he should not be known as the seller to the heretics. So David put the problem to Louis Mintz, a friend and supporter of Louis who was also in the property business, and he agreed to purchase the property from Colman and then sell it to the New London Synagogue. That was duly executed and we became the owners of the stately old synagogue building on Abbey Road. When the transaction became known and the building was being redecorated, a supporter of the Chief Rabbi entered it surreptitiously and removed the seat on which Brodie had sat whenever he attended this, his local synagogue. Those boards were never to be defiled by offering repose to the posterior of the heretical Louis Jacobs!

Reflecting now, almost half a century later, I readily concede that I may have been too passionate in my pro-Jacobs advocacy in the columns of the *JC*. But my plea in mitigation is that at the time I was in my energetic forties, aflame with principle, opposed to the arbitrary exercise of authority and appalled at the injustice done to Louis Jacobs. I doubt that my approach would be any different now, though I would probably be more diplomatic in its expression.

17

A Semester in New York

By the time I assumed the editorship of the *JC*, I had visited the United States about ten times on lecture tours sponsored initially by the American Jewish Committee and subsequently in response to invitations I regularly received from other organisations. Nearly all my lectures were to Jewish groups, I travelled extensively and, even when on what were called 'one night stands', I took every opportunity to learn about the interests of community leaders and the structure and activities of Jewish organisations. American Jewry was said to number some six million (there never have been accurate statistics), about half the total world Jewish population. It was, I think, natural that I should have decided that the *JC* would have to cover that aspect of contemporary Jewish life far more fully than had previously been the case.

We had, in New York, an excellent correspondent in Richard Yaffe as well as a 'stringer' in Washington and, between them, they could be relied upon to report for us every item of significant Jewish news in the United States. But I wanted more than that and I discussed what could be done with my friends in New York during a visit in 1959. During that stay, I travelled to Boston to visit the newly established Brandeis University, not a Jewish university though a considerable proportion of its undergraduates and faculty were Jews. There I was introduced to Dr Abram Sacher, its first President. He, in turn, introduced me to a young man named Martin

Peretz who had just graduated from Brandeis and was teaching at nearby Harvard. Martin was bright, articulate and ambitious, knowledgeable about Jewish affairs, interested in journalism and keen to write for the *JC* which I encouraged him to do. His first contribution, an appraisal of the disproportionate number of Jewish 'best seller' writers in the United States, appeared just a few weeks after my return to London and I gave it prominence on the feature page.

It was so well received that I suggested he write a weekly feature, something like a 'Letter from America', but he was reluctant to commit himself to that degree of regularity. So I assembled a group of excellent Jewish writers to form a panel of contributors to a new weekly feature to be called 'American Survey'. The members of the panel were Oscar Handlin, Martin Peretz, Richard Yaffe, Albert Vorspan and Rabbi David Silverman and the first piece which was by Handlin was published, by a happy coincidence, on my forty-fourth birthday. The series ran for a considerable time and ended only when some of the contributors became unreliable in adhering to their deadlines.

As well as fulfilling lecture engagements, I spent as much time as I could when in the States in establishing contacts with Jewish leaders and institutions. Through my closest friend, Rabbi Wolfe Kelman, I saw a good deal of the Jewish Theological Seminary and its faculty. The Seminary was founded in 1886 as an orthodox but westernised rabbinic school in an attempt to counter the growing influence and attraction of the reform movement. It began to flourish when the leadership was taken over by Dr Solomon Schechter who came from Cambridge where he had been the Reader in Rabbinics. It was particularly interesting to me since Schechter favoured the religious approach of the London United Synagogue which, at that time, was described as 'progressive conservatism'. That was the beginning of the peculiarly American phenomenon of

Conservative Judaism, (its official name was the United Synagogue of America) a denomination to the right of Reform Judaism and to the left of orthodoxy.

I spent as much time as I could with Dr Louis Finkelstein, then the Chancellor of the Seminary, and we became good friends. George Bernard Shaw once had something to say about the good looks of the bishops of the Church of England. In his opinion they were among the handsomest bunch of men in the world. That thought passed through my mind when I met Louis and another head of a Jewish theological seminary, Dr Nelson Glueck of the (Reform) Hebrew Union College in Cincinnati. He and Louis were two of the finest looking men I had met in the United States. Louis Finkelstein was distinguished in appearance, tall, fine featured, bearded and with a presence and personality which made him stand out in any company. He was also a distinguished scholar and for several years had been coming to London in the summer to work in the British Museum Library and staying at a small hotel close to the library in Bloomsbury. At that time a kosher restaurant existed on New Oxford Street, a few minutes walk from his hotel and he regularly lunched there. I frequently joined him and noted that, on each occasion, he ordered the same menu – chicken soup, roast chicken, lokshen pudding and a glass of tea. It never varied. One year he broke from his customary pattern and took a short trip to Paris to meet Bernie Mandelbaum who was then Vice-Chancellor of the Seminary. Bernie told me later that he had taken 'Finkie' to a kosher restaurant on the Rue Rosier and that he had ordered chicken soup, roast chicken and lokshen pudding and that, on leaving the restaurant, had remarked to Bernie that he didn't know why people were so enthusiastic about French food.

I was assured on excellent authority that when President Truman visited the JTS and Louis Finkelstein presented him with a miniature scroll of the Pentateuch, the President began his response with the words, 'It's just what I wanted.'

My work in London, at that time and subsequently, was by no means limited to office hours. In addition to a full day spent at my desk, I was busy most evenings and weekends attending some of the numerous meetings and functions of the Jewish community and, in addition, often travelled to the provinces to meet correspondents and readers and speechify. By the middle of 1968, having held the post for almost ten years, I was beginning to feel the need for a break. I talked it over with David Kessler and he readily agreed that it would be a good thing for me to take a sabbatical from the pressures I was finding stressful.

I had, some while earlier, been invited by Louis Finkelstein to spend a semester as a Visiting Professor at the Jewish Theological Seminary. It was an open invitation which, he assured me, I was free to take up whenever I had the time. This seemed the ideal thing to do for my sabbatical, it would not be strenuous and I always enjoyed being in New York. When I told Louis that I could come for a semester at the end of 1968 he flatteringly received my decision with enthusiasm.

So I rented a small apartment in New York's Upper East Side and took up residence. My duties at the Seminary were not onerous, consisting only of teaching a course on contemporary Jewry – where Jews lived and how they lived, their major institutions and concerns and, of course, Zionism and the State of Israel. I enjoyed teaching my interested and interesting class and, even more, spending time with some of the luminaries on the faculty with whom I established friendly relationships and from whom I learned a great deal.

During these months I kept in touch with the London office and with the *JC* correspondents in New York and Washington. One day I received a call from Si Kenen, our man in Washington, asking if I would be interested in attending President Nixon's Inaugural Ball at the Smithsonian. I was intrigued, said

I'd be delighted, and a few days later received an impressively large engraved invitation to the event.

The day arrived and I entrained to Washington, having borrowed the appropriate attire, and presented myself on a rainy evening at the Smithsonian. Receiving the hundreds of guests was a bevy of attractive young ladies who ushered us into the spacious party area and left us to our devices. I wandered around looking for a familiar face without success until I saw Yitzhak Rabin, also wandering aimlessly, who having just arrived in Washington as Israeli Ambassador, also knew nobody there. We joined forces and, as a first combined operation, decided to find the bar. Eventually we found it and acquired drinks for which, to our astonishment, we had to pay. Yitzhak remarked that, had they saved some money on less elaborate invitations, they might have afforded giving the guests a drink.

Taking our drinks with us, we found a reasonably quiet corner in which to sit and chat. This we did, quite happily and inconsequentially, until midnight when an announcement invited all the guests to repair to the grand hall to greet the President who had just arrived. We joined the throng and waited a while until a fanfare of trumpets accompanied the steps of Mr Nixon, his wife and daughters as they entered the dais on which the band was playing.

Raising both hands to acknowledge the applause and calling for silence, the President made some appropriate and platitudinous remarks concluding with the following words which I paraphrase. The band tonight, he said, is that of Guy Lombardo and that has a special meaning for Pat and me. In 1945, on the day the war with Japan ended, Pat and I were in New York and we felt that we had to celebrate. So we went to the Starlight Roof and we danced. The band playing that night was Guy Lombardo's – applause – and, he concluded, I am sure that when the next war ends, Guy Lombardo will still be playing.

There was an audible intake of breath from the audience. What did Nixon know that we did not?

*

I was first introduced to Arthur Goldberg by Walter Reuther, then head of the Union of Automobile Workers, when I visited Detroit on a lecture tour in 1949. Arthur was the counsel for the Union and, at that time, there was little indication of the heights he would reach. In the years that followed he became Secretary of Labour under President Kennedy, was appointed to the Supreme Court by President Johnson and, at the request of Johnson, left the Supreme Court for three years service as the United States Ambassador to the United Nations. I learned from him when he visited London in 1969 that he had only left the Supreme Court under great pressure from Lyndon Johnson who had assured him that, after his service at the UN, he would return to the Court as Chief Justice. Johnson never did carry out that promise and, in recounting this episode, Arthur was understandably bitter.

On that visit to London he asked me if I could arrange for him to meet some press people with whom he wanted to discuss the situation in the Middle East and I invited some of them to lunch. We were about seven or eight in number including such press luminaries as William Rees-Mogg, Editor of *The Times*, Alastair Hetherington of the *Guardian* and Paul Johnson, then editing the *New Statesman*. Arthur was at his most effective, talking with great authority and a wealth of detail and anecdote which underlined the fact that he was at the centre of world affairs and had worked with the great people of this earth. He had acquired, since I had last seen him in action, enormous self-assurance which missed, sometimes only just, amounting to vanity or arrogance. Above all, he gave the impression of honest objectivity in his assessment and he radiated integrity.

During the time we spent together he seldom asked questions because he was clearly not interested in subjects outside his field. Nor did he possess much personal warmth. I was with him for quite a long time during this visit and had been of some considerable assistance to him, but he seemed to take it all as his due. Nor did he ever open up a personal subject such as asking my opinion, enquiring about my work or other similar topic. He was much less interested in people than in politics or legal issues. At the age of sixty-one, he seemed at the height of mental and physical vigour. I noted at the time that I did not think he would go out of his way to do a favour for a friend but would exert every effort for the betterment of humanity generally.

He came to London again in 1974 and I recall a poignant incident which he then related to me. King Feisal of Saudi Arabia had made a state visit to the United States a few years previously and, in New York, had made a reference in a speech which was considered anti-Semitic. In consequence, Mayor Lindsay had refused to attend a dinner in his honour. Arthur did attend and was, of course, introduced to Feisal who thanked him for his presence. Arthur told me that he replied that, as the US Ambassador to the UN he considered it his duty to be present during a visit by a Head of State and added, 'I have a personal reason to be glad I came.' The King asked what that was. 'Well, I'm impressed to see that you look as I always imagined our father Abraham would have looked.' According to Arthur, the King was 'greatly amused'. That may or may not have been the case, but Arthur Goldberg was pleased with himself in recounting the tale.

18

More Travels

I had never visited Israel before becoming *JC* editor. That was
not due to any lack of interest; I simply could not afford it.
Although my father and his Hasidic friends were rather disdain-
ful of *die Tsionisten* – as it was pejoratively pronounced in
Yiddish – I had in my early teens, even before my barmitzvah,
become enthused with the romance of the re-creation of
Jewish nationhood. I became a member of the first ever group,
called Gedud Trumpeldor after an early Zionist hero, of
Habonim (The Builders), a vigorous Zionist youth club which
met, ironically, in the hall of the Christian Street School. There
we sang Hebrew songs and learned about developments in
Palestine, the history of Zionism and the lives of the heroes of
the movement.

A visit to Israel, the source of so much of the news and
features in the *JC*, was, naturally, the first of my travel priorities
and in 1959 I arrived in Tel Aviv, then hardly a sight to
enrapture. In appearance and atmosphere it was, apart from its
beach front, reminiscent of one of the small Polish towns I had
visited before the war. But when I began to walk the streets and
observe what was going on in them it hit me forcefully that
everyone was Jewish and that I could just as well be in Petticoat
Lane, where I had always felt at home in my youth because
everyone I knew was Jewish. When I went out of that London
ghetto, it took some time before I no longer felt that I was
among strangers, but here in Israel there were no strangers and

Jews could behave freely and normally without a nagging concern about 'what will the goyim think?'

In 1959 the old city of Jerusalem was part of Jordan and my only glimpses of what it held came through telescopic views from strategic points in Israeli Jerusalem. I travelled as far south as I could, traversing the southern desert described in the Bible as the 'wilderness of Zin', a name more evocative of the actual scene at that time than its current name, the Negev. South of Beersheba, the stones and soil, broken by occasional clumps of shrubs and stunted trees, gradually gave way to sand, the real desert. Further south, rocks began to jut out and the scene became wilder with some startling geological formations. My destination, Eilat, was at that time a small port with few buildings but it was clearly destined to become the glamorous Red Sea resort which would attract the sun-loving tourist.

The contrast to all this was the far north and, in particular, the town of Safed high up in the hills of Galilee. The only route through the hills at that time was a road with terrifyingly sharp twists and turns but the anxiety of the journey was replaced by a feeling of deep contentment at the sight of the jewel of old Safed town. Built on terraces formed on the sloping terrain, the town occupied a dozen levels.

I was particularly interested in the old synagogues and especially the Sephardi Ari Synagogue of which there is a fine painting by Chagall. It had become quite dark by the time I reached it and the bent and ancient custodian escorted me around by the light of a candle. A combination of all these circumstances made this a mystical, eerie experience and, when I closed my eyes, I could see the medieval cabbalists whose spiritual home this had been.

I was taken by surprise at the place held by religion in the life of the country. In the Diaspora communities with which I was familiar, the majority of Jews, whatever their beliefs, had some connection with the organised religious community. They might go to a synagogue only on Yom Kippur or to participate in a memorial service on the anniversary of a parental death and, in England at any rate, nearly every Jew belonged to a synagogue in order to be buried in a Jewish cemetery. But in Israel there seemed to be no such compromises, for the division between the synagogue-goers and the non-religious section of the population, the majority, was sharp and deep. Here the synagogue-goers were content with what they had, showing no desire for change or for missionary work with the secularists. I visited many synagogues of various shapes and sizes but, oddly, the one I recall most clearly from my first visit to the country was the Great Synagogue in Tel Aviv. It was large, lofty and shabby, and crowded on an ordinary Sabbath. What stayed in my mind was the highly organised *shnoddering*, the process of procuring offerings which had to be promises since there could be no cash transactions on the Sabbath day. The tourist was soon spotted and called on by his Hebrew name to recite a blessing on the Torah scroll. The *shammas* would give him an addressed envelope in which the offering was to be posted to the synagogue after the Sabbath had ended. But, with a natural suspicion that the enthusiasm of the moment might fade, the beadle asked for the name of the visitor's hotel and the room number, and gave the assurance that he would call after the Sabbath. That was what happened to me.

I spent a highly enlightening and hectic two weeks meeting prominent figures in politics, business, religion and academia, visiting institutions and seeing the country. I lost some of my romantic notions when I learned from meeting many politicians, both in and out of government, that the practice of politics in Israel was no more or less idealistic than in other countries. The idealism seemed to me, at that time, to be concentrated in the kibbutzim many of which I visited. This was the first of what were to become annual visits.

Tea with Einstein and Other Memories

*

My next official journey abroad came soon after my appointment as Editor, as a consequence of my acceptance of a
luncheon invitation from the German Ambassador. In the
course of an agreeable general conversation he expressed his
regard for the *JC*, recognised our legitimate interest in what
was happening in Germany and asked me if I had ever visited
the country. I told him that in my early, pre-war, travelling
days, Germany was positively not on the list for Jewish tourists
so that, though I had been on the continent before the outbreak
of war in 1939, I had never considered visiting his country nor
had it occurred to me in my post-war travels. The Ambassador
gently chided me for my abstention. My paper, he said,
contained so much news and comment on what was happening
in his country that he thought it incumbent on me to go and
see for myself and he invited me to do so as the guest of his
government. I accepted the validity of his argument, thanked
him for his invitation, but assured him that my paper could
afford to pay for me. I added that I would, however, appreciate
it if he could offer me facilities to meet those to whom I would
like to talk. He agreed to my request and I lost no time in
making the journey.

I spent two weeks in Germany early in 1960 and it was an
intensely emotional experience. I found myself looking coldly
at the men and women in the street – had they been Nazis and
what were they doing during the period of the Holocaust?
Then, when I began to meet individuals, I could not avoid
wondering whether the hand I was shaking belonged to one of
the butchers or their accessories.

The start of each of these encounters followed the same
pattern. The people I was talking to knew that I was the Editor
of the *JC* and, after the introductory formalities, they would tell
me either that they had a Jewish grandparent or other Jewish
connection or that they had absolutely no knowledge of the

182

Nazi atrocities. I invariably felt some discomfort at being the cause of this embarrassment but I also knew that I would have taken it amiss if there had been no such recognition of the need to express remorse for that dreadful period of German history. The conclusion I reached was that, for my generation at any rate, the relationship between Jews and Germans was bound to be strained.

My only meeting at which this strain was absent was that with Chancellor Adenauer. He impressed me with his candour, his energy and, above all, his sincerity. When he talked about Hitler and the Jews his voice noticeably changed its timbre and I felt sure that there were tears in his eyes. He was either a magnificent actor or a truly righteous man – I had no doubt that he was the latter.

We talked at some length, primarily about the methods being employed to educate the German people about Nazism, particularly in the schools, and also about the steps being taken to exclude former Nazis. Based on the information I had received both before and during my visit, I expressed some disquiet but Chancellor Adenauer gave me the clear impression that he was sensitive to foreign, and particularly Jewish, opinion on this score.

The most interesting subject of conversation was Israel, first on the topic of reparations about which he spoke passionately, assuring me that, even when reparations ended in three years time, Germany would continue to support Israel, whichever party was in power. I asked him whether the exchange of diplomatic relations with Israel was on the cards to which he replied that it would be unwise at the present time because of his government's apprehension that Arab states would retaliate by recognising East Germany. But he concluded by saying that this was wholly a formality since both the government and public opinion looked upon Dr Felix Shinnar, the head of the Israel Mission, as the Ambassador.

During the two weeks of my visit I spoke to dozens of Germans, humble and influential, individually and in groups. Among them were Ministers of the Federal Republic and of some Länder, officials of the government and of voluntary organisations, professors, teachers, trade unionists, clergymen and, most interestingly, schoolchildren. In addition to Bonn, then the capital, I also visited Düsseldorf, Cologne, Frankfurt and Berlin.

I had specially asked to meet groups of schoolchildren for the obvious reason that ascertaining the attitude of this rising generation towards Jews and their comprehension of the enormity of the Holocaust was of far greater importance than the apologies or equivocations of the generation which had lived under Nazism. During some of these encounters, which made a great impression on me, teachers or my 'minders' were present and naturally, the responses of the youngsters were less spontaneous than on one particular occasion when I was alone with a class of fifteen or sixteen year olds. A boy stood up and said that he was bored with the attacks on the Nazis, that it was time it was forgotten, that he and his friends were in no way responsible and that many of them were critical of the Jews who were stirring things up against Germany. Several others in the class nodded their agreement. This was the only occasion when I heard sentiments of this kind expressed.

*

During the years of my editorship I travelled extensively. I was anxious to acquaint myself directly with the leadership of the many and varied Jewish communities throughout the world whose news we covered and where we had correspondents and readers. Of the countries I had never visited, South Africa was, after Israel and Germany, first on my list. I got there in 1964 spending three weeks travelling within the country and meeting a variety of interesting personalities, Jewish and non-

Jewish. Numerically, the Jewish community was a small one numbering some 120,000 but its interest and importance was out of proportion to its numbers. It had always possessed leaders, both religious and lay, of international stature. It was a prosperous community, charitable and highly supportive of the Zionist movement and the State of Israel. South Africa was also of special interest to me because at that time it was actively pursuing its apartheid policy and Jews are particularly sensitive to racial issues.

I communicated with the South African officialdom in London informing them of my proposed visit and was promised every co-operation. One of my requests was for a meeting with Mr Verwoerd, then Prime Minister and one of the most committed supporters of apartheid. I was assured that this would be arranged and was informed that, when I arrived in South Africa, Mr Verwoerd's office would be in touch with me to arrange an appointment. That promise was only partly fulfilled for, soon after my arrival in Johannesburg, I did receive a message from Mr Verwoerd's office but it was to the effect that he would not see me. When I asked the reason I was informed that the Prime Minister had received reports about my paper and that he objected to our criticisms of apartheid. I was later told that Afrikaner officialdom in Pretoria had taken a particular objection to a recent comment by the *JC* columnist 'Ben Azai' that two prominent Jewish opponents of apartheid were acting in accordance with the best Jewish tradition.

When, a few days later, I met a small group of wealthy Jewish supporters of the nationalist government, I referred to this incident. They promised to take it up with the appropriate authorities, which they did, and later informed me that, although they had not been able to change the PM's mind (or those of his officials), they had arranged for me to meet Mr Frank Waring, the Minister of Information. I had no interest in meeting Mr Waring and I told them so. But they were insistent that my rejection of what they saw as an olive branch would be regarded as offensive and would worry the Jewish community. In the circumstances, I agreed.

In the event, my meeting with Mr Waring was perfectly pleasant. He was of British descent, which made him a rarity in the Nationalist-Boer government of which he was a member, and he also claimed to have Jewish forbears. We talked generalities – and cricket – for a while and then he turned to comment on a current furore. A newsletter of the Dutch Reformed Churches of South Africa had published an article accusing Jews of being behind world communism. Mr Waring informed me that he deplored this expression of anti-Semitism of which there was no trace, he assured me, in the present government. The South African *Sunday Times* and, of course, the Jewish press, made a big story of it.

I found that the influential group which had arranged my call on Mr Waring notwithstanding, relations between the government and the Jewish community as a whole were strained. Not long before my visit, Israel had voted against the South African government at the United Nations as a result of which the government had withdrawn the privilege that the Zionist Federation had long enjoyed of unfettered remission of funds to Israel. In an effort to maintain a reasonable relationship with the government, the South African Board of Deputies, the Jewish community's most representative organisation, had declared that it 'does not enter the political arena save on matters affecting the Jewish community as such'.

Although most of the many Jews I met were cautious in expressing opinions on domestic political issues, in particular on apartheid, I had no doubt that the majority was opposed to the Verwoerd agenda. A former Chief Rabbi of Johannesburg, Louis Rabinowitz, had been fearless in attacking it but, at the time of my visit, his successor, Bernard Casper, an old friend going back to Young Sinaist days, had only been in the country for one year and could obviously not speak with the authority of his predecessor.

The English-language press was acquitting itself with distinction at that time. It was unremitting in its attacks on the government and the *Rand Daily Mail* was among its leaders.

The Editor of that paper told me that the press was free and, generally, very critical of the government; it had replaced all other organised forms of political opposition to apartheid. The Afrikaner population accepted apartheid as the natural order of things going back to the early days of the European immigration to South Africa. To them it would be a recipe for disaster to give the majority black population control. As far as the English ingredient of the population was concerned, it had tacitly agreed to leave the responsibilities of government to the Afrikaners and to be free to pursue their business activities in a prosperous country.

The Jewish community at that time was patently nervous. In that respect it did not differ from the white community generally but there was a special reason in the case of the Jews. Its members included supporters of all the recognised political parties but there were also some Jews, most of them not involved in the affairs of the organised community, who were communists and regarded as saboteurs. They constituted an uncomfortably high proportion of the total number of the young whites so involved and had given rise to a certain amount of anti-Semitic comment. Several editors of Afrikaner newspapers to whom I spoke told me that they had received violently anti-Semitic letters on the subject. Despite this cause for nervousness, South African Jewry at the time of my visit was probably the best organised of the Diaspora and the most generous. Its institutions were efficient, its public buildings and synagogues imposing and its lay leadership of first-class calibre.

By far the most agreeable hours I spent in the country were those in the company of Nadine Gordimer – this was before she had been awarded the Nobel Prize. Cool and attractive, self-effacing in manner, she assured me that writers were left alone. True, her last book had been banned and she was no longer invited to broadcast, but she had no fears for her personal safety. She was the most balanced commentator any visitor to that complex country could hope to have. But, more than that, she seemed to be acquainted with every other liberal thinker in the country and introduced me to several of them. I thus had the opportunity of meeting Chief Albert Luthuli who had been awarded the Nobel Peace Prize in 1960 for his anti-apartheid work and who, at the time I met him, was under house arrest. En route to Durban I visited Alan Paton, then in his sixties. A short, spare, weather-beaten man, he was eminently objective. He was strongly critical of the discrimination in employment, of the establishment of group areas and the general dehumanisation of the blacks. But, at the same time, he told me, the whites, including Boers, were now much kinder to the Africans in their personal dealings with them.

Enlightened South Africans – and I met many – recognised that the outside world was entitled to express an opinion on such issues as apartheid legislation and the almost unlimited police powers. However, I also came to the conclusion that one of the consequences of intemperate and emotional criticism from abroad was the hardening of resistance to change. We, the concerned outsiders, had to try to understand the fears of both white and black South Africans in the hope that a decisive body of opinion would emerge, and recognise that apartheid was both morally wrong and against the long-term interests of the state. I tried to promote that attitude in the editorial comments on the subject that I made thereafter.

*

Towards the end of 1967 I visited Tehran for the first time, primarily to meet the communal leaders and to learn something about the present concerns of this ancient community. Before leaving I communicated with the Iranian Embassy in London which offered me the opportunity of a meeting with the Shah which I gladly accepted.

The most interesting event of that visit was a non-event. On my arrival at my hotel in Tehran, I received a message that the Shah would not be able to see me at the appointed time on the following day since he had been delayed on a visit outside the capital. Could I stay on for another two days and see him then? I replied that this was not possible because of other commitments and, to apologise personally for this muddle, the Minister of Court came to see me at my hotel.

After expressing his regret, he told me that the Shah was a friend and admirer of the State of Israel but that he could not afford to make that public. Only recently he had received a delegation from the Arab League protesting at the existence of a direct flight between Tehran and Ben-Gurion airport in Israel. The Shah knew and approved of this facility but at the meeting he expressed his surprise and irritation that his staff had not informed him about the air link and promised that he would look into the matter. This same performance had occurred on previous occasions and, of course, the Shah had no intention of doing anything at all. The Minister also informed me that, although Iran did not have diplomatic relations with Israel, the Jewish state did have a Purchasing Mission in Tehran and that it was generally known as the Israeli Embassy. Finally, he asked me whether I knew his son-in-law, a Jewish lawyer in New York!

While in Tehran, some of the Jewish community's leaders invited me to dinner. We talked about current concerns, but essentially this was intended as a social occasion the outstanding feature of which was the excellence of the cuisine, kosher, naturally. The table, seating about a dozen, was beautifully laid and decorated but I was surprised to see two heaped plates of caviar. I mentioned to one of my hosts that the rabbis with whom I was familiar in Britain regarded caviar as non-kosher since the sturgeon, from which it came, did not have recognisable fins and scales. I was assured that it was accepted as kosher here and a lasting benefit I gained from my Tehran visit was an introduction to this delicacy.

*

I was particularly keen to visit the Soviet Union and regularly made applications for a visa during the years of my editorship. It was never declined, the Soviet Embassy officialdom merely did not respond. It was not until after my retirement as Editor, during the summer of 1982, that I was able to travel there and with a group of art lovers visiting the cities of Odessa, Kiev, Moscow and Leningrad.

Before leaving, I consulted some friends who were involved in the efforts to enable Jews to emigrate from Russia to Israel despite the opposition of the rulers of the Soviet Union and I took with me the names of some 'refuseniks', as those who had been refused permission to leave the country came to be known. I was advised to be cautious when getting in touch with them since communication with foreigners could be dangerous and, added one of my advisers, 'every Russian is an informer'. So, before making any visit, I would leave the hotel, make a telephone call from a public phone in the street and then either walk or travel by public transport to my destination since taxi drivers were particularly suspect as informers. Every one of these visits was an inspiration. Most of the refuseniks I met, a few individually but mostly in small groups, were highly intelligent, personally engaging and, almost always, optimistic. We conversed in English (sometimes) but mostly in German or Yiddish. Many were professionals or academics who had been dismissed from their jobs because of their applications to emigrate and had been reduced to menial occupations.

I thought I had taken every precaution to protect those I was visiting as well as myself for I was liable to expulsion if my activities came to the knowledge of the authorities. But I had clearly not been thorough enough for some months after my return to London, and after I had written and broadcast on the subject of the refuseniks whose names, of course, I did not disclose, my visit was referred to in a lengthy article in Leningrad's principal daily, *Leningradskaya Pravda*.

The main theme of the article was a justification for the denial to Soviet Jewish citizens of the right to their own culture and it included an attack on me for establishing contacts with Soviet refuseniks. It asked, 'What business had an English tourist with Soviet citizens of Jewish nationality?' And then it answered its question – 'William Frankel is the Editor of the greatest Zionist newspaper in England, *The Jewish Chronicle* ... an open mouthpiece of Israeli propaganda.' In fact I had left the editorship some five years previously.

That article in the *Leningradskaya Pravda* was the subject of an analysis in the *Wall Street Journal* by Charles H. Fairbanks, Jnr, at that time the USA Deputy Assistant Secretary of State for Human Rights. He saw it as an attempted justification for the recent formation in the USSR of a Public Committee Against Zionism and quoted from the article its attack on Zionism's 'unbridled militant chauvinism' which was 'dangerous and infectious, just like any kind of infection like leprosy, like the plague'. Fairbanks concluded that the fact that the *Pravda* article told the Soviet public 'that British Editor William Frankel ... transmitted "certain instructions" to Jewish dissident G.I. Vasserman laid the groundwork "for charges more serious than have recently been used".' Needless to say, I had no instructions to transmit; my calls on refuseniks were simply to attempt to raise their spirits by assuring them that many of their co-religionists outside the USSR sympathised with their lot and would do whatever they could to help.

19

On Becoming a Journalist

Early in 1976, I decided that the time had come for me to retire from the editorship of the *JC*, a position I had held for almost twenty years. In the long history of the paper, the length of my term of office was second only to that of Leopold Greenberg who had been the Editor for thirty years. I had decided to go because I was feeling stale in the job, had said all I had to say and no longer felt excited, as in the past, when coming to the office.

Moreover, I was mentally and physically tired. The preceding years had been wearing. In 1971 I had ended my marriage and moved to a small flat in the newly built Barbican apartment complex which was conveniently close to the *JC* office. I had taken nothing but my clothes and so had to spend some time in the tiresome but necessary activity of acquiring all the practical necessities for living. It had not been an amicable separation and, after a marriage which had endured for thirty-two years, the break brought with it much grief for us both, particularly during the divorce proceedings which followed.

I had met Claire some eight years before when I was on a lecture tour in the United States and, on a visit to Baltimore, was invited to dinner by Nancy and Morton Blaustein at which Claire and her then husband were fellow guests. We got on well and I met them both on occasion when they visited London and I went to the United States. It was after my divorce when I was in Washington that I telephoned Claire and learned from her housekeeper that she was in Reno engaged in divorce proceedings herself.

In December 1973, after living a bachelor existence for some two and a half years, I married Claire. The ceremony was in her Baltimore house and the rabbis officiating were my friends Wolfe Kelman and Herbert Tarr, respectively conservative and reform. The marriage ceremony was traditional and under a *chuppah*, though its structure, a hula hoop filled with flowers, was anything but traditional. Claire moved to London some months later and we acquired the lease of a Georgian house in Montagu Square. Thus began a new and happy domestic life.

I cannot forbear to recite a delightfully improbable incident which occurred soon after we moved into our new home. Coming home one evening, I was irritated to find a man attaching a bicycle to the railings of our house. I informed him politely, I hope, that these railings were my property and that he should park his vehicle elsewhere. He left and the following morning I found a piece of paper in my mail box addressed to 'The man who dislikes bicycles' and then:

> Be grateful, Sir, the one you spoke to then
> was born and bred a gentleman,
> who knew that parking by your door
> was not in breach of any law,
> But by his courtesy and *gentillesse*
> Agreed to lighten your distress
> To move his steed from this abode
> And wheel it right across the road.
> Remember as you lock your door
> The days, perhaps, when you were poor,
> Relieved perhaps once to have found
> That pavements are still common ground.

I was suitably humbled and kept the piece of paper, cheered that only in England could such a response have been elicited.

*

In April 1976, I decided to tell David Kessler of my intention to resign on my sixtieth birthday the next year. He was, as he had always been, understanding and helpful. We talked about a successor and I told him that, a year or two back, when I had appointed Geoffrey Paul as my deputy, I had had the thought that he might eventually succeed me. I had, in fact, given Geoffrey an indication of my intentions and he was happy with the prospect. David was satisfied that Geoffrey would ably fill the post and offered it to him. After some tripartite discussions, we all agreed that it would, for a variety of reasons, be undesirable to enter into a ten months' transition period before the actual date of my resignation. The agreement we reached was that I would take leave of absence in June, that Geoffrey would then become Acting Editor and that his appointment as Editor would be announced simultaneously with that of my retirement the following February. Everything went off satisfactorily and according to plan and, on 3 February 1977, the *JC* hosted an elegant farewell party for me at the Stationer's Hall.

I knew, of course, that when I left the editorial chair, I would perforce return to the obscurity from which I had emerged when I moved into it. Editors, even of small newspapers, are courted and the *JC* occupied a respected position in national life as well as being a most, if not the most, important element in the life of the Anglo-Jewish community. It was also held in great esteem throughout the Jewish and journalistic worlds and, as Editor, I had found a welcome and friendship wherever I travelled.

All this would now change, I mused. I did not intend to retire from work at sixty. It was time to change, to attempt to do other things, but I was in no hurry to make decisions. For one thing, it occurred to me that when it was known that I had left the *JC*, some offers might come my way and I did not want to exclude that possibility by too quickly committing myself to other work. I needed some time and space to reconsider my position and decide what it was that I really wanted to do.

I have never planned my career. Every major element of it came about by chance, the random element. I have had day-dreams, seen myself addressing a rapt House of Commons or living it up with the great and famous, but whatever has happened to me in my career was a consequence of some fortuitous event. I read law because I happened to be in Cambridge escaping from the London Blitz. I moved from the Bar to the *JC* because I happened to meet David Kessler in New York in 1957 and now, just as I was contemplating the next transition, I received an invitation from the Australian Jewish community to spend several weeks in Sydney speaking in support of a communal fund-raising event.

It came from the then lay head of the Sydney Jewish community, Hal Goldstein, whom I had previously met in London. He was a manufacturer of refrigerators and it was a delight, when I eventually reached Sydney, to see the name Goldstein in prominent capital letters on the refrigerators in the celebrated Opera House where more familiar words, like Frigidaire, might be seen in other countries. Hal was engaging, unaffected and well organised. The proposition he made me was that, since Australia was half way round the world from London, he would provide me with two round-the-world air tickets and would cover all our expenses during the time we were in Sydney. Claire and I discussed it at length and decided that we would spend three or four months travelling and, during that time, think about and try to adjust ourselves to the different life we would be living on our return to London.

So, early in July 1976 – it was around the time of the Israeli raid on Entebbe – we took a flight from London to our first stop, Teheran. It was a different city from the one I had first visited some ten years earlier. The ayatollahs and mullahs were in the ascendant and the Shah and his entourage were nervous.

Some of the people I had met on my previous visit who had been open and forthcoming in discussing the political situation with me were now inhibited. It was graphically illustrated when a journalist acquaintance I was meeting examined every item on and under the table in the restaurant in which we were sitting in case of hidden microphones. From Teheran we travelled to Isfahan and Shiraz, both exquisitely beautiful.

Our next stop was India and early one morning in mid-June we arrived in Delhi and checked in at the Oberoi Hotel where there was a message awaiting us. It was from Mr Cushrow Irani, then Managing Director of *The Statesman*, India's oldest English-language daily, published in Delhi and Calcutta. He had been informed of my visit by the International Press Institute of which we were both members and the message was an invitation to dinner that evening. I telephoned to accept.

At the appointed hour, his car, an immaculate Ambassador (then the most popular car in India, an adaptation of the Morris Oxford), pulled up at the hotel and the turbaned driver ushered us through the opened rear door. We were driven to a house set in a pleasant garden in one of the broad streets of New Delhi, one of the houses built for the ruling classes during the Raj. There Cushrow and his wife Threety welcomed us and the bonding was immediate. By the time the evening was over Claire and I regarded them as our friends. Cushrow was affable, extremely well informed and, once he got on to the over-whelming subject of Mrs Gandhi's Emergency which was then in force, his passionate flow of words was practically unstoppable, not that I would have wanted to stop him. The press had been virtually silenced, foreign correspondents had been expelled and only Cushrow's *Statesman* and, to a lesser extent Ramnat Goenka's *Express*, were standing up to the authoritarian Prime Minister. Threety had a bag ready packed and placed near the front door for Cushrow to take if the police were to call suddenly and arrest him.

Sri Lankan-born Threety Irani was dressed in an elegant sari and was charming, beautiful and highly intelligent. They had three lively and attractive daughters, much the same ages as Claire's three girls in America, coming close to marriageable age and, though wearing the symbol of modernity, blue jeans rather than saris, content to leave it to their mother to find them suitable husbands. There was so much to talk about, and we had so much in common, that their house in Delhi became our base during our several weeks of travel in India. Cushrow and Threety remained among our closest friends though, sadly, the opportunities for meeting have declined.

We travelled to the regular tourist destinations in northern India ending our stay in Kashmir. On our last night there, we attended a sound and light performance in the gardens of Shalimar and that was to have an unusual and, for me, important sequel. All the insects in Kashmir appeared to have converged on Shalimar and decided that Claire was their prime target. She suffered bites from head to toe. The following day we returned to Delhi, staying the night with the Iranis before taking off for Hong Kong the following morning.

Before we left, Cushrow invited me to take a bundle of documents detailing the iniquities perpetrated during the Emergency which had not received much publicity in India because of Mrs Gandhi's press muzzling and only occasional comment abroad since most foreign correspondents had been expelled. I assured Cushrow that when I returned to London I would see to it that the documents were delivered where they could do some good.

By the time we reached Hong Kong, Claire's exposure to India's insect life had manifested itself. She had lost her sense of balance, was too weak to walk and was running a high temperature. We were staying at the opulent Peninsula Hotel, one of whose owners, the late Horace Kadoorie, saw to it that the hotel's doctor was in attendance and that everything humanly possible was done to speed her recovery. Nevertheless it was some days before she was able to move out of the hotel and, despite her protests, I was not inclined to leave her and wander about in the city while she was still in bed. So I stayed in the room and, for want of something better to do, began reading the papers that Cushrow had handed to me.

I have never considered myself a writer. I do not pretend to possess any literary talent and the writing I had done until that time had been largely confined to legal opinions in which clarity of expression rather than style was the criterion and my writing style for the *JC* was no different. Throughout the nineteen years of my editorship I had, perhaps, written half a dozen leaders and contributed an occasional article, generally after a visit abroad. I had also written some book reviews (mostly on American Jewish subjects on which I was considered an expert because of my AJC connexion) for *The Jewish Chronicle*. Nor did I consider myself a journalist – when I became Editor of the paper, I regarded my function as offering ideas, exercising judgment and controlling an organisation rather than writing myself. However, sitting in the Peninsula Hotel, reading the factual and documented accounts of what was currently happening in India, I came to the conclusion that I should not wait until my return to London which would be many weeks ahead. So I telephoned William Rees-Mogg, then Editor of *The Times*, with whom I was acquainted, told him what I had and asked him whether he would be interested in a report from me. He was very positive. Would I telex as long a piece as I wished? I asked him to attribute it to 'A Special Correspondent' rather than give it a personal by-line to ensure that Cushrow Irani could not be identified as the source since my association with him must have been known to the authorities.

I sat down and, between handing Claire glasses of water, read and wrote. My first report appeared on the front page of *The Times* a couple of days later headed 'Censors tighten their grip on the Indian press'. Rees-Mogg was happy about the piece and asked for more. Before leaving India, Cushrow Irani had told me that, although his telephone was bugged, in characteristically Indian fashion, the 'buggers' went off duty at midnight and did not return to their task until 6 am the following day. I could, therefore, safely call him during those six hours and he would keep me up to date with what was going on. And so I telephoned him from Hong Kong, Bali, Sydney and then London for updates from which I produced further reports which duly appeared in *The Times*. Indeed, so welcomed were my pieces that I was even encouraged to write one on Australian politics during my stay there. Being a feature article and not from India, it could bear my own byline, the first time my name had appeared as a contributor to that eminent newspaper.

Back in London, I received a telephone call from Rees-Mogg early in 1977. Mrs Gandhi had, suddenly and unexpectedly, called a general election. *The Times'* correspondent had been expelled from India during the Emergency, so would I go and cover the election campaign? I protested that I was not really a journalist to which William replied that I was not being asked to be a reporter but to write some feature articles, which my previous experience had shown that I could do, to give a general flavour of what was going on. I accepted the offer on that footing and, for the first time carrying a press card, left for Delhi early in February 1977.

With the respect, indeed reverence, with which *The Times* was held in many quarters in India and with the support of Cushrow Irani at *The Statesman*, I was able to get about and see almost everyone I wanted. The most interesting of these interviews was with Mrs Gandhi who had declined to see any foreign correspondents but then made an exception for me because, as she pointed out when I thanked her for the privilege, she had inherited a high regard for *The Times* from her father, Jawaharlal Nehru, India's first Prime Minister.

During the 'on the record' period of the interview, she was formal, unsmiling and distant as, with no discernible hesitation, she gave me some answers I knew not to be true. One of them was in response to an occasion when I was in Bombay a few days earlier and had talked to an important and, I believed, completely honest industrialist. He had, among other things, told me that he had been visited by an emissary of Mrs Gandhi asking for a donation to her election campaign fund. He knew that a refusal would be damaging and, reluctantly, coughed up a substantial gift of rupees. Without mentioning any names or places, I put this to the Prime Minister and she replied, with every appearance of candour, that her campaign was being funded exclusively 'with the *paise* of the poor'. I also put it to her that the election campaign was heavily loaded in her favour since she had an effective party machine working for her while her political opponents had only just been released from prison, with no money and no organisation. Her unblinking response to this was that, quite the contrary, they had the advantage of being seen as martyrs.

After the interview, we sat and chatted over a cup of coffee. She reminisced about her happy days in England, her admiration for the British political system and for *The Times*. One or other of us turned to the subject of Israel (she must have been told that I had been the Editor of *The Jewish Chronicle*) and she professed to be an admirer of what the Jewish state had achieved, assured me that she was friendly but that her public stance had to take into account the fact that India had 90 million Moslems. That gave me the opening to tell her that I had just been to Cochin and had visited its beautiful 400-year-old synagogue. Since there were, at that time, only a handful of Jews left in Cochin, I thought that a good way to preserve this unique building would be to re-erect it in the grounds of the Israel Museum in Jerusalem which had done this sort of thing before and, would, I was sure, be happy to do it for the Cochin

Synagogue. She looked at me sternly and responded with 'It's part of Indian history too.' I forbore to reply that India's record of maintenance of ancient structures was not encouraging.

I relished my temporary association with *The Times* which obviously pleased the paper too because, during my fourteen days in India, nine longish reports, all with my byline, were published, several on the front page. On my return to London, William Rees-Mogg invited me to his office and there I was introduced to his deputy, Louis Heren, a journalist whose work I had admired from the time he was that newspaper's correspondent in the United States. We got on instantly. He was also an East-Ender having been born in Wapping and we had attended the same school, St George's-in-the-East Central. He was a few years younger and we had therefore not known each other at school but the teaching staff was the same and we reminisced happily for a while. The point of the meeting came when William invited me to accept a retainer as 'Special Adviser to the Editor', my duties being to write occasional features and leaders on subjects of Jewish interest and to attend the weekly editorial meetings. I was flattered at this first truly journalistic appointment, thrilled to be associated with a newspaper I had read since school days and one of international eminence and I accepted without any hesitation.

The weekly editorial meetings, which took place on Tuesday mornings in the Editor's office, were attended by the most senior members of the editorial staff, a dozen or so at most. For these meetings, Rees-Mogg moved from behind his desk to a cane-seated rocking chair in front of it from which he, informally but authoritatively, conducted the proceedings. The hour-long discussion was centred on one subject, of which the participants had previously been notified, and it was generally of a very high standard, tending towards the academic. I doubt if such gatherings were held in any other newspaper for the atmosphere was more that of a meeting of dons at a university rather than of working journalists responsible for producing a daily newspaper on which the more junior staff members were working at that very moment. Nothing could have been further from the frenzy which surrounds scenes in newspaper offices depicted on the screen.

I enjoyed them – indeed I would have paid to have sat in on them instead of being paid to be there! And I also enjoyed writing regular features as well as the occasional leading article. Though it was never expressly mentioned, I became aware, early in the relationship, that one of the reasons William had recruited me was to balance the influence of some of the senior journalists who were strongly pro-Arab. There was only one other Jew at the Tuesday morning gatherings and he was always silent and clearly embarrassed when the subject of Israel came up. I doubt whether I influenced editorial policy but I occasionally felt it necessary to draw the attention of the Editor and his deputy to instances of what I considered bias and, just possibly, my representations may, in some instances, have had some positive result.

One of the pleasures of my all-too-brief stay at *The Times* was the deepening of my friendship with Bernard Levin, its consummate columnist. I had been an admirer of his writing from the time I first read him in the *Spectator* in which he wrote under the nom de plume of 'Taper' and when as Editor of the *JC* I decided to introduce that sort of informed and sparkling comment on current affairs in my paper, my first thought was to turn to Bernard. Initially somewhat dour in manner, he became quite animated when I put the idea to him and seemed keen to undertake the assignment. But then came the knotty problem of his fee. This was in 1958 when our top fee to contributors was £3 per hundred words. I offered him £5, in my ignorance thinking this was fair if not generous, but he wanted double that and we parted without agreement.

Bernard sometimes came to my home for dinner and on one

such occasion he regaled us with what he assured us was a true story about his aunt – I think she was named Sadie – who was addicted to the Irish Sweepstake. Sadie, he told us, would painstakingly peruse every winner on the printed lists which contained hundreds, if not thousands, of names. He once asked her how many tickets for the Sweepstake she had bought and was flummoxed when she said she didn't buy any. 'Well,' he responded, 'if you don't buy tickets, how can you expect to win a prize?' To which she responded, 'Bernard, if I'm *beschaert* (Yiddish for fated) to win, I'll win.'

All in all, I relished my *Times* experience but the pleasure was not long-lived for in 1980, rather than continue operating (at a substantial loss borne by its then owner, Roy (Lord) Thompson) under the dominance of an overbearing and un-scrupulous printers' trade union, the management of the paper decided on a lock-out and *The Times* ceased publication for several months. During that time, secret negotiations were taking place with Rupert Murdoch who acquired ownership of Times Newspapers and resumed publication from premises in Wapping equipped with the modern production methods which the union had vetoed at the Gray's Inn Road offices.

When publication resumed under the editorship of Harold Evans, I was told by the new Deputy Editor, Charlie Douglas-Home, that Evans had decided not to renew any of the recipients of retainers, of whom I was one, but that they would be glad to have occasional features from me. Some time later I met Harry Evans and he asked me why I had stopped my association with the paper. I told him what Charlie had told me and he emphatically denied that he had made any such decision, asserting that this was yet another instance of Douglas-Home's duplicity. I have no idea who was telling the truth. I did write a few pieces for *The Times* after this and one such article was prompted by a visit to the theatre.

One of our most pleasurable breaks after my retirement from

the *JC* was to spend a few days in Stratford-on-Avon, staying at the lovely Wellcombe Hotel, and to see two or three plays. In 1984, Claire and I with Selma Hirsch, an old friend from New York, saw a new production of the *Merchant of Venice* with Ian McDiarmid in the title role. I had last seen that play at Stratford many years before with a young Peter O'Toole brilliantly playing Shylock – he was an unknown then.

This latest visit was, as always in Stratford, an enjoyable and memorable occasion but in this instance, the excellence of the production of *The Merchant* was marred, as all three of us agreed, by the portrayal of Shylock as a rapacious Jewish villain, a depiction which inspired the audience to react with glee at his downfall. There was laughter and applause as, after the loss of Jessica, Shylock cries out, 'O my ducats! O my daughter!' There was more vocal glee at the prospect of Shylock's conversion to Christianity.

The reasons, all three of us felt, for the audience reaction and our discomfiture was the actor's portrayal of his role as well as the anti-Semitic writings and drawings from previous productions of the play which were reproduced in the programme. I am not sure what Jews looked like or how they talked in Venice in the sixteenth century, but it was certainly not the appearance presented by McDiarmid clothed in black caftan, sporting a ragged beard and dangling side-curls. To add verisimilitude, his gestures were those of a caricature Jew while his guttural accent fortified the image of a *shtetl* Jew of Eastern Europe in the twentieth century. We all thought that he greatly exaggerated Shylock's arrogance when on top and his cringing when vanquished. How I felt about this presentation and the response it provoked from the audience can best be judged from a few passages from the article I wrote for *The Times* article which appeared on 17 April 1984:

'Shylock in the *Merchant of Venice* is the medieval stereotype of the evil and bloodthirsty usurer. When Shakespeare wrote it in 1596, Jews had not been allowed to live in England for three centuries and scholars agree that, in all probability, the Bard had never met one. He copied the contemporary stage figure of the Jew as the equivalent of Satan, even dressed to look like the popular image of the devil adorned with a large hooked nose ...

'It has generally been assumed that those who read Shakespeare or see his plays are either knowledgeable and sophisticated adults or children in a classroom where problems are explained so that neither is likely to be infected by the anti-Jewish prejudices of the sixteenth century. As a further insurance against that danger, many of the great actors who have played Shylock from Keane and Irving to Olivier and O'Toole, have successfully given the character some dignity, nobility or tragic quality.

'Ian McDiarmid's portrayal of the role in the production of *The Merchant* which opened at Stratford last week disregards this recent convention. He plays the part as it might have been in Shakespeare's time – comic, villainous and avaricious, cruel and insolent in success, servile in defeat – everything, in fact, apart from the hooked nose and devil's costume ...

'... since my school days, prejudice against Jews has led to fearful consequences and there is now less disposition to ignore anti-Jewish stigmas however venerable their source. Even the most sympathetic presentation of Shylock does not prevent *The Merchant* from being anti-Jewish, but for a long time now, Jews have been reluctant to invite accusations of philistinism or paranoia by pointing this out. Mr McDiarmind's "Jewish" portrayal challenges that reticence ...

'I do not for a moment suggest that *The Merchant* should not be read or performed. Nor is it practical to insist that actors playing Shylock should follow recent precedent in softening his villainy. But even actors and directors most dedicated to their art might possibly agree that other factors exist of no less consequence than artistic freedom of expression. I wonder whether Mr McDiarmid did think about them. If he did, his Shylock suggests that the post-Holocaust inhibitions towards public anti-Jewish presentations are fading.'

Mr McDiarmid did not like it at all. I was told that he had telephoned *The Times* and threatened an action for defamation. The BBC called me and asked if I would discuss my article with the actor on radio. I agreed but he refused. He later wrote a letter taking me to task which *The Times* published and there the matter rested.

By way of a footnote to this episode, I was invited soon after to the Chichester Theatre where Sir Alec Guinness was to open in the same play. After the performance, I was taken back stage and introduced to the distinguished actor. He told me he had read my *Times* article but made no other comment and I have no idea whether his treatment of the part was in any way affected by what I had written. He played the fall of Shylock with pathos and restraint and there was not the slightest indication that the audience response was one of satisfaction.

*

When other journalistic assignments came my way I ceased to write for *The Times* and the first came from one of my former colleagues on that newspaper who had taken up a post on the *Los Angeles Times*. He asked me to write a weekly 'Letter from London' which I was happy to do but that did not last long. The *LA Times* London correspondent was distinctly vexed by the arrangement and must have made his displeasure known. At about the same time, I received a letter from the Editor of the

Asian Wall Street Journal asking for a fortnightly column which I enjoyed writing for some years.

A third invitation came from my friend Cushrow Irani who came to London to close *The Statesman*'s office in Fleet Street which had become unaffordable, as had retaining a full-time correspondent. Before returning to India, he asked me if I would help him out by writing a weekly column 'giving the flavour of London' for a couple of months until he appointed a part-time correspondent. I agreed and, validating the maxim that there is nothing as permanent as the temporary, I supplied a weekly column for just under twenty-one years. When I began spending half the year in Washington, I suggested to Cushrow that he should replace me with someone who was in London all year round. But his response was that I should continue writing my column from whichever city I was in.

There was so little feedback from my Indian readers that I began to doubt whether there were any. That is, until some-time in the autumn of 1999, when I was spending part of the year in Washington and I received an invitation from Justice Ruth Bader Ginsburg, who knew of my Indian connection, to join her at a reception at the Supreme Court for a visiting group of Indian judges and lawyers. She introduced me to all the visitors as 'William Frankel, a London barrister' and they were uniformly and formally polite. That changed when I ended the round of introductions and spoke to a gentleman who happened to be the Indian Solicitor General. Making con-versation, I asked him where in India he was from and he replied Calcutta. That prompted me to tell him that we had something in common since I was a contributor to *The States-man*. He embraced me enthusiastically, 'So you're *that* William Frankel; we all read you.' I was reintroduced to a number of the other visitors as *that* William Frankel and the formality gave place to warmth.

My weekly column for *The Statesman*, and occasional articles requested of me by various publications, were providing a regular pattern for my working life in addition to being an occasional commentator on various BBC news programmes. During the same period, I edited an annual *Survey of Jewish Affairs* which was published by Basil Blackwell for the Institute of Jewish Affairs. All in all, with my travels and my involvement with a variety of Jewish activities in a voluntary capacity, my post-editorial years were happily and agreeably varied for, in addition to my new profession as a journalist, I returned to my old one as a lawyer.

It was certainly too late to think of returning to the Bar and, in any event, I did not want anything like a full-time occupation but one day I ran into an old friend, Sebag Shaw, who by that time had been elevated to the High Court bench. Talking about what I was now going to do, he asked whether I would be interested in sitting on a tribunal which called for a qualified lawyer as its chairman. I said I would be and, with his recommendation, I was appointed President of a Mental Health Review Tribunal and Chairman of a Social Security Appeals Tribunal. On average, I spent a day of each week performing these functions.

The first was, by far, the more interesting. Under the Mental Health Act then in force, individuals detained in mental institutions could apply for their release to a tribunal once a year. Each tribunal consisted of the lawyer chairman, a psychiatrist and a lay man (or woman) possessing some experience in social work. The applicant could be represented but generally appeared in person. We heard him or her, the psychiatrist of the mental institution and any other witnesses the appellant wished to call. I sat many times in Broadmoor and heard fascinating cases which must remain secret. One of the abiding impressions this experience made on me was to enhance my recognition of the limitations of psychiatric treatment.

Both my chairmanships came to an end when I reached the

age of seventy-two when retirement was mandatory. By that time, I had learned something about both mental health and social security and, I believe, remained compos mentis and could have continued to serve advantageously. I made this point when I replied to Lord Hailsham's letter – he was Lord Chancellor – thanking me for my services. He was then in his eighties!

20

Some People I met

I first met Kitaj (he preferred to be referred to thus rather than by his first name Ron) sometime in the late 1970s. The eminent artist who had lived in London for many years and had been elected a Royal Academician, was born in Cleveland, Ohio, and we met through a common friend, Rabbi Daniel Silver, rabbi of the most important reform congregation in Cleveland. I had once visited its house of prayer, an imposing edifice bearing the simple – and self-important – name of 'The Temple'.

Daniel had succeeded his father, the famous Rabbi Abba Hillel Silver, a towering figure in American Jewish life. I had met Silver *père* many years earlier when I was taken to see The Temple on one of my lecturing visits to the city. In the corridor we encountered the great man himself and I was introduced to him. Trying to act the courteous Englishman, I expressed my sense of privilege at meeting him and my disappointment at not being present when he, the renowned preacher, was perform-ing – or words to that effect. He was pleased and responded with a gracious flourish, inviting me into his study to listen to a tape recording of his previous Sabbath sermon. It was not what I had in mind but I sat through it, I hope politely.

Although bearing a strong physical resemblance to his hand-some father, Daniel was a totally different personality. He was kind, contemplative, scholarly, courteous and diffident. We met in London because his wife (and now, alas, widow) had been born in Birmingham, Alabama, and was a youthful acquaintance of Claire's. It was, I imagine, through their association with the arts (Adele was then holding an important post at the Cleveland Art Museum) that the Silvers knew Kitaj and that, consequently, we got to know him.

When we first met him, Kitaj was living with Sandra Fisher in Chelsea. She was also a painter and an American, much younger than he and as gentle and sweet-natured as she was beautiful. One day, in 1984, Kitaj telephoned to say that he and Sandra wanted my advice and could they come over to see me that day? They both arrived at my home to tell me that they had decided to marry, primarily because Sandra wanted to have a child.

The advice they sought was about the place for the wedding for, by that time, Kitaj had become actively interested in Judaism and was reading widely on the subject. I had gathered from him, well before this occasion, that his father had died when he was very young and that he had become so attached to his stepfather that he had taken his surname. Although his parents were Jews, they had not been practising and he had grown up knowing very little about the Jewish religion, history or culture. In recent years, possibly under the influence of Daniel Silver, he had been studying these things and had collected a respectable Jewish library.

Both he and Sandra wanted a Jewish wedding ceremony in a synagogue, but they were anxious that it should be a beautiful synagogue and did I know whether such a sanctuary existed in London? I had no hesitation in extolling the beauty of the old Spanish and Portuguese Synagogue in the heart of the City of London and I showed them some pictures of its interior in books on my shelves. The synagogue had been completed in 1701 and was modelled on the ancient and magnificent building in Amsterdam from which many of Britain's Sephardi community had emigrated. Not quite as large as its Amsterdam model, the London synagogue in Bevis Marks, a street close to the boundary between the City of London and the East End, is of splendid proportions, lit by great candle chandeliers (a gift from the Netherlands community) and dominated by its finely constructed Ark at the eastern end which houses the Torah scrolls. At the other end of the synagogue is the *bima*, the platform on which stands the reader's desk and, behind it, the seats of the (all-male) choir. It would, I assured Kitaj, be a noble setting and I suggested he see it.

Claire took them both to Bevis Marks and they were enchanted. I then spoke to Rabbi Abraham Levy, the senior minister of the Spanish & Portuguese community, and he was happy to make an appointment to see the Kitajs and to discuss marriage arrangements in the old synagogue. A day or two later, Rabbi Levy telephoned me to say how much he had enjoyed meeting them and that it was a *Kiddush Hashem* (a sanctification of God's name) that the marriage of two such remarkable people would be held in his synagogue, adding that it would be a privilege to conduct the ceremony. A date was fixed and Claire and I were invited to attend what was to be a small, private occasion.

Shortly after these events I entered the Harley Street Clinic for a coronary by-pass which turned out to be eminently successful and, after the normal period of hospitalisation, I returned home to begin my convalescence. I was still in bed and finding talking difficult when Kitaj telephoned to say that a problem had arisen about his forthcoming wedding.

The story he told me was that, in the course of his discussion on procedure with the officials of the synagogue, he had been asked to furnish some proof that he and his intended wife were Jews. In the case of Sandra, that was simple for she had in her possession the *ketubah* (Hebrew marriage contract) of her parents. Kitaj had no such documentary evidence and was told that it would suffice if he obtained a letter from a responsible Jewish source in Cleveland, his birthplace, to the effect that his parents were both known to be Jews.

So Kitaj had written to his friend Daniel Silver who had promptly replied with a letter in the terms that had been suggested in London. This letter had gone to the ecclesiastical authorities of the Spanish and Portuguese Synagogue (its rabbinical court, not Rabbi Levy) who had decided that, since Rabbi Silver was not an orthodox but a reform rabbi, his letter could not be accepted and, in the absence of any other evidence of Kitaj's Jewish ancestry, the marriage could not be performed in their synagogue.

I immediately telephoned Rabbi Louis Jacobs, my friend and by now the Minister of the independent, traditional, New London Synagogue, who was as appalled as I was by this turn of events. He described the decision as absurd since, according to Jewish law, the evidence of a Jew was acceptable unless there was some good reason to doubt its veracity. The mere fact that the witness was a reform Jew was not, in his view, a reason for invalidating such evidence. I asked Louis whether he would be prepared to conduct the wedding in his own synagogue and his assent was unqualified.

Having imparted this information to a relieved Kitaj, I telephoned Rabbi Levy to ask whether the information I had received was accurate and, apologetically, he confirmed it. After I had expressed my disappointment and disapproval, Rabbi Levy told me that he was equally unhappy with this turn of events but, 'William, you know what the orthodox community would do to me if I went on with it.' I could not deny that acting contrary to the ecclesiastical ruling would open him to criticism but I added that I considered him one of the more enlightened spirits of the orthodox community and that I hoped he would reconsider. He did and the marriage took place at Bevis Marks.

Rabbi Levy, stately in his silk hat and robes conducted the traditional ceremony with charm and dignity. The bride was radiant, the groom handsome and the best man, David Hockney, performed his duties with aplomb. Among the small congregation were Kitaj's fellow artists of the London School including Frank Auerbach and Leon Kossoff. I had taken my camera and, since I was pretty well seat-bound after the operation, Claire took the pictures. It was only when I returned home that I discovered there was no film in the camera.

In 1991, the year of the *JC's* 150th anniversary, I was Chairman of its Board of Directors. One of the paper's celebratory projects was the production of a special supplement and, without my knowledge (there was no reason why I should have been told), the Supplements Editor had invited Kitaj, who he considered to be the most important Jewish artist in Britain, to provide the cover drawing. Kitaj declined on the ground that it was not his sort of thing but, assuming that I was behind the invitation, telephoned me to explain why he did not feel he could accept the assignment. I told him that I was unaware that he had been asked but thought it an excellent idea and suggested that even some sort of appropriate scribble from him would add to the prestige of the publication. His response was encouraging; he did not promise anything but, if some suitable idea occurred to him, he would do as requested.

A few days later a messenger arrived at the office with a small roll of canvas. On it Kitaj had made a crayon drawing of a bird's head (copied from an ancient Haggadah manuscript), its claws holding an open book with 1841 on one page and 1991 on the facing page. Below was his bold signature. It was perfect and reproduced brilliantly. I thanked Kitaj and asked him to let me know his fee. No, he replied, there would be no fee. So I asked him if he would sell the original to the paper. That he also declined but said that he would be willing to give it to me personally in exchange for a few of my Jewish books. The transaction duly took place.

In 1994 a long anticipated and carefully planned Kitaj retrospective opened at the Tate Gallery. For Kitaj and Sandra it was possibly the most important event of their artistic lives. He had been given, so I was told, carte blanche by the gallery to exhibit everything he wanted and it was an enormous show. The last picture before the exit was a large oil painting entitled 'The Wedding' and it portrayed Kitaj and Sandra as well as Rabbi Levy and other figures under the *chuppah* (marriage canopy) in the Bevis Marks Synagogue.

That retrospective turned into a disaster for the Kitajs. The critics were, almost universally, hostile – they did not like the work, they objected to the captions Kitaj had written for every painting explaining its meaning (a helpful practice the Tate often followed in exhibitions) and they made it clear that they did not like Kitaj. He was crushed and angry, telling us (and no doubt others) that the critics were anti-American and anti-Semitic. It was not long after this that Sandra suffered a cerebral haemorrhage and, within hours, she died. We attended the funeral service at the small Westminster Synagogue in Knightsbridge conducted by its Rabbi Friedlander and among the congregation was Hockney who had flown in from California. Kitaj and son Max were composed but afterwards, when we talked, he was bitter. Sandra had been killed by the malevolent critics; he had had enough of this country and would leave. He did stay on for a year or two after Sandra's death but, as good as his word, he then left London for California and we did not hear from him thereafter.

*

At general election times it had long been the practice at the *JC* to circulate to the leaders of the three main political parties a number of questions of specifically Jewish interest and to publish their replies. When the October 1974 general election came around, I thought I would make a change, since written answers tended to be obfuscating rather than clarifying, and the idea occurred to me that a livelier response would emerge if the party leaders were personally interviewed. I decided to do the interviewing myself and a few weeks before the date of the election I went to Transport House in Smith Square, together with a reporter and recording machine, for an interview with the then Prime Minister, Harold Wilson.

When we arrived, Transport House looked a mess with lots of scruffy-looking people either hanging about or moving apparently aimlessly conveying a general impression of cheerful disorder. Nobody we asked knew about the interview and it took a considerable time before someone was found who knew why we were there. Eventually we were shown into a shabby room furnished with a few odd chairs and a dilapidated table, a couple of cupboards and, everywhere, piles of papers and posters. Harold Wilson joined us a few moments later, in his shirtsleeves, puffing his pipe, very cordial and relaxed. He first apologised to me for having 'stolen' our columnist, Gerald Kaufman, by taking him into the government.

It was he, not I, who asked the first question and that, to my surprise, was whether there were many Jews in Bath. I told him that my son was living in Bath but that there were a few other Jews and I asked him why he had put the question. Wilson explained that Christopher Mayhew was standing as a Liberal in Bath and he made it clear that this was a man he despised. From further conversation I understood the reason to be that when Mayhew was in the Labour Party and attended meetings of the parliamentary group, he would invariably ask questions of Wilson revealing his (Mayhew's) hostility to Israel. What, said Wilson, irritated him no less than the substance of the questions was the unpleasant manner in which Mayhew put them, never referring to him (Wilson) either as Mr Wilson, Wilson or Prime Minister but always as 'the leadership'.

In the interview that followed, Wilson replied very frankly to the questions and with every evidence of his sympathy and friendship for Israel. Since he was at that time still Prime Minister, I readily agreed to his request to submit a proof of the interview to the Secretary of the Cabinet. When the copy was returned to me, a number of replies to my questions made by Wilson which I had considered particularly interesting and important had been deleted. An example was my question, 'You have mentioned renewed arms supplies ... do you make a distinction between arms to the so-called "confrontation states" and those more distant from the war area, such as Libya and Saudi Arabia?' to which the reply was, 'We are endeavouring to meet the Israeli requests for Centurion tanks which acquitted themselves so successfully in the Yom Kippur War. In general, our supplies to the Arab states are related to the degree of confidence we can have that they will not be used against Israel in any future fighting.'

I met Harold Wilson on a number of occasions, all formal or business, which provided little opportunity for anything but the most impersonal of conversational exchanges. The first opportunity I had to spend any time with him was early in 1973 when he was Leader of the Opposition and I invited him to lunch at the Athenaeum. He was an easy conversationalist and, almost from the beginning of our meeting he saw to it that some kind of intimacy was established between us. He was patently more interested in talking than in listening – but that may have been because he found nothing interesting in what I had to say. Not that I said very much; he provided few conversational openings and, on the rare occasions when I did say something, he would respond with a perfunctory smile and acknowledgement and then return to his own line of conversation most of which was about his recent visit to Israel.

Describing it as one of the most exciting weeks of his life, he was at pains to point out that he had been received in Israel as though he was still Prime Minister and that Golda Meir, then Prime Minister, had given instructions to that effect. It was a surprise to me that a former Prime Minister should be so insistent on these points of prestige. And this anxiety to be treated as a Prime Minister was repeated in numerous other references to his reception in Israel as well in a surprising amount of 'name dropping' of the eminences who had come to see him in Downing Street. Everyone would, I imagine, assume that a former Prime Minister knew many important people and it surprised me that he should have felt so insecure.

With a remarkable display of memory, he took me through all his engagements in Israel mentioning the names of those he had met. He was clearly greatly moved by a party which had been given for him on Christmas Day at which he had met some two dozen Russian Jews whose migration to Israel had been assisted by what he described as his 'Pimpernel' activities. Drinking his second whisky, Wilson asserted that he was sure the Israelis wanted peace and that he had communicated this view to the Egyptian Ambassador in London whom he had told that if the Egyptians sat down with the Israelis, they would be amazed how much they would get. He had found Moshe Dayan surprisingly 'dovish' – he had actually implied that, as part of a peace settlement, even the Golan was negotiable. Wilson thought that this was unimaginable in practice. He went on to tell me that, before the Six Day War, his idea of a maritime consortium to break the Sharm blockade had been sabotaged by Lyndon Johnson 'who had got cold feet'. He was sure that King Hussein's Jordan would be the first Arab state to make a deal. Hussein had come frequently to see him at No.10, unexpectedly and without aides, and they had had long and intimate conversations.

Wilson spoke with some venom about Roy Jenkins who was

then receiving a very good press and suggested that the *JC* try to get Jenkins to commit himself on Middle East issues which he had so far been at pains to avoid. He was clearly envious of Jenkins' treatment in the press, so superior to that he was getting, and was vitriolic about the *New Statesman* and its then Editor, Anthony Howard, whom he regarded as conducting a vendetta against him.

One of the subjects which cropped up was currency decimalisation which had taken place during his Premiership and, as the change had been followed by steep inflation and price increases, I wondered whether he had any second thoughts. He replied that Jim Callaghan, then Chancellor of the Exchequer, had made such an emotional appeal for the retention of the historically sanctified pound sterling that the cabinet went along with him. Wilson concluded that had the cabinet followed his advice to abandon the pound and substitute the ten shilling note as the currency unit, the value of a new penny would have been nearly the same as that of the old, whereas the new penny at 2.4 times the old made it easy to inflate prices by that percentage.

The abiding impression after two hours of virtually non-stop talking by Harold Wilson (perhaps he was unusually loquacious on this occasion because his aperitif was followed by a third whisky at the meal) was that he was not sure that he was a great man and that he felt he had to try to impress.

Two days after my first meeting with Harold Wilson, before the 1974 General Election, I had an interview with Ted Heath, then leader of the Opposition. The meeting took place at the Conservative Party headquarters which were, like those of the Labour Party, also on Smith Square. The contrast between the character of the two offices could not have been more emphatic: the Conservative premises were clean and freshly painted, the furniture was tasteful and the workers, young and debutante-looking girls and tall and well dressed males, all appeared to know what they were doing.

I was escorted to an elegant office on the first floor with good antique reproduction furniture, an opulent fitted carpet and a crystal chandelier. William Whitelaw was in the room – it might have been his office which Heath used on occasions like this. I was reasonably sure that Whitelaw had no idea who I was, but he must have assumed that he should have known me and engaged me in companionable, albeit pedestrian, conversation until Heath entered. Whitelaw then sidled out – there was no communication between them and I was later informed that they were not on good terms since Whitelaw had strongly advocated the previous election which had resulted in Heath's defeat.

Mr Heath was well dressed in a check tweed suit and looked extremely healthy. It was 11 a.m. and his first words to me were 'Is it too early for champagne?' and I replied that it was never too early for me. (At Transport House I had been offered a cup of coffee by Lady Falkender which arrived in a cracked cup.) An obsequious aide produced elegant glasses and a cold bottle of bubbly from a discreetly hidden refrigerator and, during the interview which followed, we both enjoyed sipping the excellent fizz.

During the interview, Heath took time to consider his replies to my questions which he delivered at dictation speed and, when I sent him the proofs for any corrections he wished to make, they were returned without even a comma altered.

*

To my great surprise I received an invitation from the Egyptian Embassy in November 1975 to a press conference with President Sadat who was on his way home after a visit to the United States where President Ford had received him warmly. It was the first time since the creation of Israel that the *JC* had been recognised by any Egyptian government institution and so I decided to attend personally together with a reporter. Most of the questions were on the subject of Middle East peace and Sadat's responses put all the responsibility for its absence on the policies of Israel. He was asked whether he would be ready to meet Prime Minister Rabin to which he replied 'not while he occupies my land'. Towards the end of the questioning I rose, said that I was the Editor of the *JC*, that I greatly appreciated the invitation which was the first of its kind and asked whether I should attach any significance to it. Sadat's reply was rambling and non-committal but, before sitting down, he flashed me a broad smile.

So I was not totally taken by surprise when, in 1977, he made his famous offer to come to Jerusalem and talk peace. I happened to be in New York at the time and was lunching with Yitzhak and Leah Rabin and Vivian Herzog who then represented Israel at the UN. The Sadat offer was naturally the major subject of conversation. Rabin was unimpressed; he did not trust Sadat, thought that the offer was merely a public relations gesture and that it should be declined by Israel. I took the opposite view saying that it would be a test of Sadat's sincerity to invite him to Israel. If he came, it could only do good but that if he wriggled out of it, that would prove his unreliability.

After the Sadat visit had actually taken place, I was again in New York and spent some time with my old friend Rabbi Arthur Hertzberg who, at one of our meetings, told me that he had to leave since he had an appointment with Rabin and asked me if I would like to join him. I did and, during our conversation, I asked Rabin whether he had changed his opinion about the Sadat visit. He emphatically denied that he had expressed the critical view I had remembered.

*

Willy Brandt, the former Chancellor of West Germany, was the principal guest at a dinner given by the British Friends of the Diaspora Museum in January 1982. He had been asked to speak on a topic related to his own view on contemporary Jewish issues and gave a most thoughtful address which was also a tribute to the quality of the audience. Indeed his presence was a great encouragement to the Friends of the Diaspora Museum. However, in the course of his speech he made the point that 'substantial parts of the Arab world' were ready to accept Israel and concluded that Israel was making a rapprochement impossible. His remarks caused some embarrassment to the sponsors of the dinner and it was felt would make our task of encouraging support for the Museum more difficult.

As I was the Friends' Chairman at the time, I raised the matter with him in my letter of thanks, asking for evidence to support his claim. In the ensuing dialogue Willy Brandt emphasised that he was a 'true friend of Israel' and was it not 'the attitude of a true friend to speak openly if he thinks there is danger for a wrong course of orientation'? To support his claim that 'substantial parts of the Arab world' were ready to accept Israel, he cited the recent 'Saudi-Arabian peace plan' and private 'serious' hints. My own view was that, though welcome in substance, the Saudi plan amounted to very little and indeed had been rejected by the whole Arab world. I pointed out to him that the only actual peace process on the world's agenda at that time was Camp David. Although agreeing with him that some of the actions of the then government of Israel, for example the bombing of Osirak and Beirut, and the building of settlements on the West Bank, had not been helpful, I pointed out that these were the consequences and not the causes of the state of war which all Arab countries insisted on maintaining against Israel. He certainly saw my point but regarded the debate as a chicken and egg situation and advocated starting a peace process without preconditions.

*

My favourite holiday is cruising. I love the life on a comfortable cruise ship, not the least of its attractions being the presence of all the holiday comforts like sightseeing, entertainments, eating and drinking well — all there without the necessity of rushing around. And of all the cruises I have enjoyed, the best were the music cruises. I had heard of the unique and unadvertised music cruise then run by the French Paquet Line but was unable to enjoy one until after my retirement from the *JC*.

On one particularly memorable cruise in the 1980s, among the artists on board the *Mermoz* were Mstislav Rostropovich and Isaac Stern. One day the ship's newspaper contained an announcement from Mrs Stern that the Jewish New Year would fall in two days' time and would all those passengers wishing to attend a service come to the ship's cinema. At that meeting I was delegated to conduct the service. The day before I ran into 'Slava' on deck and he greeted me, as he did most people, with unaffected warmth. That encouraged me to ask him if he would introduce the service with some music. His first reaction was that he did not have any suitable music on board but that if something occurred to him he would come.

Fifteen minutes before the service began, Slava arrived trundling his cello. He first played a short piece by Bloch then informed his audience that when he was young and in Moscow a Jewish friend, later killed during the war, had written a piece for him. He performed this with such combined pathos and passion that there was scarcely a dry eye among the congregation. Finally, he declared, 'We Russians and Jews are all the same people and we all love Tchaikovsky,' and went on to the music. The service that followed was something of an anticlimax but the occasion will, I am sure, always remain in the memory of those of us who were privileged to be there.

21

Israel's Early Prime Ministers

When I was about ten, a friend took me to one of the weekly sessions of a new youth movement called Habonim (The Builders). There we were taught Hebrew songs and dances by enthusiastic leaders who inspired us with romantic stories of the 'Halutzim', the young pioneers in their kibbutzim in the Land of Israel, preparing the way for the return of the Jewish people to their ancient homeland. I became a Zionist and, in the process of my Zionist education, heard for the first time the name of prominent figures in the movement.

The outstanding public face of Zionism was that of Chaim Weizmann who became Israel's first President. But the dominant figure was Ben-Gurion, the long serving leader of Mapai, the Labour Party, the most powerful constituent of the Zionist movement. It was he who became the driving force behind Israel's Declaration of Independence in 1948 and he can truthfully be described as the founding father of the Jewish state.

Many years after my first meeting with BG in Cambridge in 1941 and after I had become Editor of *The Jewish Chronicle*, I renewed my acquaintance with him. BG was then Israel's Prime Minister and he held that office until 1963. On each of my visits during this period, our Jerusalem correspondent made an appointment for me to see the great man who briefed me on current issues. Ben-Gurion was always extremely forthcoming and laudatory about the *JC* which he said he saw regularly.

Though always friendly, he never touched on any personal

subjects. The only exception occurred during a visit I made to Israel in the summer of 1961 with my son John who had just celebrated his barmitzvah. I spent as much time as I could showing John the country and he stayed with friends in Tel Aviv while I went about my business. At one point I had telephoned BG's then secretary, Yitzhak Navon (who later become President), asking if I could come and see the PM during my brief stay in Jerusalem. Yitzhak said that BG was particularly busy at that time and could only give me half an hour. I told him that would be fine since it was only a courtesy call and an appointment was made for 12 noon. I arranged with my friends for John to be brought to the Prime Minister's office at 12.30, wait outside until I emerged, and we would then lunch together.

My meeting with BG began punctually at noon and was still going strong at 1 pm with the PM in full flow. At the first available opportunity, I interrupted to say that I would not detain him any longer since there was a hungry young man awaiting me outside. He called out to Yitzhak to bring John in.

After the introductions, he observed to my son as, so I was told, he invariably did to young Jewish visitors from abroad, that he hoped he intended to settle in Israel. John replied that, although he was enjoying his visit, he could not come to live in Israel. 'Why?' asked BG reproachfully, to which came the answer that it was because there was no cricket in Israel. Ben-Gurion was uncomprehending, having no clue what the game was. I did my best to explain and the Prime Minister recovered rapidly suggesting to my son that this made it all the more important that he should come to Israel and introduce cricket to the nation.

On the occasions I visited Ben-Gurion at home, his eccentric wife Paula invariably made an appearance, usually to bring in cups of coffee. On a visit to Sdeh Boker, where BG had gone to live after his retirement, she remained in the room listening to the conversation and, at one point, broke into it to ask me if I was Jewish. BG spluttered that I was the Editor of *The Jewish Chronicle*. She merely shrugged her shoulders. Ezer Weizman, nephew of Chaim Weizmann, who later himself became President, once told me that at one point when he headed the Air Force, he had to call on Ben-Gurion at his home. When he did Paula answered the door and Ezer explained his business. She turned and called out, 'Ben-Gurion, there's Weizman to see you – not the one who's dead.'

BG was often referred to by Yiddish-speaking Israelis as *a persoenlichkeit obber nisht a mensch* – a personality but not a decent human being. He could be tough and even spiteful as in his treatment of Chaim Weizmann who once told President Truman that he was not allowed by BG to put his nose into anything other than his handkerchief. Not only was he adamant in refusing Weizmann any semblance of authority as President of Israel but was petty enough to leave no room for his signature on the Declaration of Independence because Weizmann was not in Israel that day.

But BG was not implacably obstinate and on occasion recognised the need for compromise. In one of our conversations he defended his agreement to perpetuate the religious status quo which had preserved the orthodox monopoly. He did so reluctantly, he said, but at the time of the creation of the state, he was fighting the British and the Arabs as well as the Stern Gang and the Irgun and he could not possibly add to these pressures by becoming involved in a domestic religious war.

He regretted, too, the electoral system adopted by Israel, for proportional representation had resulted in a multiplicity of parties and the inevitability of more or less unstable coalitions. He would much have preferred an adaptation of the British constituency system and the 'first past the post' elections. But the political party machines had insisted on the continuation of the long standing election procedure of Zionist congresses and that was another war he was not in a position to wage at that time.

It was one of BG's strengths that, in the early years of statehood, he had gathered around him a small group of able young men who became his inner political circle. They included Shimon Peres, Abba Eban, Moshe Dayan and Yigal Allon Had he been able to retain their loyalty, the history of Israel might have been very different from what it has been. But after his 1965 breach with Mapai (which later became the Labour party), only Peres and Dayan remained loyal to BG in a new party called Rafi. The defections were a source of immense disappointment to him and, in conversation, he did not hide his distaste for those he regarded as deserters lacking in principle. Self-criticism was never one of his characteristics and on the occasions we met and talked about the present and the past, there was never an indication that he bore any measure of responsibility for the defections. It has, for many years now, been an almost instinctive reaction on my part to every development in Israel's history, to speculate on what BG would have done. In general, he comes out well from these futile imaginings.

*

During my editorship I had occasion to meet the three immediate successors to Ben Gurion: Moshe Sharett, Levi Eshkol and Golda Meir and there was a brief encounter with Menachem Begin. Sharett, formerly Shertok, was Israel's first Foreign Minister and second Prime Minister. A man of formidable intellectual attainment, his linguistic apparatus was quite spectacular and there were few of the major modern languages that he could not speak fluently. He was a very orderly man, neat and methodical; the sort of administrator who one imagined would be likely to know the precise number of paper clips on his desk. He set the tone for the Israeli Foreign Ministry which, for decades after his departure, retained something of the leisureliness and gentlemanly qualities of the old school of Western diplomacy.

Being the senior member of the Cabinet at the time, it was natural that he should succeed to the premiership when, in December 1953, Ben-Gurion resigned out of sheer physical exhaustion. Sharett remained in that office for only two years returning to the Foreign Ministry when BG felt fit enough to take over again. That too did not last long.

The circumstances which led to his dismissal by BG in 1956 were to have a resonance almost fifty years later in the controversy over Prime Minister Ariel Sharon's response to the Palestinian intifada. Sharett had always been a man of moderation, attuned to the gentle art of diplomacy and totally hostile to the Israeli policy of massive reprisals against the incursions of Egyptian *fedayeen* which was alienating Western public opinion. But BG, Moshe Dayan and many other members of the Labour Party as well as the whole of Begin's Herut Party, believed that Sharett's moderation had achieved nothing and had only intensified the belligerence of General Nasser, then the Egyptian leader. Sharett was obviously going to be an obstacle in the way of implementing the measures which BG was preparing to break the Egyptian blockade of Akaba. When the French sounded out Israel on the prospect of collaboration in an attack on Egypt, Sharett had to be got rid of and in June 1956 the tougher Golda Meir, then Minister of Labour, replaced him.

Sharett was shunted off to the political sidelines and appointed Chairman of the Jewish Agency and the World Zionist Organisation and it was in that capacity that I got to know him. He was, by then, a dispirited individual, admitting to me that he had never quite mastered the large and entrenched bureaucracy of which he was now the nominal head. Nor could he understand the attitudes and structures of the Diaspora Jewish communities which had changed from those of the pre-war Jewish world with which Sharett had been closely involved. At a meeting with him in Jerusalem in the early 1960s, he had talked to me about the new wave of Jewish writers in England and showed himself to be familiar with much of their work. He got in touch with me later to say that he would be visiting London early in 1963 and was anxious to meet some of them. I promised to arrange this for him and in February invited a dozen or so young literati including Shaffer, Wesker and Freddie Raphael to dine with him at the Athenaeum. As I have previously mentioned, most of them were pretty well alienated from the organised Anglo-Jewish community and I hoped that some would be sufficiently impressed by this intellectual leader of Zionism to change their attitudes. In the event, the occasion was an abject failure. The writers were underwhelmed with Sharett while he could not understand their concept of Jewish-ness.

Sharett was only too well aware of the failure for, a few days later, he wrote me a long letter which began, 'I want to thank you most cordially for having convened that highly gifted and, to me, most intriguing bunch of people to break bread and exchange thoughts with me. Permit me now to say a few frank words on the subject.' And then he continued:

'On the following morning I had quite a hangover which has not been completely dispelled to this day. The plain truth of the matter is that I did not hit it off with those fellows. Maybe Shaffer, who kept silent but occasionally nodded assent to me, was the exception – yet even this is probably wishful thinking on my part ... As for the rest, it was abundantly evident that they were disappointed, if not to say disgruntled, and in any case found most of the things I had to say of little consequence.

'For myself, I thought I was trying to discuss the meaning of contemporary Jewish life in the free world – a vast and intricate subject of which to me Israel's future is the pivot in one way or another. The query that remained hanging in the air at the end of the proceedings was, according to my impression, whether those around the table seriously cared about the problem – not necessarily as far as Israel, but as far as their own identity was concerned ... The attitude of cold disdain displayed around the table towards "fund-raising for Israel" made little sense to me and signified a displaced fastidiousness concerning matters of finance which could not be the result of serious thinking.'

Poor Sharett had talked to these intellectuals in the same style as he, no doubt, addressed meetings of Diaspora Jews where fund-raising was virtually the only area of common interest.

If Sharett as Prime Minister was a short break within the Ben-Gurion era, the third Prime Minister, Levi Eshkol, marked its end. He took over the Premiership in 1963 when Ben-Gurion suddenly resigned in consequence of the Lavon affair, a political scandal which for a while preoccupied Israel's politicians. (Pinchas Lavon, a clever but arrogant Mapai politician, had a flair for making enemies. In July 1954, when Britain was negotiating a Suez Canal deal with Egypt, Israel launched a campaign with the object of frustrating an agreement. That operation, authorised unilaterally by Lavon, failed and the subsequent inquest became known as the Lavon affair).

BG had hand-picked Eshkol as his successor believing he could be fairly easily handled but the new Prime Minister soon became his own man. He was neither a charismatic figure nor a cultivated diplomat but an experienced political operator, practical and down to earth, a homely man and a natural conciliator always ready to compromise. There was a story around at that time that, on being asked whether he would like tea or coffee, Eshkol replied 'half and half'.

In May 1967 Nasser ordered the evacuation of the UN Peace Keeping Force from Egyptian territory, deployed his troops in the Sinai and blockaded the Straits of Tiran. Eshkol's response was wavering and unsure and his popularity plummeted. But with the outbreak of the Six Day War, the waiting and tension over, Eshkol recovered his stature as a national leader. Afterwards, when conditions might have been created for a settlement with the Arabs, the Eshkol coalition government, unable to reconcile the different views of its members, was paralysed. When the Prime Minister visited President Lyndon Johnson the following year, he could only tell his host that he led a national coalition 'which has decided not to decide'.

But he did keep the coalition together through his engaging personality. My friends close to the cabinet liked to tell me how he addressed his ministers as *kinderlach*, the Yiddish for 'my children' and always had an apt Yiddish joke or anecdote to relieve tension. On one of my visits to Israel at that time I asked him what his government intended to do about the occupied territories and he answered in Yiddish. '*Mir zenen areingekrochen in a blotta*' – 'we have crawled into the mire'. On my way home from Israel, I stopped off in Paris to see Nahum Goldman, the leader of the World Jewish Congress, who was recovering from a bout of ill health. I repeated Eshkol's comment on the occupied territories and Goldman added his story about *blotta*, a feature of every *shtetl*. 'A beggar in a *shtetl*, walking in his galoshes through the mud, spied the local *gvir* [rich man] walking nearby but not wearing galoshes. So the beggar asked him why he was not wearing them to which the *gvir* replied, "'If I don't wear galoshes I won't walk in the *blotta*."' It was a characteristically Goldman comment on the situation.

On another occasion I asked Eshkol why Israel was spending many millions in subsidising a domestic textile industry when its products could be purchased for much less in the world market, he recalled that the Jews had been the successful entrepreneurs of the textile industry in Lodz and that this kind of work was a *yiddisher geschaeft* – a Jewish trade which had to be encouraged.

Eshkol died in harness in 1969 and the party chose Golda

Meir as his successor. She had relinquished the Foreign Ministry several years earlier because of ill health but the recuperative effects of power were never demonstrated to greater effect, for taking office as Prime Minister appeared to have gained her a new lease of good health. She always gave me the impression of being the archetypal Jewish mother, invariably asking after my own health and enquiring about my family. But this politeness soon gave way to substance and after the brief formalities our conversation almost immediately turned to Israel's current concerns.

I often noted in our conversations how frequently she would introduce her views with the words 'I simply cannot understand.' That was absolutely true. Subtle arguments seemed to be beyond her and she often dismissed them as 'just like a professor'. Her attitudes were so simple, so straightforward and self-evident, that she could not understand how anybody of goodwill could fail to accept them. If they did fail, they could not be people of goodwill.

I never received any indication that she had any constructive ideas on either the future of the occupied territories or on the outlines of a peace treaty with the Arabs (at that time they were not described as Palestinians). At one of our meetings, in June 1969, I asked her directly whether she had a policy for the occupied territories other than the continuation of the present military occupation. She said that she had not. The only alternative to the present situation was annexation to which she was opposed. She saw no choices other than those of occupation and annexation.

She was quite convinced that opposition to Israel could only be the result of anti-Semitism. On one occasion when she was in London for a weekend, Arthur Lurie who was then Israeli Ambassador asked me if I would lunch with them and then spend the afternoon talking with Golda while the Luries siestad. After lunch Golda and I repaired to the drawing room, she kicking off her shoes and stretching out on a sofa. We talked and, at one point, I dwelt on Israel's inefficient and amateurish public relations. I mentioned that with the outbreak of war in 1939, one of the first actions of the British government was to set up a Ministry of Information. Israel had been constantly at war since its foundation, I argued, but still had no organised set-up to counteract the hostile publicity emanating from its enemies. We talked round the subject for a while until she abruptly ended the conversation on the subject by informing me that setting up a government department for this purpose would be a waste of time and money because 'whatever we do, the goyim will hate us'.

I had only one brief personal encounter with Menachem Begin, the first Israeli Prime Minister not to come from the ranks of the Labour Party. He had been the leader of the Irgun Zvai Leumi, a militant group which had undertaken an underground struggle against the British rulers of what was then Palestine and which had, no doubt, contributed to the British departure. Not long before he had achieved the premiership after the Israeli Labour Party's election failure in 1977, he visited London with, I was told, the intention of enhancing his image in Israel by meeting notable figures in the British government and the Jewish community. I had recently introduced a weekly political column in the *JC* and the first columnist was Gerald Kaufman, a successful journalist who later was elected a Labour Member of Parliament. His column immediately preceding Begin's arrival was a recital of the visitor's history and advising against anyone shaking his blood-stained hands. Begin's visit was not a success and he left the country somewhat ignominiously. Some months later, on a visit to Israel, I met him. His manner was cool to the point of hostility and he accused me of wrecking his British visit through the Kaufman column. I told him that I had not editorialised on the subject and that an independent journalist who was given complete freedom to express his opinions, provided that they were neither defamatory nor obscene, wrote the column to which he had taken offence. Begin left me in no doubt that he did not accept this as justification and our meeting concluded on a note of frigid politeness.

22

London and Washington

My life style was completely transformed after I returned to London from the round-the-world adventure which followed my retirement as Editor of the *JC*. For the previous half century I had performed regular and well-defined duties, whether as an employee in the offices of the organisations in which I had served or as my own man in my chambers in the Temple or in the editorial chair. Now I was on the loose, as it were, but not yet sufficiently relaxed to contemplate either a hedonistic life of leisure or merely casual involvement with the various voluntary bodies with which I was associated. So, to keep all options open, I began my new life by acquiring a security blanket in the form of a rented room in the Pump Court chambers of a barrister of my acquaintance. I was not a member of chambers since I had no intention of returning to practice – I was simply the tenant of a room. That did not last long for the room was later needed for a working barrister, a much more desirable situation for the clerk of the chambers whose income was in no way enhanced by a tenant who merely paid rent.

It was not long before I was kept busy with professional occupations like writing, broadcasting, sitting on my tribunals and membership of the Board of Directors of the *JC*. I had one other, albeit brief, part-time appointment. After the lamented death of Terence Prittie, I acted as Director of 'Britain and Israel' until a worthy successor to Terence could be found. We found it impossible to recruit anyone of his stature and, in any event, by that time other groups had come into being to present the Israeli case and 'Britain and Israel' faded out of existence.

Chief of my voluntary activities was my chairmanship of the Institute of Jewish Affairs (IJA), an academically respected research organisation and think tank on Jewish affairs. It had been founded, and was financed by, the World Jewish Congress (WJC). The relationship between the London committee of the IJA and the WJC based in New York was extremely cordial, primarily because the London group, then housed in an elegant house on New Cavendish Street, was encouraged to proceed with its work without interference.

But then there came a time when this happy association foundered as a result of the IJA being requested to undertake a task that we in London saw as a piece of political propaganda. We declined and that led to a personal visit by Edgar Bronfman, President of the WJC. By that time, Jacob Rothschild had succeeded to the title of Lord Rothschild and had accepted the Presidency of the IJA. We met Bronfman at Jacob's office and, after a somewhat acrimonious discussion had concluded with our refusal to act as the WJC requested, Mr Bronfman informed us that the WJC would discontinue its financial support.

We were not deterred and immediately undertook some fund-raising activity in which we were initially greatly helped by the American Jewish Committee which contributed generously to our research programme during the transition period. As a final chastisement for our disobedience, the WJC claimed title to the name Institute of Jewish Affairs and we changed ours to the Institute for Jewish Policy Research (JPR) which continued and enhanced its unique and valuable contribution to contemporary Jewish life.

At about this time, I was commissioned by the Thames & Hudson publishing house to write a book about Israel on the lines of Anthony Sampson's celebrated *Anatomy of Britain*. The book that emerged, *Israel Observed – an anatomy of the state*, was published in 1980. I found the experience rewarding. Being committed to a deadline for the completion of my manuscript, I was driven into the discipline, which I had not previously known I could maintain, of writing a certain number of useable words each day and, during this period, I rose early and did not sit down to breakfast until I had completed my quota. It also compelled me to make another longish stay in Israel where I worked from the Mishkenot Sha'ananim, the splendid guest-house administered by the Jerusalem Foundation. Finally, through this assignment I got to know Anthony Sampson who patiently explained to me his writing method for his famous series of 'Anatomy of Britain' books without which I doubt if I could have produced what my publishers wanted.

During the first few years of my retirement from the *JC* editorship, I remained in close touch with the friends I had made there, in particular with Tony Mandelson who would frequently drop in to see me in my room in the Temple, keeping me in touch with my friends in the office and their current concerns. Towards the end of the 1980s, David Kessler decided it was time to relinquish the chairmanship; he had then become an octogenarian, and appointed (formally it was the Board which did so) Ellis Birk as his successor.

It was during Ellis' tenure, that my successor Geoffrey Paul decided to retire and a new Editor had to be found. It was not an easy task for there was no obvious candidate on the staff and advertisements did not produce a wealth of talent and experience. Of those who responded, Ellis was most impressed with Ned Temko, a young and engaging American journalist then working in London for the *Christian Science Monitor*. I liked Ned and was impressed by his professional qualifications but was doubtful if he was right for a position which called for an intimate knowledge of the Anglo-Jewish community. But Ellis was keen and the Board approved the appointment. Whether it was for that reason or not, David Kessler cooled towards Ellis' chairmanship and, when his three-year-term had expired, he asked me to take over. I spoke to Ellis about it and he took the view that his continuation in that office would not be tenable in the face of David's opposition.

So I became Chairman in 1991 and my first public appearance in that capacity was in December of that year when the JC celebrated its 150th anniversary with a reception at the London Guildhall attended by many national and communal leaders. Lord McGregor, then Chairman of the Press Complaints Commission, enthusiastically lauding the contribution of the paper to national life, gave the toast to the JC and I responded.

This was the only occasion in the long history of the paper for one man to have held (not concurrently but consecutively!) both the editorship and the chairmanship, and I confess that I enjoyed the first better than the second. But the chairmanship of the company was, in its different way, no less stressful and called for some two or three full days each week in the office. But there were some moments of pleasure and satisfaction. One of them occurred when, sitting at my desk, I received a visit from a charming lady, Dr Risa Domb, the Lecturer in Modern Hebrew at Cambridge University. Earnestly and with animation, she outlined to me her idea to create a Centre for Modern Hebrew Studies at the University for which she had already received approval from the authorities – all that was needed was the funding. Her enthusiasm was contagious and I promised to help in any way I could.

The scheme appealed to me for several reasons. I thought it highly desirable that Israeli culture should have a place in one of the world's great centres of learning. I was also mindful of the fact that, since my days in Cambridge, only a minority of Jewish undergraduates were interested in the synagogue and I felt that a Centre for Modern Hebrew Studies could offer the others an alternative Jewish interest. Finally, I was thankfully aware of the enormous benefits that Cambridge had brought me and felt good at the prospect of making some contribution in return.

We formed a Board, including some of Cambridge's most eminent Jewish academics, and then a fund-raising committee with what seemed at the time an overly ambitious target to provide an endowment for the Centre. This committee met some half a dozen times and we all relished the opportunity of exchanging reminiscences, but what we did not accomplish was raising any serious money. There was nothing for it but for me to go for it myself. So I approached a few of my affluent friends in both England and America who I knew to have charitable trusts. My pitch to them was that I had never asked them for money before and that I was only asking them now because I felt strongly about the cause and knew that they would not have to put their hands in their personal pockets.

Some substantial donations were coming in but it was hard going and the turning point was the result of a fortuitous encounter. I was a guest at a lunch for a prominent Israeli statesman, and seated next to me at the table was a young man whose name – Gerald Leigh – I recognised as having been on a list of Jewish Cambridge graduates. I spoke to him about the Centre project. He appeared interested and asked if I would write to him on the subject and he would put it to his fellow trustees of the family's charitable trust. I did and he did and the result was a staggering gift of almost half of our remaining target.

In 1994 my three-year tenure as chairman of the *JC* Board ended. It had been a pretty turbulent time and David Kessler, by that time not on the Board but never reluctant to assert his authority as the principal shareholder and the creator of the Kessler Foundation, ensured that I followed the Ellis Birk precedent and did not offer myself for re-election.

By that time I had been married to Claire for some twenty exhilarating and joyful years. Her three daughters, all by then happily married and beginning to raise families, were living in the United States. We were visiting them once or twice a year and they came to stay with us in London, but I occasionally felt that Claire might wish to be closer to them. She had never spoken of it, but the niggling thought in the back of my mind was that she might prefer to return to live in the United States.

So I put it to her that it was her turn to decide where we would live and that now that I was free of the professional responsibilities that necessitated living in London, I was ready to move with her to the States if that was her preference. I was delighted with her response that she was not at all anxious to leave London permanently; she had made many good friends there, loved our home and all the advantages the city had to offer. The conclusion was that we agreed to undertake the experiment of dividing our time more or less equally between the two countries.

But how were we to divide our time? There was no disagreement on which time of the year to be out of London – obviously the winter months – and so we planned to leave in October and return in April in time for the cricket season! But where would we live in the States? It would have to be a choice between Baltimore, Philadelphia and Washington where the three girls lived. Our choice fell on Washington, a city both of us enjoyed.

During one of our regular lunches, I told Isaiah Berlin of this planned change in our life-style and he held up his hands in horror. 'Nobody has a *home* in Washington – they are all transients. I spent four and a half years there and I know.' I would have said the same thing after my first visit to Washington in 1949 but much had changed in the subsequent half century. In 1994 it was no longer provincial and the city had expanded considerably; fine new buildings, monuments, museums and restaurants, with a respectable choice of concerts and theatres, had made Washington in every respect a worthy capital of the world's only superpower. Changes in administrations necessarily brought about the arrival and departure of political appointees, but the transients were far out-numbered by the permanent residents.

The apartment we acquired in Washington has a plaque outside its front door recording that it is an historic site having first been occupied by Senator William Borah of Idaho. I had come across this name long before in my studies of international relations. Senator Borah was an arch-isolationist who, almost single-handedly, had frustrated President Wilson by successfully opposing American participation in the League of Nations after the First World War. After we moved in and Claire was researching for some writing she was doing about Eleanor Roosevelt, she read that Alice Roosevelt Longworth, the daughter of President Theodore Roosevelt, had had a long running affair with Senator Borah. At one point she had given birth to a daughter and was minded to name her *DeBorah* but her husband had objected.

Washingtonians, we learned, are extremely hospitable and it was not long before we had acquired an interesting circle of friends. With the invaluable aid of e-mail, I was able to continue my association with the activities in London with which I was involved and Washington was never dull, for politics, its sole industry, was always fascinating in its machinations and complexity. An old friend introduced me to the Institute for Learning in Retirement attached to the American University and I was invited to teach a course there – which I continued to do for several years – on the subject of contemporary Britain – my classes consisting mainly of well-informed and agreeable retired professionals, most of them enthusiastically philo-British. Questions were invariably pertinent and probing and I gained at least as much as my students from these occasions, helping to keep what remained of my grey matter in reasonable working order.

As I pen these words in my eighty-ninth year my mind, I suppose predictably, occasionally adverts to a mental balance sheet of my life. My working life does not occupy my thoughts to any considerable extent. A question which, from time to time, crosses my mind is whether I should have left the Bar for I loved the work, the camaraderie within the profession and the life of a barrister generally. It was the telephone call from Barnett Janner which prompted the decision to make the change but there was one other, previously unuttered, factor which weighed with me. It was the feeling that, as an East End Jew, there was little hope that I would ever be appointed to the High Court bench, the aspiration of most of my Bar contemporaries. At that time, these judges were almost entirely public school and Oxbridge products. Had I waited I might not have left for soon after, my friend Morris Finer, whose background was similar to mine, became Mr Justice Finer.

But then, would I have enjoyed sitting day after day and listening? I doubt it. And, on the other hand, my years as Editor were satisfying and sometimes exciting. Whether I achieved anything I do not know, but there can be few who could confidently claim to have a positive answer to that question.

Index

Index

Index